The
EVERYTHING®
Psychic Book

Dear Reader:

Has anyone ever told you that you have a psychic gift? Have you been trying to suppress thoughts or premonitions that sneak into your mind? Did you have experiences early in your life that you still can't explain?

You are psychic. Everyone is. Sometimes your special abilities may seem more like a curse to you. They did to me. I spent a great deal of my life without being able to understand what was going on inside my mind.

Fortunately, when I discovered self-hypnosis, I discovered things about myself that I never knew before and began to accept my own special gifts. Your gifts may be different, because they have been given to you for a unique purpose—to help guide you through your life.

Life can be an incredible adventure. Once you discover and tune in to your psychic abilities, you will gain awareness of the amazing things that happen around you. This book will help you discover your psychic gifts, to use them with the help of psychic tools and lots of intuitive exercises, and to figure out what fits you best. And this adventure is bound to be simple, fun, and very enlightening!

Michael R. Hathaway

The EVERYTHING® Series

Editorial

Publishing Director	Gary M. Krebs
Managing Editor	Kate McBride
Copy Chief	Laura MacLaughlin
Acquisitions Editor	Bethany Brown
Development Editor	Julie Gutin
Production Editor	Khrysti Nazzaro

Production

Production Director	Susan Beale
Production Manager	Michelle Roy Kelly
Series Designers	Daria Perreault
	Colleen Cunningham
Cover Design	Paul Beatrice
	Frank Rivera
Layout and Graphics	Colleen Cunningham
	Rachael Eiben
	Michelle Roy Kelly
	Daria Perreault
	Erin Ring
Series Cover Artist	Barry Littmann

Visit the entire Everything® Series at everything.com

THE
EVERYTHING
PSYCHIC
BOOK

Tap into your inner power and
discover your inherent abilities

Michael R. Hathaway, D.C.H.

Adams Media Corporation
Avon, Massachusetts

Copyright ©2003, F+W Publications, Inc.
All rights reserved. This book, or parts thereof, may not be reproduced
in any form without permission from the publisher; exceptions
are made for brief excerpts used in published reviews.

An Everything® Series Book.
Everything® and everything.com® are registered trademarks of F+W Publications, Inc.

Published by Adams Media, an F+W Publications Company
57 Littlefield Street, Avon, MA 02322 U.S.A.
www.adamsmedia.com

ISBN 13: 978-1-58062-969-0
ISBN 10: 1-58062-969-5
Printed in the United States of America.

J I H G F E

Library of Congress Cataloging-in-Publication Data
Hathaway, Michael R.
The everything psychic book / Michael Hathaway.
p.   cm.
(An everything series book)
ISBN 1-58062-969-5
1. Psychic ability. I. Title. II. Series: Everything series.

BF1031.H2955 2003
133.8–dc21

2003002636

This book is available at quantity discounts for bulk purchases.
For information, call 1-800-289-0963.

Contents

Astral Projection and Telekinetic Powers / 129

Psychic Work in Your Sleep / 143

It's in the Cards and the Stars / 155

A Plethora of Psychic Tools / 169

The Art of Dowsing / 183

Creative Psychic Talents / 197

Dedication

To all my psychic friends and the metaphysical coffeehouse.

Top Ten Psychic Abilities

1. **Astral projection:** Being able to have out-of-body experiences, during which you may visit different realms, like the Akashic Book of Records (see Chapter 7).

2. **Clairaudience:** Psychic sense of hearing—whether it's voices, music, or any other sounds that those around you cannot detect.

3. **Clairsentience:** Psychic sense of feeling, both in terms of touch and emotion. You may get a certain psychic feeling or actually touch something that you cannot see.

4. **Clairvoyance:** Psychic sense of sight—seeing invisible entities, images, or the auras of people or objects.

5. **Divination:** Using psychic intuition as well as divination tools—the Tarot, runes, astrology, crystal balls, and so on—to get information about the future.

6. **Dowsing:** Using a dowsing instrument like a pendulum, Y-rod, L-rod, or bobber to detect underground water, look for missing people, and conduct other psychic activities.

7. **Psychic communication:** Being able to communicate with your spiritual helpers, such as fairies, angels, souls of loved ones who have passed away, and other spiritual entities.

8. **Psychic healing:** Using alternative-healing methods to work on healing auras, balancing the chakras (the body's energy fields), and repairing the mind/body connection to set your patient on the path of recovery.

9. **Retrieving memories of past lives:** Using your psychic talents to be able to retrieve memories of your soul's past lives.

10. **Telepathy:** Communication with people over long distances via the power of the mind.

Introduction

▶ HUMAN BEINGS HAVE BEEN ATTEMPTING to learn the answers to the puzzles of the Universe since the beginning of existence. The ancients looked at the stars, to many different gods, and even at the entrails of sacrificed animals for guidance into the future. The Bible is filled with words from great prophets. All other tribes and societies throughout history have had those who claimed the ability to see the future, to heal, and to have other powers and insights from the world of the unknown.

Today, people are just as interested in the unknown as ever. Many of you want to be able to communicate with relatives and friends who have passed over to the Other Side. You want to know what the purpose of life is all about. And you may wonder if you have some sort of psychic ability like Sylvia Browne, John Edward, or James Van Praagh.

You may have the feeling that you are missing your life's calling, and you want to get yourself back on track. There is something gnawing at your insides, but you don't know what to do about finding out what it is, much less how to go about addressing it. It may be that day after day and year after year, you continue to feel you are drifting without a central focus for your life.

You may have had an early psychic experience that left you with the feeling of something that has yet to be resolved. That experience may have terrified you, and you live in fear of it happening again.

If any of these questions linger with you, you may find the answers and perhaps a new beginning to your search for the meaning of life in this book. Yes, you do have special psychic abilities. There is no one else on earth who has exactly the same gifts that you do. As you progress through this book, you will have an opportunity to gain insights about yourself that you have never discovered before. You will be guided through the easy step-by-step process of understanding how your mind is different and special. You will have a chance to try out many different psychic tools that may help you develop a special intuitive ability.

You will learn about the importance of being comfortable with your personal Belief System, the one that is truly yours, that you were born with. It can help guide you and protect you as you go through life. You will consider the possibility that you have a soul, and will come to realize that this life experience is very important to your soul's journey.

Many how-to books are written from the individual viewpoint of the author. If your mind is similar to the author's, a book like that may work well for you. If, on the other hand, you are different, reading a book with a limited point of view can be frustrating. *The Everything® Psychic Book* is designed to help each of you discover and develop your own psychic abilities, no matter how different they may be.

There is an amazing world of self-discovery and an incredible opportunity for personal and soul growth waiting for you just ahead. It is now time to give yourself permission to start your adventure with your psychic abilities. Ⓔ

Chapter 1

What Is Psychic Ability?

This chapter will provide you with an introduction into the psychic world and what it means to be psychic. You will learn how psychics have played a role in the history of the world since ancient times. You will also learn about the levels of consciousness, about psychic intuition, and about going into a trance. At the end of the chapter, you will have the opportunity to experience what it feels like to connect to your third eye in order to center yourself and balance your mind.

An Overview of Psychic Abilities

Did you know that you are psychic? You are, even though you may not think so. Many people do not understand this special ability. It is often unwelcome and misunderstood, not only by the psychic himself, but by family, friends, and strangers alike.

Everyone is psychic. You were born with at least one special gift already imprinted in your soul. Everything that you have experienced so far in this lifetime has helped develop your ability. Your psychic ability, like any other talent or characteristic, is a product of your physical self, your environment, your relationships, and your inherited genetics.

FACT

The word "psychic" comes from the Greek word *psyche,* "spirit" or "soul." In Greek mythology, the soul is personified by Psyche, a girl who loved one of the gods and suffered through many trials because of it. Through her suffering, she became a great soul (or soulful). Everyone gets his or her psychic information through an individual connection with his or her spiritual side. The way you make your connection is different from anyone else's way.

Unfortunately, the idea of being psychic often conjures up the image of gypsy fortunetellers or pay-per-minute telephone psychics. Many who claim to be psychic are really ready to fleece you out of your hard-earned money with their "mystical insights." They are masters at tricking their clients into giving them information they can use as if it came from the realm of the psychic.

Similarly, many books talk about developing and using your hidden psychic power as if it were a force that could help you control the world around you. You may be told that you can manifest your destiny, enjoy perfect health, and find wealth and prosperity with the powers you have within. As a result, many try to misuse their gifts for self-gain rather than for benefiting the Universe and helping their souls progress along the journey of understanding.

Free Will

Each soul has a map to follow during its lifetime. The map should be used as a guide to learning life lessons and resolving old karma. Whether or not they choose to follow this map is each person's individual choice.

Some people see life as a battlefield. They are constantly facing one crisis after another. They find themselves drained of any creative energy that could help them move forward. They do not know how to step back and find a different view of their own situation. They do not understand that their own failure to recognize their intuitive guidance system, which is in place and waiting to be set in motion, is what creates part of their dilemma.

You can't turn your psychic gift on and off like a water faucet. Once the tap is opened (whether knowingly or unknowingly), it may be difficult to shut the flow off again. Sometimes even when you want to turn it on, nothing comes through. It is a connection with the portion of yourself that flows from the soul. It is your free will to choose to become in tune with your psychic ability.

The Psychic Process

Because it is different for every person, it is impossible to explain exactly what the psychic process is like. No one else has a mind that is identical to yours. Many psychic courses designed to help enhance intuitive abilities are presented in a model that the instructor uses. If you, the participant, are not of a similar mind, your initial enthusiasm can easily turn to frustration.

Your mind receives external stimuli through five different senses: sight, sound, touch, taste, and smell. You remember past experiences internally through these same five senses. Each of you, however, processes these memories in different ways.

Remember that you are the keeper of your own ability. It is there waiting to be set into positive use. No matter what you read or others tell you, it is your soul that knows the answers. The goal is for you to be able to identify and become comfortable with your own special psychic abilities. In you, as in everyone, they are truly a gift to be shared with the world.

Early Psychics

Psychic traditions have existed since the beginning of recorded history and were present in one way or another in ancient cultures throughout the world. The royalty of many cultures used divination to seek guidance in war and to forecast natural disasters such as drought and floods. Ancient Chinese diviners cast bones and yarrow sticks and interpreted the way they fell. The prosperity and lifestyle for many of the diviners to the court greatly depended on the success of their predictions.

In the ancient Middle East, the psychic powers were practiced by the prophets, as described in the Old Testament of the Bible. In Africa, the ancient peoples used trance states, achieved through the use of hallucinogenic plants as well as dancing, singing, and chanting, to contact the spirit world. The Egyptians communicated with their dead, forecast future events, and aligned their pyramids with star formations. Aristotle discovered the Egyptian technique of palmistry, which is still practiced today.

The Greeks used oracles at sacred locations to give prophecies of the future. The Romans sacrificed animals and studied their entrails for events yet to come. They also looked to the stars for messages from beyond.

Native American Psychics

Early American psychic practices have also been documented. The Aztecs in Mexico used astrology and oracles, while the Incas in Peru received their information from patterns they saw in grains of corn and coca leaves. Native Americans from what is now the United States and Canada followed many practices similar to those of the Africans, including singing, dancing, chanting, and using hallucinogenic substances to connect with the Great Spirit. When males reached puberty, they would enter the wilderness to meet the Great Spirit, who would be there at the end of their lives to help them move on to the next world.

Shamans, priests, priestesses, and medicine men, as well as others trained in their culture's mystical traditions, set out through their minds on sacred journeys to other realms in order to retrieve revealing information for the future. The key to these journeys was the ability of the travelers to be induced into a deep trance state.

Nostradamus

Nostradamus was the best-known psychic of the Middle Ages. He wrote almost a thousand prophetic verses in combinations of several different languages, including French and Latin, in a verse form known as quatrain, with each stanza consisting of four lines that rhyme alternately. The real key to the writings of Nostradamus may never be totally understood.

FACT

Nostradamus was a French physician (1502–1566). His work, *The Centuries,* was published in 1555 and brought him fame as well as an appointment to Catherine de Medici's court as her personal astrologer. *Centuries* is still analyzed today by scholars looking for references to the world's future.

The Spiritualist Movement

After the Middle Ages and the Renaissance, during the Age of Reason, beliefs in supernatural powers waned, but they were reborn again with the help of the Spiritualist Movement. The groundwork for the movement began with Emanuel Swedenborg (1688–1772). Swedenborg was fifty-six when he first began to pay attention to his psychic abilities. He learned how to go into deep trances and communicate with the dead and the angels. Then he would write down the communications he received. Some of his trances lasted up to three days.

Swedenborg believed in God and in the existence of heaven and hell, but he thought that individuals choose the heaven or hell that they visit in the afterlife. Their behavior on earth determines their afterlife experience. The Church of the New Jerusalem was established as a direct result of Swedenborg's writing and teachings.

Mesmer, Braid, and Davis

Another contributor to the Spiritualist Movement, Friedrich (or Franz) Anton Mesmer (1733–1815), developed the theory of animal magnetism, claiming that there is an invisible fluid inside the human body that can be moved about to create healing while the patient is in a trance or "mesmerized." Mesmer was wrong about the existence of the fluid, but healing could and did take place as a result of the suggestion heard by the patient in an altered state of consciousness.

Dr. James Braid (1795–1860), a Scottish physician, developed Mesmer's ideas into the basis for modern-day hypnosis. His theories were set down in his book *Neurypnology,* published in 1843.

QUESTION?

What is hypnosis?
Hypnosis occurs when you enter an altered state in which your unconscious mind accepts suggestions without resistance from the conscious mind. If you aren't familiar with hypnosis, you may want to read *The Everything® Hypnosis Book,* which can help you understand in greater detail what happens during hypnosis and how to use the hypnotic process.

Another influence in the Spiritualist Movement was Andrew Jackson Davis (1826–1910). He was known as the Poughkeepsie Seer, and he had the ability to see through the human body to locate diseased organs. Davis believed that he was able to channel Swedenborg.

The Fox Sisters

The Spiritualist Movement was really brought to the forefront by the Fox sisters, Kate (1841–1892) and Margaretta (1838–1893). The sisters claimed that they were able to manifest spirit communication through the rappings of a peddler who had been murdered and whose bones were found in the Fox home. The public became enthralled as they gave demonstrations of this "psychic" manifestation throughout the country.

The sisters were later exposed as frauds and confessed that the rappings of the murdered peddler were actually produced by them, cracking their toe and knee joints. Even so, the movement of Spiritualism was underway both in the United States and in Europe. Spirit rapping gave way to séances, table tipping, trance writing, and spirit communication through a medium. Many of these techniques are still practiced today in the Spiritualist Church.

Edgar Cayce, Father of the New Age

The largest impact on the advancement of psychic knowledge was made by a man named Edgar Cayce (1877–1945), who is now considered to be the founder of the New Age movement. Cayce spent much of his life trying to understand what he did while he was in a trance. While in trance, he spoke about currently unknown civilizations, in which the soul hadn't yet developed a physical body and was free to travel about without the restriction of gravity and to communicate through thought. You may have soul memories of those early times that can help in your psychic development.

An Unlikely Psychic

Cayce was an unlikely candidate for reaching the pinnacle of acclaim that he still enjoys today, over a half century since his death. He began life in rural Kentucky's tobacco country. He was close to his grandfather, Thomas Jefferson Cayce, who was said to have special psychic abilities.

Tragedy stuck one day when young Cayce witnessed the death of his grandfather in an accident with a horse. After the incident, young Edgar would visit his grandfather's spirit in one of the barns. Cayce's grandmother and mother encouraged him to continue these visits and to tell them about his experiences.

Many calamities befell young Edgar. When he was three, he fell against a fence post and punctured his skull on a nail, possibly deep enough to reach his brain. His father poured turpentine in the wound, and Cayce recovered in a short period of time. At fifteen he was hit on the spine by a ball and began to act strangely. After his father sent him to bed, he entered a hypnotic trance, telling his father what to do to cure him. Because his father followed the directions, he awoke the next morning his normal self.

When he was in his early twenties, he lost his voice. A traveling stage hypnotist temporarily helped him, and he learned to enter a self-hypnotic trance aided by a local man named Al Layne, who had taken a mail-order course on the subject. While in this altered state, Cayce was able to give himself the cure for his voice blockage. His throat turned bright red, he coughed up some blood, and his voice returned. Over the next year Cayce's voice would need further treatment on a monthly basis, and Layne, intrigued by Cayce's diagnostic abilities, experimented with his subject, hoping to uncover answers to his talent.

FACT

In 1901 Edgar Cayce began to give readings for clients. Over the next four decades he produced a body of work that consisted of over twelve thousand readings that were carefully transcribed and are still being studied today. These readings were on health, past lives, ancient mysteries such as the lost continent of Atlantis, and predictions for the future.

Edgar Cayce and Extrasensory Perception

In 1933, Edgar Cayce and his supporters formed the Association for Research and Enlightenment for the purpose of studying, researching, and disseminating information about extrasensory perception, or ESP, as well as dreams, holistic health, and life after death. The center was located in Virginia Beach, where it still remains today.

Cayce was able to use his psychic abilities in four different areas: precognition, retrocognition, clairvoyance, and telepathy. He had the ability to see into the future and give predictions of events to come. He could look into a person's past to find the origins of an existing health condition. He had the physical ability to see through objects and could see the inside of the human body. He was also able to enter another mind and know what the person was thinking. He could sleep on a book and remember its contents when he awoke.

Levels of Consciousness

There are three levels of consciousness that play a role in psychic experiences. The conscious, the unconscious, and the Universal Mind can either work with or against each other, and each person must learn to balance the messages received from these three minds.

The conscious mind consists of only 10 percent of the total mind. It is in charge of reasoning, analyzing, and making critical decisions. In order for the conscious mind to be efficient, it needs to be able to maintain an objective viewpoint. This, however, is often very hard for the conscious mind to do, because it is constantly receiving input from the unconscious and the Universal Mind.

ALERT!

When the unconscious mind takes control over the conscious mind, the individual's ability to make critical decisions is severely impaired. The result is often an action that is regretted later, when the conscious mind regains its objective perspective.

The unconscious mind is the storage facility. It retains and recalls memories that are sent up to the conscious mind at a time when it perceives that an action is needed. When this occurs, the conscious mind often accepts the suggestion and automatically sets it into motion.

The Universal Mind is the place where spontaneous insights come from. It is a direct link with the history of your soul and your guidance system, which keeps you in line with your life map or life purpose.

The Universal Mind also includes knowledge of your karma. In Buddhism and Hinduism, the word "karma" is used to relate the actions of one lifetime to each other and to make sense of how these affect subsequent lives. Unresolved karma can manifest itself through the Universal Mind, presenting an opportunity for the conscious mind to bring about resolution. You may receive intuitive warnings of possible confrontations related to karma.

Your Psychic Intuition

There are three types of psychic intuition: deductive, random, and goal-focused. Deductive intuition comes from the unconscious mind; random intuition comes from the Universal Mind; and goal-focused intuition works with all three minds. Your mental makeup determines the type of intuition that is yours. Each person has a unique form of intuition that may be a blend of any of the three types.

Deductive Psychic Intuition

Deductive psychic images come from your unconscious mind's ability to take in external sensory stimuli. That's not as complicated as it sounds. Your five sensory receivers—eyes, ears, mouth, skin, and nose—are constantly bombarded with stimuli in the form of external pictures, sounds, tastes, tactile sensations, temperature changes, and smells. You take in a lot of information that you are not consciously aware of because it is absorbed by the unconscious mind, where it is stored.

When your conscious mind has a question about something that it cannot answer, this question will also go to the unconscious mind, which will mull over the problem and rely on its stored data to come up with a response. In the meantime, your conscious mind usually goes on to another subject and forgets what it was looking for. But your unconscious mind stays hard at work. All of a sudden, out of nowhere, a psychic insight appears. Your unconscious mind has come to a logical psychic solution to your problem, one that your conscious mind hadn't thought of.

Random Psychic Intuition

Random psychic intuition is different from deductive psychic intuition in several ways. It comes from your Universal Mind and may be totally unrelated to anything known or connected consciously or unconsciously to the psychic image. It could be about something that has, is, or will take place anywhere in the world. In other words, random psychic intuition can take place in any of the three phases of time—past, present, or future.

A random psychic experience often comes at a time when it is unexpected or even unwanted. It can be very powerful and leave you dazed and confused. This disorientation may last only a few moments, but its effects are powerful enough to last a lifetime. The experience itself may continue to live on in your mind long after the image first appeared.

Not all random psychic experiences are negative. It is possible that you might have a pleasant premonition; then later, you might realize that what you saw as nothing more than a happy daydream has become a reality. It may be that you suddenly get a set of numbers in your head that leads to a big sweepstake jackpot win. Or a song may begin to play in your head that you haven't heard in years, a song that later you may unexpectedly hear on the radio or television.

Random psychic intuition happens when you are in a light trance state. It occurs when your conscious or critical mind is open to the images that are sent up from your unconscious and your Universal Mind. A random psychic trance can be triggered by external or internal stimuli. Once the intuitive trance process begins, it is hard to disengage from until it has run its course.

When you ask a fortuneteller to give you an answer about a specific problem in your life, the psychic will connect to her intuitive Source and focus on the requested information. Then she waits for her mind to download the information requested.

Goal-Focused Psychic Intuition

Goal-focused psychic intuition is a combination of deductive and random intuition. Using this method, you can make a conscious effort to gain certain insights through psychic intuition. You can attempt to use your intuitive ability for a specific goal. Focused psychic intuition is the kind that is normally employed by professional psychics and others who already understand and use their intuitive abilities on a consistent basis.

Professional psychics who work with the police will often familiarize themselves with some of the facts of the case they are working on. Examining a piece of evidence or a photograph from a crime scene could provide intuitive information, and an actual visit to a specific location may also lead to new clues. Some of the information may be drawn from deductive intuition, and some may be generated at random, but all clues gathered are related to the specific goal of the psychic trance.

Entering a State of Trance

When your conscious mind's ability to think clearly is interrupted, you enter the state of trance. All people, whether they know it or not, go in and out of trances many times a day. When you are in a trance, your critical reasoning becomes confused. The power of suggestion, whether it's by your unconscious mind or by someone else, takes control of your thought process.

You can be guided or induced into a trance in several different ways. The trigger can come either through external stimuli—if, for instance, you were to enter a specific location—or through internal stimuli, such as thoughts or feelings. Trances can be positive or negative, and they can continue to influence you long after your initial experience. You can remain in a trance state for a few minutes or for days. The state will continue until something interrupts it. Once you recognize the trance state, you have the choice of remaining in it or not.

Sometimes a trance experience can be so powerful that the individual loses total touch with reality. This is more likely to happen when the person is in a highly suggestible state. The images that are received into the conscious mind can occur with such strength that the individual's reality shifts into the trance reality.

Moving Through Time

Your mind moves through three different phases of time: the past, the present, and the future. Everything that you have experienced in your lifetime—your past—is deposited in the memory bank of your unconscious mind. Sometimes the information is held there for years before it suddenly comes back up to the conscious mind. When you experience these memories again, you have actually entered a memory (also called a past) trance. The stronger the memory experience, the stronger the trance.

Your memories of the past help you construct trances relating to the future. When you experience a future event, you are entering a future trance state. The stronger you experience this image, the stronger the trance experience will be.

Your mind also experiences the present. In this time phase it can distort speed and distance. Sometimes a minute seems like an hour, and sometimes an hour seems like a minute. In athletics, being in the present is called "being in the zone."

QUESTION?

Have you ever driven down the highway and become so absorbed in thought that you actually went right by your destination?
You were in a state of trance when this occurred. Even though you were not totally aware of your location, you were still driving your vehicle safely. This phenomenon is called highway hypnosis.

It is easy to get caught up in such a deep trance that you are unaware of what time phase you are in. To break the trance, you must be able to balance the three phases of your mind and be aware of each one.

Psychic Trances

Psychic trances occur when your conscious mind is flooded with information that cannot be deduced by critical reasoning. Usually, this information comes from the unconscious and/or the Universal Mind. Quite often this information comes at a time when you are least expecting it. If you are not prepared, a psychic trance can catch you by surprise and may cause a great deal of mental chaos. Many people try to block this information. However, it often finds its own way to the surface again.

We all enter psychic trances. Some have a great deal of meaning, while others seem to be there just to verify that you are capable of experiencing something unexplainable. Perhaps you knew the telephone was going to ring, or you thought of a song just before it played on the radio.

Finding Your Balance

To avoid the chaos, you need to have an inner balance of mind. Create a place in your mind where you can escape for a few moments, and learn to relax there. For some of you, this may seem like an impossibility. If relaxing for you at this time is difficult, don't worry. As you progress through the book, you will learn how to find your balance.

You may already be familiar with the term "centering yourself." Many situations in your life can keep you from being centered. You may be kept off balance by the people around you, the environment, or by psychic information when it pours through the unconscious mind. It is easy to be overwhelmed by all the stimuli, both external and internal. To help deal with life's uncertainties, you need to learn how to center yourself.

Connect with Your Third Eye

Your third eye is actually your pituitary gland. It is located in the center of your forehead, above your two other eyes. It secretes hormones that affect many of your bodily functions, including your growth and your metabolism. All three of your eyes together form the points of a triangle, a symbol that is found throughout ancient history, especially in the society of the pyramid builders. Perhaps they were aware of some lost ancient secret that helped them connect to the eye of the soul.

If for some reason you are uncomfortable about connecting to your third eye, don't feel that you have to try. All the exercises in this book are designed for you to have a positive experience. If at any time you are not comfortable, you may simply stop and return to a more positive feeling.

Focus Upward

An easy way to center yourself is to make a connection with your third eye. Those of you with a religious background may connect with your third eye when you pray. Another way to do it is through meditation. Another approach of connecting with your third eye is by doing the following exercise.

For a moment, look upward with your two physical eyes as if you were trying to see your third eye. If for some reason this is impossible or hard for you to do, that's okay; it is not actually necessary to move or see through your two eyes to experience this. You may keep your two eyes open or closed while you peek up under your eyelids. Some of you may want to squint slightly and feel your third eye.

When you try this, you may feel a slight pressure in your third eye. It may feel like it is swelling or even vibrating. You may have a feeling of warmth or coolness, or you may perceive a certain color. Whatever you experience is okay—it's also possible that you won't feel anything at all.

Each of you will connect to your third eye in a way that is natural and correct for you. Remember, there is no one else exactly like you. No one else will have the experience that you have when you communicate through your third eye.

Now Breathe

Now let's add something else to help you center when you connect to your third eye. You may want to take a moment and find a comfortable place to sit or lie down. If any of your clothing is tight, you may want to loosen it a little. It is not absolutely necessary, but it may help you to become a little more centered. When you have done this, you may allow yourself to feel a connection with your third eye.

For a moment, allow yourself to get comfortable with the sensations you are experiencing as you make this connection. When you're ready, take a deep breath at a level that feels right for you. It may not be easy for you to inhale deeply, and that's okay. What is important is for you to breathe at a pace that helps you strengthen the connection with your third eye.

Continue to breathe slowly for a few minutes. It doesn't matter whether you keep your eyes open or closed—whatever way feels right for you is correct. Your mind may just drift away. It may also be very active, with lots of thoughts suddenly popping up, or it may focus on one thing.

Some people get frustrated trying to learn to meditate. They are instructed to quiet their mind, but they find it impossible to do. If your mind is that way, don't worry about it; just breathe and focus on your third eye.

After you have experienced the results of this exercise for a length of time that is comfortable for you, you may take a deep breath. As you exhale, release the connection with your third eye and come back to the surface of your mind refreshed and relaxed. The more you practice this, the easier it will be to make a positive connection. Focusing on your third eye is a great way to begin connecting to your psychic mind.

Chapter 2

Early Psychic Experiences

Psychic development begins at an early age. In this chapter, you will learn how to dig deep into your memory and remember the psychic powers you may have had as a small child but that you gradually repressed as you entered adulthood. Reclaiming these memories will help you reclaim your psychic gifts, which are unique to you and may include psychic dreams, near-death experiences, déjà vu, past-life influences, incidences of automatic writing, and other products of your psychic intuition.

Trying to Remember

Can you remember your first psychic experience? Some of you can probably recall it clearly, while others may have little or no recognition of any psychic experience at all. Chances are that it came at a very early age. You may be able to find an older family member or acquaintance who can remember that you talked about some incident that you have consciously forgotten. It could have been a series of circumstances or a single event.

All of those past experiences are stored in your unconscious mind. Even as you read these words, you may call to mind something that you haven't thought about in years. Some of you may have powerful memories connected to "unexplainable experiences" in your past. As you progress through these pages, the goal is for you to be able to define and reconnect with your special psychic gifts.

What Do You Recall?

Do you remember your early psychic experiences? Maybe you weren't aware at the time that what had occurred wasn't part of reality, that is, until you shared the information with others. Or maybe it was clearly a psychic event. Here are a few tips for trying to remember your early psychic experiences:

- Allow yourself to be open to recalling psychic memory flashes, and don't overanalyze them.
- Don't expect to get all of the memory at once.
- Keep notes of your psychic memory flashes so that you can refer back to them.
- Once you have an idea of a possible psychic flash, talk to others who might have been aware of it at the time it happened.
- Use basic relaxation techniques to help you focus on your early psychic memory.

Here is an easy relaxation exercise that may help you remember early childhood psychic memories. If you would like to try it, find a place to sit or lie down, and let yourself get comfortable.

When you're ready, you may take a deep breath (again, at the level that is comfortable for you) and allow yourself to focus toward your third eye. As you breathe in and out, you may tell yourself that in a few moments you will count from five to zero. When you reach zero you will be very relaxed, and your unconscious mind will be open to recalling early childhood memories of psychic experiences. Any memory you may recall will be for positive insights, and at any time you want, you may always open your eyes and come back to full consciousness, refreshed and relaxed.

ALERT!

Whenever you are connecting to your third eye, give yourself the suggestion that you may always end your connection by opening your eyes, taking a deep breath, and connecting to your conscious mind.

Count Down

As you count yourself down, you may feel yourself sinking deeper and deeper, feeling more and more relaxed with each count. It is a very pleasant feeling, and you look forward to the next number as you count yourself downward. As you focus on your third eye, you may allow yourself to relax more and more as you open up your psychic memories. You may allow any muscles that you feel are stiff to relax. If you are ready, take a deep breath, exhale, and start counting:

5. Breathe in and out, and feel yourself relaxing more and more with each breath. Let yourself relax your muscles. As you mention the next number to yourself, you may feel yourself connecting more and more strongly with your third eye. You may feel yourself going deeper and deeper into your unconscious mind, opening up to your early psychic memories.

4. Feel yourself going deeper and deeper as you feel the connection to your third eye becoming stronger and stronger. You may breathe in and out, slowly, relaxing more and more with each breath. You may feel yourself getting closer and closer to your memories of your early psychic experiences.

3. As you breathe slowly, you may feel yourself relaxing more and more. You may feel yourself going deeper and deeper into your unconscious mind. As you get closer and closer to zero, you will be more and more connected with your unconscious mind. You will be ready to come in contact with your early childhood psychic memories.

2. You are getting closer and closer, as you sink deeper and deeper. You are relaxing more and more, and your psychic memories will be ready for you to access when you get to zero. As you breathe in and out slowly, you will allow yourself to relax more and more. You can feel your connection to your third eye more and more.

1. You are almost there. You may feel very comfortable, relaxed, and safe. You know you may always come back to a conscious state any time you want by opening your eyes, taking a deep breath, exhaling, and feeling relaxed and positive. You may allow yourself to go deeper and deeper as you count slowly backward from five to zero, each number ten times stronger than the last.

0. You may feel the connection to your third eye even more strongly than before as you are now ready to access the unconscious memories of your early childhood experiences. Anything you see, feel, hear, taste, or smell will help you to remember your early childhood psychic experiences.

ESSENTIAL

While you are in a relaxed and comfortable state, you may let your unconscious memory recall images from the past that are about your early psychic experiences at a pace that is good and comfortable for you. Be aware that you can open your eyes and come back to full consciousness any time you want, feeling relaxed, calm, and refreshed.

Count Back Up

When you are ready, you may count slowly back up to your conscious mind. When you reach five, you will remember any images you may have recalled relating to early psychic experiences.

1. You are coming up and slowly releasing your connection to the third eye as you count toward five.
2. Breathe slowly and comfortably, as you count yourself back up.
3. You are getting closer and closer to the surface of your conscious mind.
4. Slowly release your connection to the third eye.
5. Now you may come fully back to the surface of your conscious mind as you release your connection to the third eye. Take a deep breath, open your eyes, and exhale. You may feel relaxed and positive about your connection to any early childhood psychic memories that you may have recalled.

Each time you perform this exercise, you may have different results. Don't expect a specific outcome. Each time you try, you may find more and different memories coming up to the surface of your conscious mind. Once you open the communication channel and continue to connect to it, the flow will become easier to access.

Near-Death Experiences

Have you ever had a near-death experience? Was there ever a close call, during which you were inches or moments away from potential death? Did you survive a bad fall or a blow to the head? Did you have other traumatic experiences when you were young in which your mind was an important key to your survival?

Near-death experiences come in many different ways, but going through such an experience may have "jump-started" your third eye into being more open to psychic intuition.

When you go through a traumatic experience, all of your senses experience a surge in the intensity of the power of their perception. In some cases, your view of the world changes dramatically. You know something's different, but you're not sure what it is.

Children and Near-Death Experiences

A near-death experience in early childhood may often go unnoticed.

Kids get into all kinds of trouble. They fall from trees, get trapped underwater, trip down the stairs, survive a car accident, or tumble off the playground swings. In some cases, such a close call may grow out of an unconscious need to escape a traumatic situation such as abuse or an emotionally unstable family.

FACT

Edgar Cayce had several early-life experiences that could have contributed to his psychic development. His skull was pierced with a nail at age three; he watched his grandfather die from a horseback accident; and at age fifteen he was hit in the spine with a ball. This later experience seemed to help connect him to his psychic healing knowledge.

Can you think of events in your life that may have affected your psychic ability? You are the sum total of your life to this very moment. Each new, passing moment will bring about change. As you learn to become in tune with your life, you will be more aware of your psychic abilities.

Early Childhood Dreams

The dreams you had in your childhood could very well have been psychic in nature. Dreams, like other psychic experiences, may deal with past events or future events, or they may provide insight into situations that are occurring at the time of the dream. Dreams are a great way to receive psychic information because the conscious analytical mind is at rest, and you are open to communication from your unconscious and your Universal Mind.

Think about the dreams you had as a child. Do you remember any? If so, can you recall if they had a theme? Did you have a certain dream that occurred over and over? Can you identify the historical time period and/or location of any dreams?

Did you have symbolic dreams that may not have made sense when you had them, but that you might better understand at this point in your life? Did you have any dreams that identified situations in your life before you experienced them? Did you have recurring nightmares? Did you have dreams that were different but followed a related theme?

Did you have dreams in which dead relatives or others who had passed over communicated with you? Did you have angels, guides, or other beings or animals come to you in your sleep to comfort you and/or offer you advice? Did you ever have dreams of flying or going to places that you had never been before? Do you recall any other types of dreams that may have been of a psychic nature when you were a child?

If you would like to investigate the subject of dreams, consult a copy of *The Everything® Dreams Book* by Trish and Robert MacGregor (Adams Media Corporation, Avon, MA).

You can investigate the answers to these questions in a relaxed state, as you contact your third eye. Trust your intuitive mind to give you the right answers. If you cannot remember anything, it's possible that you did not use dreams as a part of your early psychic development.

Second Sight

When you were a child, did you ever see things that were invisible to others? Did you have "imaginary friends" to play with? Could you find your way to or around a place where you had never been before?

What other experiences that might not be explainable to others did you have as a child? Did you ever have a visit from fairies or guides? Do you recall any contacts that could be considered otherworldly, such as with beings from another planet?

FACT

Here is an example of a second-sight experience. Mary remembers that as a girl, she played in the woods with other children. They taught her how to play their games. It was only later that she learned their games and clothing were from the Revolutionary War period.

A Sense of Déjà Vu

Did you ever, as a child, go to a strange place and know you had been there before? Did you experience something and feel that it had already happened? Childhood déjà vu is a phenomenon that can happen naturally. As a child, your view of reality is different because your early psychic experiences aren't limited by the boundaries that society has set for adults.

Sometimes déjà vu is so strong that second sight engages, and the experience becomes so real that the person having the experience loses touch with reality. This happens to a child more easily than to an adult, but such experiences often stay with a child into adulthood.

Past Lives

During childhood, we may still have memories from our past lives; these memories are gradually forgotten as we grow older. Do you recall any early childhood memories that can give you clues about your past lives? Did you know things about family members from different lifetimes? Did you ever act as if your role in the family were different than it should have been? Did you ever tell your family stories about other lifetimes?

Chances are, some of your psychic intuitions have come from what you've retained from your past. The more of these soul memories you can recall, the more you will find a connection to your psychic gifts.

Other Psychic Talents

When you were a child, did you have a natural talent for doing something? Did anyone ever remark that a particular ability of yours seemed developed far beyond your age? Did it seem as if you knew how to do something without anyone else showing you? Did you have a special athletic talent?

Did you draw or paint at an early age? If so, were these scenes from your childhood, or did they seem to be inspired by something you had never actually experienced in this lifetime? Did you have a musical talent?

Were there music styles or certain compositions that affected you in different ways?

Do you remember hearing voices? Did you have a guide or an angel who talked you through bad times and gave you encouragement? Or did the voice seem to come from an object you held dear—a doll, a baby blanket, or even your favorite chair?

> Your psychic talents may go beyond sight and hearing, although these are the more common senses for psychic power or recollection. Some of you may remember being able to sense energy fields or auras, or certain smells. And some of you may have at times felt unexplained emotions that had no real-life explanations.

The Function of Your Psychic Gifts

Now that you have had an opportunity to examine your childhood experiences of psychic intuition, think of how these gifts may be reclaimed and made a part of your present life. Some of you may use your intuitive abilities daily, and some of you may not, but it's never too late to reawaken your psychic powers. It is possible that you may be a little leery of getting in touch with your gifts. Remember that they are a natural part of your total self, no different than your physical body.

Chapter 3

In Tune with Your Guides

Your psychic gifts have been given to you for a specific purpose. But what is that purpose? How can you figure out what it is you were meant to do in this life-time? The answer lies in your life map. This is something each person is born with, and we each have the choice of whether to follow it or not. It is up to you to examine what you believe in and then to find the guidance you need, both in the Universe and within yourself, if you're going to find your life map and follow it on your life's journey.

Your Life's Purpose

You have probably thought about your life and its purpose in the greater scheme of things. Many people have asked themselves whether there is anything more to life than being born and living until we die. Most of us wonder whether we all have souls or whether there is some other element to our existence that transcends this life and our physical bodies. To answer these questions, some people turn to religion, but they don't always get the answers they are seeking.

The answer to your life's purpose lies in your soul. Imagine for a moment that in the beginning of the soul's journey, it had no physical form. Each soul had all the knowledge of the Universe but not the experience that goes with it. Each reincarnation of the soul had a specific goal in which to gain the experiences. Each lifetime also provided a chance for advancement, as the soul learned an additional lesson.

QUESTION?

How does the soul know what lesson is to be learned in each lifetime?
It relies on its guidance system, which contains all the knowledge from lifetimes past. The knowledge of your soul can help you grow in wisdom and experience. It can also help you as you progress through your present life.

When the soul learns all the lessons of the Universe, it will progress to the rank of "old soul" and will again return to its initial form of pure energy. In that state, it will continue to exist among the souls that have not yet reached that level on their journey.

The Choice Is Yours

The lesson you have been given to learn in your lifetime can be made yours if you follow your life map. The choice of learning or not learning that lesson is up to you—that's the power of free will. Your conscious mind may choose to work toward self-gain and the satisfaction of your ego rather than the goal of focusing on your life lesson. If you choose to disregard your life map and seek to satisfy your ego, it may be necessary to repeat your lesson in a future lifetime.

Unfortunately, many people choose to use their psychic ability for self-gain. They forget that their talents are given by the Universe to benefit the whole. Some even use their "powers" to inflict pain or to control others. If an individual abuses these gifts, then there will be plenty of opportunity for that person to make restitution in future incarnations.

You have been given the opportunity in this lifetime to let yourself get back in tune with your life map. You may be aware of karma that needs to be resolved. The more you are open to your life map, the more you will be guided to find the way.

The Power of Religion

To find your life's purpose, you also need to examine your beliefs and what guides you through life. What do you believe? Do you practice a specific faith, or do you adhere to basic spiritual principles? If you were asked to explain to someone else exactly what your belief structure is, could you do it? Would you be comfortable explaining it, or do you feel awkward or unable to reply? It's all right not to have the exact answer. In fact, some people think they know what they believe in, but it may turn out that it's not the right concept for either themselves or others.

You may have had a situation in your past where you had great faith in something that never worked out. Did your faith or what you believed in fail you, or did you fail it? It could be that the failure itself was really a success. Perhaps this failure was an opportunity to get in touch again with your inner guidance system. It could be that the outcome you were looking for was not the outcome that was a part of your life map.

Rituals of Belief

Man's belief in the power of communication with the Divine did not begin with the Christian doctrine. It has been part of human society since the earliest of times. Man has worshiped the heavens and the sea. He has created mystical figures and animals and built idols.

Mankind has celebrated the changing seasons and prayed for bountiful harvests. He has built temples over sacred earth energies and pyramids aligned with the stars. He has even created living gods on earth and endowed them with absolute and supreme power—emperors, high priests, pharaohs, and dictators.

Man has even killed his own kind in hopes of evoking great miracles through his gods. Human sacrifice is known to have taken place in many cultures in not only ancient but also recent history. It was the belief of self-sacrifice and great rewards in the afterlife that motivated the kamikaze pilots of World War II and the terrorists of today to give their own lives while hoping to kill many others at the same time. Do you think these people are following their life map? Or were they led astray, off their life paths?

QUESTION?

Do you pray? If this is the case, to whom or what?
Many churches have prayer chains or lists. Whenever there is a concern, there are individuals waiting to pray for divine help. It is not uncommon when a prayer chain is activated for miraculous results to happen.

Authoritative and Permissive Faiths

There are two types of religion: permissive and authoritative. Although they both have the same goals, there is one major difference between them. The difference has to do with how a particular belief system's objectives are accomplished. One kind of philosophy (the authoritative) uses the power of intimidation, while the permissive type encourages you to find your own path to the common goal.

Many people who are trying to discover their Belief System turn to instant answers. They purchase books and attend churches or other meetings in their quest to make a connection with the Divine. They spend big money to let others provide them with the right answers.

They may find exactly what they are looking for, or they may go away empty and unfulfilled. It is very easy to become confused with all the advice that is out there—to give up the search for a belief and to sink back into old ways and patterns.

Authoritative Beliefs

Authoritative beliefs are governed by the fear of failure. If you stray from the doctrine, you will surely be among the damned, sentenced to spend eternity in hell. Worse even than the fear they inspire, these types of beliefs are dominated by rules that are almost impossible to follow to the standard that is required for success.

Authoritative religion expects its members to accept the absolute doctrine they are given to follow. There is no room to challenge, and questioning isn't tolerated. Very often the hierarchy of this form of belief becomes quite wealthy through the gifts and support of the faithful members.

Generally, authoritative religions don't accept that individuals should have or use psychic abilities. These gifts are thought to be the work of the devil. In early colonial times, most famously in Salem, Massachusetts, young women with strong psychic powers were labeled "witches" and burned at the stake. Today, some religious cults have gone so far as to punish and even kill members that they think are "possessed by the Devil." It's no wonder that many people are reluctant to reveal their psychic gifts to others.

Permissive Beliefs

The premise of permissive belief is that you yourself know how to reach the common goal of connecting to the Divine and living your life in harmony with it. This type of belief gives you the opportunity to learn from your mistakes and to make corrections. Permissive beliefs are always optimistic about what you may accomplish in the future, regardless of your past.

Permissive religions don't rule by intimidation, and they recognize the individuality and gifts of each person. The reason for their willingness to recognize and trust the good in people is they accept that your gifts were given to you for a higher purpose, one that can be used to benefit mankind as a whole. Permissive religions have room for many different types of beliefs, as long as they all work toward a positive goal.

Permissive beliefs accept the use and development of psychic talents because they see each individual as a complete person, with mind, body, and soul. Furthermore, these beliefs advocate working with and staying in tune with your inner guidance system.

Your Inner Guidance System

Your inner guidance system is your connection to the Universal Mind as well as the sum total of all the wisdom and experiences you've accumulated up to this point in time. Remember that your inner wisdom and experiences come from your soul and that they transcend this one lifetime. The purpose of your inner guidance system is to help you stay on course with your life map.

Think of your guidance system as your conscience. It lets you know when something you may have said or done or left undone is inappropriate. Of course, you have the power to override your inner guidance system, and chances are you do it all the time. Everyone does. Have you ever caught yourself saying, "Why didn't I listen to myself?" It is only natural to get caught in the battle between your ego and your conscience. One is authoritative and looking for instant satisfaction, while the other wants to do the right thing.

Your inner guidance system is loaded with intuitive knowledge. It knows the answers to your deepest questions, and if you will take the time to listen, you will hear them. It is better to have doubt than to race blindly forward with a false sense of security. Remember that the drive of your free will is the stuff that resurfaces in your karma of the future.

Building Trust and Confidence

It takes time to build trust and confidence in your inner guidance system. It is the same as developing any other skill. It takes patience and the willingness to risk making mistakes as you work toward your goals. Many people are overwhelmed easily and give up because the end goal seems unobtainable.

Over the past twenty years there has been a movement to help individuals build confidence in themselves to face challenges in life that they never thought they could. Businessmen participate in fire walks just to prove to themselves they have what it takes. Outward Bound programs challenge participants on treks through the wilderness, over the ocean, or up steep rock cliffs. The common goal is to help you realize that you are capable of facing any situation in life, whether it is career-oriented or personal.

The key to developing your trust and confidence is to start with one step at a time. If you only focus on an obstacle that is too big to climb, you will never have the opportunity to get to the top. If you work toward a small and easily achievable goal, when you reach it, you will have accomplished your short-range objective. You will then have more confidence that you can make it to your next goal. And before you know it, you have accomplished your long-term goal.

These small reachable goals are usually in tune with your inner guidance system. Each step of the way provides a balance. Giving yourself permission to take a small risk, and knowing that you have a safety net created by past success, you will become better and better at reaching toward the unknown. There is a great thrill of adventure when you are traveling in sync with your life map, in tune with your inner guidance system.

Paying Attention

As you learn to pay attention to the messages from your inner guidance system—and to be on the lookout for the external assistance you receive—you will become more accepting of the unknown. In fact, you will eventually find yourself expecting to get a communication or validation that confirms you are on course with your life map. Your confidence will come as you identify your own psychic channels when you progress through the chapters in this book.

Paying attention does not mean that you race about trying to force the validations. They will come to you at the time you need them, which is not necessarily the time you think you need them. Most people feel pressured to find the answers they think they should know. It is possible that there may be others involved in the work you are doing for the Universe, and they may be out of sync with their potential.

When you create false messages and signs for yourself, you may get confused and miss the real message. This is especially true as you develop your psychic talent. You may try to read into something that isn't there. Many people who first discover their psychic abilities put their antenna up higher than is needed, and they get interference.

When you follow signs that aren't signs, you may run into resistance. Pay attention—the roadblock that frustrates you so much may really be there to help you get back on the right path.

QUESTION?

What is resistance?
It is something that holds you back from what you want to accomplish and may actually be working in your best interests. Your psychic development can work hand in hand with resistances rather than in conflict with them. Remember the hologram concept. Everything has more than one dimension. Be sure to look at both views.

Take Time to Listen

It is important to pay attention to your inner guidance system. As you have read, every moment can bring new messages to guide and protect you. The messages may come to you in one or more of the five senses. You might get a picture in your mind or hear a voice in your head. You may get a feeling that something is right or something is wrong. You may think of someone you should call, write to, or visit. You may get a feeling that you should do something, and though you act on the feeling, you don't know why you did it until afterward.

Your messages may come to you at any time, including when you're least expecting them. It could happen while you are asleep, or while you are walking, reading, or watching television. It is very easy not to pay attention, but the more aware you are, the more open your line of communication to your inner guidance system will be.

Developing Your Connection

To tune in to your inner guidance system, you need to practice. The more you focus on developing your intuitive gifts, the more they will respond to you. If you can find a regular time once a day when you can focus on communicating with your unconscious and your Universal Mind, you will develop a habit of connecting to your inner guidance system. You will add a posthypnotic suggestion to help you with this automatic process.

If you would like to try this exercise, find a comfortable place, either sitting or lying down, loosen your clothes, take a deep breath of air, and slowly exhale. You may now focus on your third eye. As you slowly breathe in and out, you may be aware that you have many muscles; some of them are tight, and some of them are relaxed.

The more you allow the tight muscles to relax, the more relaxed you will become. In a few moments you may count down from five to zero, feeling yourself going deeper and deeper with each number. As you go deeper and deeper, you will feel your connection to your third eye becoming stronger and stronger.

Feel the Connection

As you feel the connection getting stronger, you will be aware that you are receiving a beam of light and energy that is flowing into your third eye from the Universe. This beam is good and positive, and it flows freely into your inner guidance system, carrying the wisdom of your soul.

If you are ready, you may start with the first number:

5. You are going deeper and deeper into the Universal Flow. Breathe slowly in and out as you feel the connection through your third eye getting stronger and stronger.
4. You are feeling the Universal Flow as it is received by your inner guidance system. You feel more and more relaxed with each count.
3. You may feel the vibrations of the Universe. As you go to the next number, you are more and more in tune with the flow.
2. You are getting closer and closer. Your breathing relaxes more and more. You are going deeper and deeper.
1. You are almost at the point of a deep and powerful connection to the Universal Mind. You look forward to the last number as you take another breath and go deeper and deeper.
0. You are one with your Universal Mind and your inner guidance system.

Now that the connection is complete, take a few moments to enjoy the strength and peace of the Universe. You may think of many thoughts or concentrate on just one. If you need help or guidance or have a worry, ask the Universal Mind to provide assistance and affirmation that you are in tune with your life map.

Enjoy the Connection

You may receive visual images, hear voices, get a certain feeling, or experience a certain smell or taste. You may get many pieces of information or experience nothing at all. Whatever happens is right for you at the time. Allow yourself to feel good, as you remain connected to the Universal Mind.

If you have a specific belief, you may communicate with it. Give yourself a key word or a touch with a finger to remind you later of how you can experience this positive feeling any time. When you're ready, count yourself back up to five, awaking relaxed and in tune with your inner guidance system. It is possible that you may have answers when you return, or they may take time. Remember—always be ready to receive.

Your own answer may come from within yourself in the form of a dream, or it may just "pop out" of your unconscious mind. It could come when you are offering advice to others, and yet the message may be for yourself. It could appear as a recurring thought that you just can't get out of your mind until you address it.

External Messages and Synchronicity

In addition to your channel of internal communication, you have an external guidance system of old souls who have completed their life journeys and wait to assist you. As Edgar Cayce said, the external guidance system is an "invisible empire" that exists around you.

Your external guidance system comes from the outside. It is a form of external communication from another person or entity. For instance, you may see auras or energies around others that allow you to receive helpful information. Or you may get a warning from a particular person or even from a geographic location.

Remember, these communications from the Universe can materialize at any time in almost any form imaginable, from a cloud in the sky to an encounter with an animal. All you need to do is pay attention.

Experiences of Synchronicity

One kind of external guidance experience is synchronicity. Have you ever found yourself in the right place at the right time? For some reason, exactly when you most need it, the phone rings with an answer to a dilemma. Perhaps it's an unexpected amount of money that you receive just in time to hold off a financial disaster. It could come in the mail, from a lottery ticket, from a long-forgotten debt someone owes you, or as a gift.

It could be that there's an item you desperately need, one that has been in your mind and possibly in your prayers. Sometimes what is needed materializes in such a subtle way that it is hardly recognized. You might be wishing for a new car when what you actually needed was the secondhand car you received.

It is very easy to overlook synchronicity. It happens so naturally that it may not even be noticed. It's like watching a magician intently so that you may learn the trick. The magic happens right under your nose while you are focused on something else.

Someone Is Watching Over You

Are forces like synchronicity and the other external forms that your messages take all just coincidence, luck, or fate? Or is there something else involved? Perhaps you already know that someone is watching out for you. Or maybe you don't believe that there is anything at all.

Do you think that there is a being or a force that the Universe centers upon? Is there a divine purpose or a higher ideal for mankind to get in touch with? Is there a general plan for the cosmos?

ALERT!

It's all right to believe your own way. After all, that belief is already inside you. It is okay for you to compare anything you read in this book to your own feelings. The important thing is that it feels right for you.

If you have something or someone looking out for you, do you know who or what it is? You may know exactly, or you may have no idea. Just the possibility that there is something creates the opportunity for hope. You may be comfortable in a specific religion and have conversations with the Divinity to whom you turn for guidance. You may go to the seashore or the mountains and communicate with nature.

Other people believe in guardian angels who are said to watch over us. You may connect these angels to someone in your family or a friend who has passed on to the Other Side. They may come to you in your dreams, or you may feel their presence, especially in times of need.

Many Catholics accept the belief in patron saints, and they rely on these saints for help. Some saints are known for bringing about specific miracles, such as healing. There are shrines for these saints filled with crutches as testimony that the cure was instantaneous. (E)

Chapter 4

Keep Yourself Grounded

The most important aspect of your psychic growth is developing the ability to keep yourself grounded or balanced. To do that, you need to let go of your fears and discover the support of your Belief, a divinity or higher power whose existence you believe in, whether because of your religion or personal conviction. At the end of the chapter, you will learn an exercise for surrounding yourself with the protective golden light of the Universe and tethering yourself to the ground with the golden thread.

Letting Go of Your Fears

Opening up to your psychic ability can be overwhelming if you are not prepared. This problem is especially evident in children and teenagers. Their first encounters usually happen without warning, and they are left confused and afraid of the unknown. Many spend the rest of their lives trying to run away from their natural gifts.

When Josh was young, he was given the opportunity to try dowsing with a forked stick. The pull of the stick was so strong that it scared him. He dropped it, and ran away. When he finally tried again as an adult, he had lost his ability to dowse. Many others have had similar experiences with different kinds of psychic talents. Perhaps you are one of them.

ALERT!

It is very easy when you first start developing your psychic gifts to become overwhelmed with what you encounter. If that happens, you need to stop, take a deep breath, and go back to a nonpsychic activity.

Internal Self-Doubt

Opening yourself up to self-doubt can lead to confusion. The doubt begins when you do not have a clear belief that your psychic abilities have been given to you for the good of the Universe. You can create the doubt in yourself, or others can create the doubt in you.

Often, self-doubt is the result of fear. It is in your human nature to try to avoid the unknown, which by nature includes some potentially dangerous situations. But when you run from fear, it follows you and grows in proportion to your retreat. Most often you are afraid without knowing what you are afraid of. It is this fear of the unknown that can paralyze your psychic development.

Fear of the unknown can eat away at your whole being. It can prevent you from moving forward along your life map. It can bring you face to face with old unresolved karma. Fear can rear its ugly head at any moment. It can manifest itself through your unconscious mind.

When you are hit by a fear that comes from psychic intuition, you may feel very alone because you are highly aware of your difference from others and cannot confide in anyone. Many suffer in silence for years, and sometimes they take their secret fear of the unknown to their graves. As you continue through this book, you will have the opportunity to understand and resolve any fear of the psychic that you may have.

The Influence of Others

Equally damaging is advice from well-meaning people who are consumed by their own fears. If you confide in them, these people may tell you that your psychic gifts are weird or even evil. They are quick to advise you about something they do not understand. The fears of others are just as toxic to you as your own—they will contribute to your own fears and may smother your psychic gifts.

A negative reaction can increase your self-doubt. As long as you let yourself be open to the fears of other people, you run the danger of internalizing them. An unbalanced and ungrounded person may absorb another person's fears instantly, losing self-confidence that is replaced with self-doubt.

As you learn how to ground yourself and find your balance, you will be able to react to fear in a different way. You will learn to move aside and get out of the line of fire of other people's fears. You can find security in your psychic intuition and learn to trust your personal guidance system. You can replace doubt with trust.

Staying Focused

Have you ever looked at a hologram? A hologram is a picture that contains two (usually contrasting) images. If you stare at the one, you won't be able to see the other. The key is for you not to focus on what you are looking at until the second image emerges from the first. Some are easy to see as you turn the picture. Others require that you let your eyes go out of focus until you see the images. Some of you may not be able to see two distinct pictures. Inversely, some of you may see two images in a picture that has only one.

Every set of eyes sees differently. Some people are colorblind, some are near-sighted, and some have trouble focusing. Many famous artists paint in distinct styles dictated by the way they see, the way they experience their reality. An art critic seeing the work through his own eyes can't always understand the artist's perspective.

ALERT!

Magicians misdirect your attention while they complete their magic tricks. You are seeing only what they want you to see. If you knew how the trick worked, it would be simple to see. You can allow the same thing to happen to you mentally when you misdirect your attention and focus on the wrong image.

Big Picture, Little Picture

There are two ways to focus the mind: the big picture and the little picture. As with a hologram, if you focus on only one, you may fail to see the other. As you have already read, when you focus on fear and self-doubt, you may fail to see love and the strength of the Universe. When you fail to separate your role from that of the whole Universe, you can lose focus of your own life map.

If you can only see the big picture, you are detaching yourself from your inner guidance system. You may be keeping yourself at such a distance that you are unable to take an active role in the work of the Universe. It is possible that you will not take the risk of self-improvement even though you know that is what you need to do. This inaction may cause you to feel paralyzed and unable to get on track with your life map.

When you only see the little picture, you become responsible for all of the Universe's work. You keep repeating karmic patterns over and over again and fail to see how you have an opportunity to learn, grow, and change. You are weighed down with the responsibility of not only solving your own problems, but everyone else's too. If you are like this, then you already know that others will constantly bombard you with their problems. They leave feeling better while you are left cleaning up their mess.

Divine Assistance

To help you keep grounded and in balance, you can count on some help. If you participate in an organized religion, you can rely on the divinity or divinities of that belief system. In fact, many psychics belong to an organized religion. Your psychic ability is a part of your very soul, as ancient as any religion. God, as that being is understood by most modern religions, is a part of all that is good. The Divine works for the betterment of mankind—that is, God's role is that of the Universal Mind.

It is also possible that you cannot define exactly what you believe. It may be that you see God as a part of nature—the oceans, forests, mountains, and all living things on the earth and in the sky. That is okay as long as you believe that there is something, somewhere in the Universe, that is a positive force that watches over you and others. Whoever that being or higher power is, that is your Belief.

Can You Explain It?

If you do not have an organized religion, what or whom do you believe in? Do you believe that there is a Divinity somewhere in the Universe? Do you believe that you have a soul? Do you believe in the powers of good and evil? Do you believe that you have a purpose in life?

Can you define your Belief in your own words ? Take a few moments to consider your answers. How would you explain your Belief to anyone else? How comfortable are you defining your Belief?

Remember that it's okay not to have definite answers for these questions. This exercise is to help you become aware and work toward identifying your Belief. It is already inside you. You were born with it, and all your actions and thoughts are either in tune with it or not.

Do you believe in miracles? And if you do, how often are you aware of them happening around you? Are you aware of them daily or only occasionally?

Communication with Your Belief

Do you rely on angels, saints, or other beings to work their good? Do you look to something to protect you from both the known and the unknown? Can you turn there when you are faced with an unknown fear?

Do you communicate with your Belief on a daily basis, just when you remember to, or only at times when you are asking for something? Do you feel that you and this higher power are compatible and in tune with each other, or do you feel as if you are in conflict?

An Exercise of Contemplation

Here is an exercise to help you contemplate your Belief. If you choose to try it, take a few moments to get comfortable; then allow yourself to take a deep breath, exhale, and relax. You may count yourself down from five to zero and feel yourself connected to your inner guidance system. (Each time you relax, it is always different—sometimes in a deep focus and sometimes not.)

As you count yourself down, you may suggest that with each count you will feel more and more relaxed and in tune with your inner guidance system. You may allow yourself to feel a connection to your Belief, whether you know exactly what it is or not. If you are still unsure, then allow yourself to be open to the positive flow of the Universe. When you reach zero, give yourself some time to feel a positive connection to your Belief. If you have concerns for yourself or others or for the development of your psychic gifts, you may turn them over to your Belief for resolution and guidance.

After you have spent some time contemplating your Belief, you may take a deep breath, exhale, and count yourself slowly upward to five and the surface of your mind. When you get back to five, take another breath, exhale, and come back to your conscious mind. It is okay to include this communication in your daily relaxation exercises.

Anchor Your Connection

You can give yourself a mental or physical anchor while you are relaxed and connected to your Belief. Put your thumb and finger together and squeeze lightly. As you do this, you may suggest to yourself that whenever you repeat this action, you will feel connected to your Belief. The level of connection will always be at the focus level that is positive and aware. In other words, if you are driving a car, you will always be alert and awake when you trigger your anchor.

The same effect can be obtained if you use a verbal anchor. A verbal anchor may be a specific word as simple as "Believe." Other types of anchors may be auditory (a specific sound), olfactory (a certain smell), or mental (the memory of a particular smell). It could even be the positive feeling you get when you are in a special place.

QUESTION?

What is an anchor?

An anchor is a neurolinguistic program (NLP) word for the process of recalling and experiencing a suggestion given while in a relaxed trance state. A touch or key word is introduced and practiced so that when it is used after the trance state has ended, the same result will be experienced again. NLP is a hypnotic technique that can bring about positive changes by installing new positive mental images in the unconscious mind.

An anchor is a way to instantly experience a positive connection to your Belief. The more you practice making this connection, the easier it will be for you to make. If you consciously practice triggering your anchors, you will begin to do it automatically within a short period of time. The more comfortable you become communicating with your Belief, the more confidence you will have in it. It is part of the key to your psychic development.

It is possible that you may already be using negative anchors, probably without any conscious awareness on your part at all. They can trigger your self-doubt. When you are connected to your psychic ability, a negative anchor may trigger and bring back an old fear or doubt. If this is the case for you, then you may use your positive belief anchor to reframe a negative one.

One concept of NLP is that the brain is like a computer—it operates on the program that has been installed in it unless a different program is installed. A "reframe" is the installation of a new mental program. This is accomplished when the unconscious mind is open to the new suggestion.

Work with Your Belief

Once you have become comfortable communicating with your Belief, you are ready to begin working with it. To begin, this means establishing a communication connection that can either remain open or be opened instantly, whenever you wish, by triggering your belief anchor(s). Your Belief is part of your inner guidance system, and when you are open to its communication, you are also working with your psychic abilities.

As you develop a partnership with your Belief, you will also become more in tune with your life purpose. This partnership is necessary for your life work—what you do during your lifetime that provides an opportunity for mankind to benefit in ways that help you and others progress in their life maps.

A great way to connect with your Belief instantly is to go through your third eye. Just feel the vibration in the middle of your forehead and believe. Take a deep breath, and exhale to add to a relaxed positive state. It is something you can do anytime. No one around you will be aware of it, except perhaps another psychic who may be observing your aura.

For those of you grounded in the Christian faith, do you know what the centermost verse in the entire Bible is? It is from the Book of Psalms, verse 118:8, and it states, "It is better to trust in the Lord than to put confidence in man."

Ask for Protection

It is very important for your psychic development to be protected by your Belief. Protection is the key for finding balance. It keeps you grounded and free from being paralyzed by your fears. Protection is the strength of your connection to your Belief.

Protection happens as you learn to cloak yourself in the strong, flexible fabric of your Belief. Protection is connecting yourself to your Belief and filling yourself with Universal Love, no matter what transpires around you. Protection takes place when you work with your invisible team. Proof of protection comes with the miracles that take place around you.

Protection can come in the form of a golden light that flows from the Universe. It is something that you can always take with you. You can connect with it by using your anchors. It too is part of your inner guidance system, and it keeps you in tune with your life map. Your psychic intuition is part of your inner guidance system, which also can protect you.

The Golden Light of the Universe

You can do the following exercise to receive the golden light protection from the Universal Mind, which can help you find your balance. This light comes through your Belief. It can help you dissociate and step back to get the whole view of any situation that you find yourself in or need to address. If you are ready to try it, find a comfortable place, take a deep breath, exhale, and allow yourself to relax. You may first try this exercise by counting down. However, as you learn how to develop an anchor, you can connect with your golden light anytime you want.

Once you become comfortable with your golden light, it can become part of your partnership with the Universal Mind and a powerful tool to keep you grounded and in balance. The golden light may be any color you would like, or it can be just a clear positive energy. It can give you the feeling of being wrapped in a beautiful secure blanket, just as you may have experienced as a child.

The golden light protection exercise is designed to help you develop a safe and secure feeling in your Belief. You are free to incorporate any image that helps you reach that state.

Count Down and Spread the Light

As you breathe slowly in and out, you may be aware that you have many muscles throughout your body. Some are tight and some are loose. Each time you feel a muscle stiffen, you may relax it, and as you are doing so, you may relax more and more. You may be aware of different muscles stiffening and relaxing as you experience this golden light exercise.

Feel yourself connecting to your third eye as you slowly focus on your breathing. You may be aware of different sounds around you. You may notice that you have many different thoughts coming into your head, and if so, that's okay. You may feel your third eye as it is connected to your Universal Mind and as it opens to the Universal Flow. As you count yourself down, feel the beautiful golden light surround you and spread throughout your body:

5. You may feel and see in your mind's eye a beautiful golden light that starts to flow through your third eye and down over your forehead, your face, and the back of your head. It flows all the way down to your neck. It is a wonderful, secure, and loving light filled with all the positive vibrations of the Universe.

4. You may now feel this golden light spreading over your shoulders, down your arms to your elbows, and down your forearms, wrists, and through to your fingertips. It is a wonderfully relaxing, safe, and secure feeling. You feel the energy of the Universe flowing through and over and around your head, shoulders, arms, and fingers. As you slowly breathe in and out and feel the Universal Flow, you will go deeper and deeper into a safe, secure, and relaxed state.

3. You may feel your golden light spreading slowly down over your chest to your waist. You may feel it as it flows over the upper half of your body, wrapping you in a beautiful secure blanket of golden light. As

you breathe slowly in and out, you will become more and more comfortable with this loving flow of the Universe. You are going deeper and deeper.

2. You may feel the golden light spreading down to your knees. You are in a beautiful and secure capsule of Universal Love and positive energy. As you breathe slowly in and out, you will relax more and more, and go deeper and deeper into your connection with the Universal Mind.

1. You will feel the golden light flow all the way down from your third eye to your ankles. You are almost totally immersed in the love and positive energy of the Universe. You feel comfortable, safe, and secure as you go deeper and deeper, marveling at the beauty and love of your golden universal light.

0. You are now totally immersed in your beautiful and secure golden light sent to you from the Universal Mind. You may feel this flow going through your whole body and surrounding you as a golden blanket of yellow light. Take a few moments and enjoy this beautiful, loving energy.

There are several ways in which you can experience the golden light exercise. You may read it out loud to yourself, memorize it, have someone else read it to you, or tape it and play it back to yourself.

Universal Protection for the Mind, Body, and Soul

While you are in this beautiful and secure state, allow yourself to feel the loving energy of the Universe as it wraps you in a protective bubble of golden light. You may connect with any of your guides, angels, or other beings with whom you have identified so far in your psychic journey. You may communicate with your Divinity, saints, or other positive religious beliefs. You may feel at this time that you are not alone in your journey through your life map, and you may know that your Universal Team will be with you to help and guide you every step of your way. (Chapter 7 describes your Universal Team in more detail.)

If you have any worries or questions for the Universal Mind, you may ask that you receive the proper help and guidance. You may ask that you will be given the proper tools to help stay in tune with your life map. You may request that the golden light protect you against the forces that would control your mind, your body, and your soul. You may ask that you receive protection against any other who would use his or her psychic gifts against you.

You may cloak yourself in the Golden Light of the Universe as you become more in tune with your psychic gifts. You may open to the Universe's guidance for the proper development and use of your psychic abilities. You may feel safe and protected by the Golden Light of the Universe as you give permission for your psychic gifts to be developed and used in a way that is good for mankind. Take a few moments as you breathe slowly in and out and feel the love and positive energy of your golden protective light.

You may give yourself a key word or physical anchor to help you connect to your light at any moment. While you are still in your protected state, try out your anchors. Practice focusing on your third eye and instantly feel the golden light start to flow. Take one more moment to feel your special connection and then slowly count yourself back up to five, opening your eyes and feeling relaxed, calm, positive, full of Universal Love, and still bathed in the Golden Light of the Universe.

ALERT!

Many beginner psychics can be startled when they first release themselves into the Universal Flow. As long as you have a connection to where you are, you will return safely. In other words, you will always know where the "ground" is.

Find Your Golden Thread

While you're immersed in the golden light, it is very natural to feel as if you can float up into the Universe. In fact you may begin to experience yourself lifting out of your body. If you're not prepared, it can really unsettle you. Similar experiences have turned away many first-time psychic floaters. As you have learned earlier in the chapter, the unknown can be terrifying.

As you feel yourself filling with your golden light, also see and feel a golden thread that extends down from the Universe and that is firmly anchored to the earth through you. This thread is strong enough to tether you to the ground. You may feel secure and safe if you begin to float up into the Universe because you will know that you can always follow the golden thread back to your place on earth. (There is a term that identifies this floating up out of your body. It is called astral projection. You can find more information on astral projection in Chapter 11.)

This is a good exercise for you to practice. Take it slow, venturing only a small distance at first until you feel safe and secure with your golden thread tether. Each time you try, you may become more confident and comfortable with your direct connection to the Universal Mind, the keeper of your soul's memories and the holder of the knowledge of your psychic gifts.

As you progress in your psychic development, you may want to review this chapter from time to time so that you may remind yourself of your Belief and the safety of the Golden Light of the Universe. Your life may be full of little bumps and turns. Staying grounded will help you navigate along your life map.

Chapter 5

Psychic Development Training

I n this chapter, you will learn about your mental makeup and how your particular mind processes the input you receive through your five senses. By identifying your mental strengths, you can use them to enter a self-hypnotic trance and conduct other powerful exercises that will help you get in touch with your third eye and the Golden Light of the Universe, so that you may make progress in your psychic development.

The Five Senses

You have five different ways of experiencing what takes place around you. You see, you hear, you feel (both by touch and emotion), you taste, and you smell. Some of you may be lacking in one or more of these sense receivers. It is possible that you might be blind, deaf, or have no sense of smell or taste.

FACT

Just as your physical genetic makeup is different from anyone else's in the world, so is your mental makeup. Understanding your mental makeup will help you communicate better, not only with yourself, but also with others. You will be able to explain your own mind and understand how someone else's mental makeup works. This will help you get your message across more easily and more effectively.

When one of these senses is lacking, another one takes over. A blind man usually has a strong ability to hear and feel. Someone who lacks the sense of taste will rely on food textures for enjoyment. Sometimes a sense is overdeveloped, and it is hard to filter out the stimulation received through that sense. The overstimulation of one sense can cause you to go out of focus and to become unbalanced and ungrounded.

As you consider how you process information through your senses, you will find that you rely on some input more than on other. You may be very strong in one sensory arena and perhaps weak or have no input at all in another. The object is to identify how your mind works, not how to modify it to fit a certain format. Remember, there is no one else like you on this earth. You are unique and special.

Sense-Imagery Exercises

To help you figure out what senses you most rely on, you may try the following sense-imagery exercises. These exercises do not require privacy. In fact, you can try them with a friend or a small group. After you are done, you can compare the differences in your responses among yourselves.

As you identify your mental makeup, take note of the positive images you can produce. These images can be an aid in deepening your self-hypnotic trances. The more you allow yourself to experience the positive feelings that they generate, the deeper you will go into trance.

Your Sense of Vision

Vision is the most commonly used sense for communication because most people are highly visual. Would you like to find out if you are, too? When you are ready, find a comfortable place, take a deep breath, exhale, and focus on your third eye. Then, consider the following questions.

Can you imagine picture images in your mind? If so, are they in color, black-and-white, or somewhere in between? Are they clear, bright, and in focus, or are they unclear and out of focus? Can you change the picture, such as seeing it in a different time, either in the past or in the future? Do you see it as a movie or as a still photograph?

Can you rewind a moving picture in your mind and watch it again, or stop it and focus on a single frame? Can you move the picture, bring it closer, push it farther away, or change the angle? Can you view it from above or from a lower position?

FACT

There are two types of visual images: experienced and dissociated. "To dissociate" means to be apart from the picture without feeling any emotions in connection with it. Some of you can dissociate from an image in your mind, and some of you cannot. It is good for you to know your image ability as you work on psychic development.

Can you see yourself in the picture? Can you see the picture without seeing yourself? Can you see yourself at a different age, either younger or older? Can you see colors around people in your imagination? Can you see energy forms or other elements in your mind?

Your Sense of Hearing

Next, you can examine your sense of hearing. Can you imagine sounds in your head? If so, what are they? Can you imagine music or sounds of nature, such as birds singing or the sounds of the ocean? Can you turn the volume up or down in your mind?

Can you hear conversations taking place in your head? Can you hear your own voice? Do these voices talk to you, and are they part of something other than yourself? Can you have a discussion with a voice in your head?

Can you see a picture in your mind and hear the sounds that go with it? Can you put yourself in the picture image and move around and hear sounds or conversations from different locations? Can you watch the image as if it were a movie or a video and still be able to hear the sound? Do you picture guides or other beings who talk to you?

ALERT!

If you have voices in your mind that are persistently negative and create bad thoughts for you, you should seek out a licensed mental health professional in your area for proper guidance.

What You Feel

It is also important to examine your feelings. Can you imagine emotions? Are you able to experience feelings such as happiness, loneliness, or sadness in your mind? Can you intensify and weaken these emotions at will? Can you imagine visual pictures that create emotional feelings in yourself? Can you disconnect your emotions from the images in your mind? Can you step in and out of the scene, feeling and then not feeling the emotions connected to it, as you wish?

Can you feel the emotions of different people in a visual image? Is it easy to be overcome by emotional images in your mind? Do you connect emotions to certain sounds or music? Do you feel emotions in certain places or objects? Can you connect seeing, hearing, and emotional feelings in the same image?

Can you imagine feeling positive, negative, or healing energy in your mind's images? Can you imagine positive energies going through your body? Can you feel energy in terms of certain colors? Can you put yourself inside one of your mental images and imagine feeling temperatures, textures, and the weight of different objects? Could you feel the length of hair or the texture of the clothes being worn?

FACT

The sense of feeling is called the kinesthetic sense. You experience your kinesthetic information in two different ways: internally, as an emotional process, and externally, as a tactile or touch experience.

Can you combine emotions and your sense of touch? Can you connect the kinesthetic sense to the visual and hearing senses? Can you dissociate and watch a visual and sound image, and yet feel the emotions and certain touches? Can you step in and out of the image and see, hear, and feel it in your mind?

Your Senses of Smell and Taste

Can you imagine smells in your mind? Can you add smells to a mind's image? Can you put yourself in that picture and move around, and experience different smells? Can you intensify or weaken smells in your mind?

Can you connect smells with emotional feelings, or with sounds, foods, nature, or other mind images? Can you connect smells and tastes? Can you picture foods and connect tastes with them? Can you imagine eating a meal and tasting the different ingredients? Can you feel different emotions connected to different tastes?

ESSENTIAL

Now it's time to put all your senses together. Can you step into an image in your mind, and see, hear, feel, taste, and smell? Can you move about experiencing a wide variety of sensory images? Can you intensify or decrease all of your imagery? Can you step in and out of all of your sensory images?

A Self-Hypnosis Trance

Now that you have explored how your imagery recall works and what senses work best for you, it may be time to learn how to use some relaxation exercises to go into a self-hypnotic trance. This self-hypnosis exercise is designed for you to count yourself downward and deep inside yourself, to a place where you feel the Universal Energy that flows through your connection to the Universal Mind. It is in that place, deep inside you, that you are connected with the Universe; through that place, you become the open channel.

This exercise is designed to help you use your sense imagery to build an even stronger link through your third eye to your unconscious and your Universal Mind. By anticipating and recalling a positive memory experience, you put yourself in your "comfort zone." This process also helps sharpen your focus on something that is positive and relaxing.

You may also incorporate trance elements of the exercises from the previous chapters. The more you focus on the image of a positive relaxing experience, the more you open yourself to the Universal Energy. Your psychic gifts are a natural part of this process. As you allow them to be open to the Universal Flow, you will get psychic messages that are much clearer.

Focusing on a Place

To begin, you may loosen your clothing and find a comfortable place to sit or lie down. Now, think of your favorite relaxing place. You may have a special place that you like to go to in your unconscious mind. This may be an actual place from earlier in your life, or it may be a place you currently enjoy. It could be an image of an activity or a sport that you enjoy experiencing or watching. It could be reading or watching television. Anything that you can feel that is positive can help deepen your focus.

This place could be outside or inside, real or imaginary—a place that is calm, relaxing, positive, and safe. If your mind works well with the sense of hearing, imagine relaxing sounds that you would hear in this place. If it would be helpful, you may also add feelings, tastes, and smells to your mind's image.

ALERT!

When you focus on a familiar and positive image, you are much more receptive to it. The more you accept its reality, the deeper into the image you can go. This process is like priming a pump. Once information starts to reach you, it will flow easier and easier. This will help you as you experience the different psychic development exercises described in the chapters ahead.

Your comfortable place in your mind may also be a place that is imaginary. It may have originated in your dreams or from another source. You may not even have an image at all, just a feeling deep inside yourself. You may see colors or feel energy or hear a relaxing sound. A relaxing smell can be a major factor in facilitating a deep self-hypnotic trance.

Focusing on Your Senses

As you focus on your breathing, imagine that you are inhaling your favorite relaxing smell. If you want, you can use a smell such as incense or a candle to help you focus on your breathing. You may remind yourself that each time you smell this relaxing aroma, you will enjoy it more and more.

FACT

If you practice a simple exercise like this every day, you may be amazed at how it can help you relax and stay in balance. It is also helpful in conditioning your mind to go into deeper trance states that are comfortable and positive.

If you have a favorite relaxing color, you may add that to your breathing by feeling the peaceful energy every time you inhale and exhale. You may also imagine your favorite relaxing music or sounds as you breathe in and out. You may feel positive waves of energy flowing throughout your body with each slow comfortable breath you take. You may feel your muscles relaxing as these waves flow through and over you.

You may picture your image in color as full and beautiful as you can imagine. You may watch your image, or you may step into it, experiencing all its relaxing feelings. You may move around in your image and experience many different things. You may sit back and enjoy yourself as if you were being entertained at a play or movie. Just enjoy yourself for a few moments, and when you're ready, take a deep breath and open your eyes, feeling relaxed and positive.

You don't need to count yourself down when you practice sensory imagery, but you can develop a scent anchor that will help you go into a light trance by recalling the smell and taking a deep breath of it. You can also use your third-eye focus to help you go deeper and get a clearer image.

Connect to Your Psychic Abilities

Now that you are able to go into a trance, you can use it to help you develop your psychic abilities. As you put yourself into a trance, you can combine your sensory image strengths that are part of your natural mental makeup with your third eye and your Belief and guidance systems. As you perform this exercise, remember that your way of making this connection is unique, and the script that you build for yourself is unique as well.

Creating a Script

A script is an induction read by a hypnotist to his subject to induce a trance state. It contains key words and a progressive, ever-deepening language pattern. As you are your own hypnotist, you have control of your own script.

You can write out your script if you want and make changes to it as you repeat the exercise. You can tape it, or you might choose to have someone read it to you. At first you may want to work on only one portion at a time, at least until you get comfortable with each section. You can always use aids, such as recorded music or other sounds, that help induce a trance for you. The more you practice, the easier it will be to enter a deeper state of relaxation.

Prepare Yourself

This exercise will require between ten and twenty minutes of your time. If you can plan a time when you are likely to have the fewest interruptions, the calm will help you develop your focus. If there are others who might try to interrupt, you might consider asking them to help by not bothering you for a few minutes.

Start the exercise by choosing a place where you can relax. Begin to get comfortable. Take a deep breath of your favorite relaxing smell and slowly exhale. As you continue to breathe in and out slowly, let your eyes and mind focus upward to your third eye. When you're ready, let your eyes close, and let yourself feel your connection to your third eye becoming stronger and stronger. Feel yourself drifting farther and farther away from your surroundings while still knowing where you are.

Spend a few moments just enjoying where you are. As you relax, you may anticipate yourself going deeper in a few moments. You may let your muscles relax as you breathe in and out. You may imagine your favorite sounds and smells and let them deepen your relaxation even more. Any conscious thoughts you have may come and go as you allow yourself to relax.

ALERT!

If for some reason an exercise makes you uncomfortable, just open your eyes and think of something positive. Then you can feel free to resume your daily activity. You may also remind yourself that you will go to a trance depth that is appropriate for the moment and that, in trance, you will be aware of your surroundings.

Counting Down

You may now feel your third-eye connection—the Golden Light of the Universe—as it prepares to spread throughout your body. You may feel very positive and relaxed as you enjoy its protective energy. If you are ready, you may begin counting downward from five to zero as you prepare to experience a pleasant memory image in all your five senses. It may be the same image every time or a different one, real or imaginary:

5. Take a deep breath and feel the golden light from the Universe begin to spread down through your third eye over your forehead, eyes, nose, cheeks, back of your head, mouth, chin, and neck, to your shoulders. You may feel yourself sinking deeper and deeper as though you were descending a stairway to the center of your unconscious and through to your Universal Mind. With each step, you will go deeper and deeper as your connection gets stronger and stronger.

4. You may now feel the golden light spread over your shoulders and down your upper arms, your elbows, forearms, wrists, and fingers, all the way to the fingertips. As you breathe in and out, you may feel yourself going deeper and deeper. You may relax more and more as you feel the protective energy of the Universe.

3. You may feel yourself going deeper as you feel the golden light spread down over the upper part of your body, over your chest and back, and all the way to your waist. You may also feel yourself wrapped in the protective bubble of Universal Energy. You may focus on your favorite sound or smell as you slowly breathe in and out. You feel the third eye and the connection to the Universe is even stronger and stronger as you feel the power of the positive protective energy that flows through you. You are going deeper and deeper.

2. The positive energy of the Universe is now spreading all the way down to your knees as you feel yourself going deeper and deeper. Any positive imagery you experience is getting clearer and clearer as you focus on the beauty and powerful energy of the Universal Mind. You may feel yourself sinking deeper and deeper inside as you continue going down to the place where you are in full contact with the Universe. It is a place where you can feel safe and protected, far away from the conscious world around you.

1. You are almost at that special place. You may feel the golden light spreading down to your ankles as you go deeper and deeper. You

feel your focus becoming clearer and clearer as you drift away from your conscious thoughts. The protective energy flows around and through you.

0. You are in a deep state of communication with the Universal Mind. You feel yourself totally wrapped in the protective energy of the universal golden light that is spreading throughout your entire body.

Develop Your Focus

Take a few moments to enjoy the protective energy of the Universe. When you are ready, focus on a positive visual image from either your memory or from your imagination. Allow this image to become clearer and clearer in your focus. You may add in your other senses, that is, your sense of hearing, feeling, tasting, and smelling. The more you experience, the more you will feel the powerful, protective energy of the Universal Mind. You are in a beautiful golden bubble of universal light.

This is an excellent method to help you strengthen your focus. At zero, you can practice getting clear images in each one of the five senses. Try changing your perspective as you experience your image. The more comfortable you become, the more it will help your psychic development.

Feel yourself moving about in your image. You may choose simply to watch, or you may experience all the positive sensations connected with it. Feel yourself totally connected to your Belief and all the universal knowledge that is there to help and guide you through your life map. Breathe slowly in and out as you focus on your positive, relaxing images. You are far removed from your conscious analytical mind.

Exploring Your Senses

Let yourself focus in on your visual image. You may be able to see colors or energy. Whatever you see, remember that it is positive and compatible with the universal golden light. Put yourself in the image, and then let yourself watch from a distance. Each time you experience it, you will see something that is important to focus on. Continue to breathe in and out, feeling relaxed and connected to the protective energy of the Universe.

Now focus on your hearing sense. Imagine sounds that are relaxing and positive. Turn the volume up or down, and slow the sounds down or speed them up. Adjust what you are hearing until the sounds are in the proper balance for you. The more you are comfortable, the more you will focus. If you can hear pleasant conversations going on within your image, let yourself listen in, and move about from different viewpoints.

Next, add in your kinesthetic sense to get the feel of the image and the moods. Experience different textures, temperatures, and emotions. Now include tastes and smells. Let yourself drift through a virtual reality of your different senses. Spend as long as you want there, feeling safe and secure as you explore the regions of your unconscious and your Universal Mind.

Anchor Your Experience

Before you leave and return to the surface of your conscious mind, give yourself word and touch anchors that will help you recreate your connection with your sense imagery. Choose a word that brings back this special feeling. Say it to yourself several times, experiencing how you feel when you are connected to your Universal Energy. Do the same thing with a touch, such as a thumb and finger pressed together.

FACT

A posthypnotic suggestion is presented to your unconscious mind while it is in a relaxed state and free from your analytical conscious mind. It adds the suggestion to your memory recall, and when you need to feel the suggestion, it surfaces in your conscious mind and is accepted without question.

While you are still in your deep relaxed state, suggest to yourself that each time you experience this exercise or use your anchors, you will become more and more comfortable with the way you process your five sense images. You may tell yourself that your abilities are given to you by the Universe to be used for the good of both yourself and others.

You may suggest that anytime you need it, the universal bubble of golden light is there to surround you and protect you. It is a suggestion you can use everyday. This will be helpful as you experience the various psychic development exercises in the upcoming chapters of this book.

Back to the Surface

When you are ready, you may begin to count yourself back up to the surface of your conscious mind, from one to five:

1. You are relaxed and refreshed as you begin your journey back. Breathe in and out slowly and comfortably. All your tensions have disappeared.
2. You continue upward. The positive images and Universal Energy are still vivid in your mind. The golden light escorts you as you continue your journey back to consciousness. You feel so relaxed and positive.
3. You are halfway there. You look forward to bringing your experiences back to the surface to assist you as you move about the conscious world.
4. You can see the surface of your conscious mind just ahead. As you come to the last number, take a deep comfortable, relaxing breath.
5. Exhale, open your eyes slowly, and come back to the surface of your conscious mind, relaxed, refreshed, and still filled with the Golden Light of the Universe.

Take a few moments to readjust to the world about you. Keep this positive experience with you as you go on about your day or evening.

Positive Effects

If you begin to use and experience these exercises daily, they can have a powerful and positive effect on your life. These exercises can help you develop your psychic abilities as well as give you balance in the rest of your daily life. They may help you deal with the challenges and resistances you face and even lead you to develop an artistic talent or the ability to heal.

The more you are aware of how your mind works and processes your sense images, the more you will learn to trust and rely on them. These are the images that may have confronted you in the past when you were unprepared for them. Now you have the opportunity to examine and study them from your safe protective bubble of golden light. The more you use your positive anchors, the more you will begin to automatically sense this bubble all around you.

The more you are prepared for the unexpected, the more the unexpected will appear to be normal. Fear is generated from the unknown. Once something new is known, it may not be fearful at all. Just remember, you do not always turn on and off your psychic abilities when you want to. They are turned on and off by the Universe.

Chapter 6

Working with Your Chakras

Much of your psychic information comes through your chakras, the energy centers in your body. In this chapter, you will examine seven major chakra centers of the human body. Then you will learn how to perform exercises that will help you open and balance these energy centers. Balanced chakras will help you in your psychic development, so let's get started!

Your Body's Psychic Energy

Energy is believed to be the basis of all matter. Under that principle, anything that can be transformed into pure energy can be transmitted through the dimensions of time. Perhaps you remember watching *Star Trek* on television. When Captain Kirk ordered, "Beam me up, Scotty!" he would dissolve into a shimmering mass of energy and be transported through space back to the Enterprise.

In a way, this is how psychic information is received—through transference of psychic energy. The psychic energy can be converted into images that may be processed through the five different senses: sight, sound, touch, taste, and smell. To get good reception, the psychic must keep her receiver well tuned.

If a psychic blocks her ability to receive, the signal or energy will not come through. On the other hand, if she isn't aware that her channels are open, she may get a stronger signal then she wanted. Knowing when and how much to open your psychic energy flow is a delicate skill that is achieved with practice and patience.

Once you learn to keep your psychic equipment in good working order, you will be able to tune in with the confidence that you will receive an energy signal that can be trusted and relied on.

The Aura Field

A field of energy called an "aura" surrounds your body. If this field is interrupted for some reason, the energy will not flow evenly. Your chakras are an essential part of this energy flow. If one or more of them is closed, then the energy is blocked at these points. Energy blocks throw your aura out of balance.

Blocked energy that is not cleared can lead to serious consequences. This can affect your mental, physical, and spiritual health. Blocked energy can also severely impede your spiritual and psychic development. As you learn to tune your chakras, you will also balance your aura and advance your intuitive gifts.

Many psychics are able to perceive other people's auras. Some sense it visually, as colors or streaks of energy. Others may feel them physically or mentally. Each psychic interprets what he or she experiences differently. You will learn more about reading auras in Chapter 17.

QUESTION?

What does the term "chakra" mean?
The word "chakra" comes from the Sanskrit word for "wheel." Hindu and Buddhist religions believe that the human body has a series of energy centers. These centers act as openings for universal energies to pass through the body's aura. Like wheels, the chakras vibrate and turn at different speeds to help receive and distribute the energy.

The Seven Chakra Centers

There are seven major chakra centers in the human body, as well as many minor ones. Note that each chakra center has a related endocrine gland that secretes hormones. The better your energy centers and your glands work together, the greater the opportunity is for your body, mind, and soul to be in harmony with each other. The seven chakra centers are the following:

1. **The base, or root, chakra (Muladara).** The lowest of the seven major centers, this chakra is located at the base of the spine and is the simplest of the seven. It relates to your physical strength and animalistic nature, as well as the senses of taste and smell. It is in the base chakra that the kundalini energy waits in coiled readiness to respond to your basic needs. (According to the Yogis, kundalini energy is the psychospiritual energy that is a powerful source of many psychic experiences.) This chakra controls the gonads.
2. **The sacral, or belly, chakra (Svadishana).** Located just below the navel, near the genitals, the sacral chakra controls sexual energy and reproduction and may affect your health when out of balance. It influences the release of adrenaline in your body and can keep it on a high state of alert when influenced by stress. This chakra also controls what is known as the cells of Leydig, testicular or ovarian cells that secrete testosterone.

3. **The solar plexus chakra (Manipura).** Located below the breastbone and above the navel, the solar plexus chakra is the center where mediums get their psychic information. The solar plexus chakra controls the adrenal glands; when it is out of balance, it can affect your stomach, liver, and pancreas.

4. **The heart chakra (Anahata).** Located in the center of the chest and in the middle of your shoulder blades, the heart chakra relates to the Universal Mind and emotions such as love, honesty, and caring. If it becomes blocked, it can affect your heart, lungs, and breathing. It also rules your thymus gland.

5. **The throat chakra (Visudda).** Located at the top of the throat, the throat chakra relates to creativity, self-expression, and the creative arts, including music, art, and writing. When its center is blocked, your throat, ears, eyes, nose, and mouth may be affected. This chakra rules the thyroid gland.

6. **The forehead, or third eye, chakra (Ajna).** Located between your eyebrows in the center of your forehead, the forehead, or third eye, chakra relates to your pituitary gland and your psychic ability. When this center is blocked, it can affect your head, eyes, and brain.

7. **The crown chakra (Sahasrara).** Located at the top of your head, the crown chakra will not open until all six of the other chakras are balanced. When it is open, you experience the highest connection to the Universal Mind by your mental, physical, and spiritual self. The crown chakra controls the pineal gland.

The Universal Life Force enters the body through the crown chakra at the top of the head. As it works its way down through your body, it flows through the other centers. As it spreads to the base chakra, it arouses the kundalini energy, which yogis believe sleeps in a coiled serpentine form.

It is the external Universal Life Force that this book identifies as the Universal Mind that you first connect with when you focus beyond your third eye to the top of your head. The Universal Life Force energy is what you feel when your third eye vibrates or swells. It is this external energy form that helps increase psychic ability.

An Exercise of Balance

It is possible that one or more of your chakras may be blocked as a result of many different situations. The cause may be stress, or it could be a mental, spiritual, or physical condition. Be aware that it is almost impossible to keep all of your chakras in balance all the time.

Once you grow sensitive to feeling the balance of your chakras, you will be able to sense when the balance is broken. At that point, you can take the steps to bring yourself back in balance.

The goal of this basic balance exercise is to open your third-eye chakra to the Golden Light of the Universe and let it flow downward through your other centers until it reaches your base chakra. When that is achieved, let it radiate upward, opening the crown chakra. This will help you begin to balance the energy throughout your body. As you get comfortable with the circulation of the Universal Flow, it may seem as if you are literally taking in this positive energy with each deep breath.

ALERT!

If the chakra is opened and not balanced, the flow of energy may be overwhelming. This is particularly true when you open yourself to psychic energy. It can pulse through you and totally immerse you without warning. Knowing how to shut down the flow is as important as knowing how to open it.

Let's Begin

You may start by getting comfortable. Take a deep breath and exhale slowly. Do this a couple more times, allowing yourself to relax more and more with each breath. If any muscle is stiff, allow it to relax as you continue to breathe slowly in and out. You may now close your eyes and focus on your third-eye chakra. If for any reason you feel overwhelmed by the energy or are suddenly flooded with psychic knowledge, you may always take a deep breath and open your eyes and return safely to your normal conscious world.

Allow yourself to feel the Universal Energy as it streams at a comfortable rate into your third eye. You may feel the warmth of love and peace from the golden light of the Universal Energy as it continues to flow downward. For a few brief moments, allow yourself to absorb this peaceful and loving feeling, as each breath brings it more and more into focus.

Feel the Universal Energy Flow Downward

You may allow yourself to focus on this loving and peaceful energy as it moves downward to your throat chakra. As the energy reaches this center, you may feel the universal vibration first relax and then open that area of your body. You may feel the love and peace that flows through the golden energy and light of the Universe from your third eye to your throat with every deep breath you take. Take a few moments to enjoy this blend of energy as it resonates with each breath, in through your third-eye chakra and out through your throat chakra.

Now allow your Universal Energy to flow downward until you focus on your heart chakra. Feel the peaceful and loving energy as it brings the warmth of the golden light and energy of the Universe to your heart. Feel the vibrations as they tune this important center around your heart. You may feel the loving and peaceful energy with each deep breath as it flows in through your third eye, down to your throat, and out through your heart chakra. Take a few moments and enjoy the love and peace as it spreads through and balances these three chakras.

Your spine is the main conduit for the Universal Energy flow. As you breathe in, focus on the love and peace that is entering through your third eye. As you breathe out, feel the love and peace flowing through the energy center that you have focused on.

Continue to Move Down

Now you may feel the peace and love of the Universal Energy as you focus it downward to your solar plexus chakra. Feel the positive vibrations of your solar plexus center balancing itself as you breathe the Universal Energy in (through your third eye to your throat and heart chakras) and out (through your solar plexus chakra). With each deep breath you take, the golden light of the Universal Energy flows downward as you feel its peace and love. Take a few moments and enjoy the special sensations created by the balancing of these energy centers.

The Power of Kundalini Energy

Now, when you are ready, allow yourself to focus the peace and love of your Universal Energy flow down to your sacral chakra. As you feel the golden light vibrations bring balance to this center, you may be aware of the kundalini energy that waits below, coiled and ready to combine its strength and power with the Universal Flow. With each deep breath, you may feel the peace and love of the Universe as it flows down through your third-eye chakra, to your throat, heart, and solar plexus, and out through your sacral chakra. Take a few moments to enjoy the peace and love of the Universe as it flows downward through your centers.

Now you may allow yourself to focus the Universal Flow downward all the way to your root chakra. Feel the power of the kundalini energy as it combines with the Universal Energy and lifts it upwards. As you breathe downward, the universal golden light flows through your third eye, to your throat, heart, solar plexus, navel, and out through your root chakra, as you feel peace and love. As you exhale, you may feel the vast power of the Universe as it pulsates throughout your entire body. As your six chakras vibrate in total harmony, they now open your crown chakra to the divine wisdom of the Universe.

Energy Flow Through Your Crown Chakra

Spend some time in this peaceful and loving state as you experience the divine energy of the golden light flowing throughout your body. Your head may naturally feel as if it is lifting upwards so your third eye can have a direct connection to the Universal Energy flow. You may slowly allow your arms to open and float up from your body. Your hands may open with their palms cupping slightly and facing upward to further receive the peace and love of the Universe.

You may feel the incredible power of the Universe as it combines with your internal and external guidance systems and your Belief. At this time, you are totally open to the peace and love of the Divine. In this state, your intuitive gifts are now in balance and harmony. You are ready to receive the appropriate knowledge provided by the Universe for your psychic development.

Count Back Up

When you are ready to come back to your conscious mind, you may count slowly from zero to five. As you continue to breathe slowly and deeply, you may bring your feeling of peace and love back to your conscious state. When you get to five, take a deep breath, open your eyes, and continue to feel the positive flow of the Universe through your balanced chakra centers. You may feel grounded in the divine love of the Universe.

This exercise is very basic. If you want to incorporate your own techniques, you are encouraged to do so. Each of you will have a different experience as you work with your chakras.

The Benefits of Massage

If you would like to help your energy centers open, you may want to consider adding light massage techniques to your balancing exercise. As you focus on your third-eye chakra, you may gently massage the center of your forehead. Move the three longest fingertips of one of your hands in a circular motion. After a few moments, let your hand return to its previous position as you focus on the peace and love that are balancing the third-eye chakra.

When you focus on the throat chakra, continue this same massage technique. Always keep your touch light as you move your hand slowly in a circular motion. If for any reason you feel discomfort, discontinue the massage and either focus on your chakra exercise without it or open your eyes and come back to full consciousness, relaxed, calm, and filled with peace and love.

ALERT!

When a blocked energy center is opened suddenly, the rush of energy can trigger a spontaneous psychic image. This often is the case when you experience massage, Reiki, or another method of healing art for the first time.

Another method of massaging your energy centers is to work with your aura. Place the open palm of one of your hands approximately two inches above an energy center. Slowly begin to circle the palm of your hand in a counterclockwise motion. You may feel pressure, heat, a tickle, or a prickly feeling as your hand moves over the spot.

Restoring Balance Through Color

Each of the seven energy chakras also has a specific color that is produced when the energy of that center is in balance. If you are visual, it may help you to balance your chakras by visualizing the proper color for each center. You may add the color imagery to your chakra balancing exercise. Here is a list of colors for each of the seven chakras:

- The base, or root, chakra is red.
- The sacral, or belly, chakra is orange.
- The solar plexus chakra is yellow.
- The heart chakra is green.
- The throat chakra is blue.
- The third-eye, or forehead, chakra is a deep indigo.
- The crown chakra is a white or pure light.

You may be able to feel energy in relationship to color. You can focus on red and go right to your root chakra and feel the base of your kundalini energy. Or you can focus on the color green and project it to your heart chakra.

As you begin to practice getting in tune with your energy centers, you may want to practice opening and balancing them in a natural progression from your third eye downward and finally back to the crown. The more you understand the vibrational level of each center, the more it can help you in your psychic development.

Sensory Imagery Exercise

Now consider using all of your five senses to help you open and balance your seven chakras. First, focus on your breathing. As you breathe slowly in and out, let your body relax. When you are ready, allow yourself to begin to focus on your third-eye energy center.

Focus on a deep indigo color as you inhale. Let this beautiful color flow over any negative colors and sweep them out of your third-eye chakra as you exhale. You may feel a certain vibration that is special to that center. You may be able to sense a certain tone that helps to open and balance your third-eye chakra.

ESSENTIAL

> Tibetan Buddhists see each chakra as a wheel with a different number of spokes. The energy level of each center turns its wheel at a different speed. Not all of the chakra models have seven energy centers. Some have more, and some have less.

As you breathe in and out, you may sense that perhaps there is a special smell or even a taste that you can relate to your third-eye energy center. Experiment using your different senses to help you open and balance your third-eye chakra and bring the strongest image into a clear focus. Now anchor that image with a touch to your third eye or with a special word or phrase. Release your connection, and practice reconnecting to your third-eye center by triggering your anchor.

When you are ready, you may focus on your heart chakra. Use the same technique that you developed for opening and balancing your third-eye chakra. Engage as many of your five different senses as you are comfortable with. They may be sight (color), sound, feeling, taste, or smell.

Once you have achieved a clear focus on your heart center, create an anchor for it. Now practice disengaging and reconnecting again. When you are comfortable with opening and balancing your heart chakra, move downward to your solar plexus. Follow the same process until you have opened and balanced your belly and root chakras.

Your crown chakra will open and balance as your six other chakras blend together in pure peace and love. You may use cues, imagery, and remembered sensations from all five of your senses to experience this Universal Flow. Let your physical, mental, and spiritual bodies feel unified in total harmony with the Universe.

The Chakras and Psychic Development

You may already have had a psychic experience through one of your different chakra centers when you unwittingly opened up to the Universal Flow. When it happened, you might not have been aware of what took place. This explanation may help you get a better perspective on what may take place when you have a psychic experience through one or more of your chakras.

The lower chakras are considered to be more primitive in the range of psychic abilities. It is through the root, sacral, and solar plexus energy centers that you open to being a medium or to communicate with the dead. You may also use these chakras when you experience psychic dreams. The lower chakra levels are considered to be more spontaneous than controlled.

The heart chakra is where you intuitively feel. If you are working with massage or other healing techniques and open your heart chakra, you may be flooded with the other person's physical, mental, or spiritual negative feelings. If you aren't prepared for the energy flow, you may find yourself internalizing it. Without an outlet, this energy will overrun yours, and it may affect your balance and even your health. If, on the other hand, you have some awareness of what might happen, you can let the energy flow through your heart chakra. Channeled this way, it has a great potential for healing those who receive the positive energy of peace and love.

When your throat chakra is open, you may have the ability to hear your guides or angels. You may receive verbal advice or even warnings about yourself or others. (You will have the opportunity to experiment with clairaudience in an upcoming chapter.) As you identify and learn to rely on the communication that comes to you through your guides, you will learn to trust their accuracy.

FACT

The ability to see psychically is called clairvoyance. When your third-eye chakra is open, you may be able to see on nonphysical planes. You may see as well as hear your guides or angels. You may also be able to see the past or future.

When the crown chakra is open, you may be able to travel to and experience different planes. It is through this center that you may be able to visit the Akashic Records, as Edgar Cayce did over fifty years ago. You may find yourself floating out of your body and experiencing the vast power of the Universal Flow.

Practice and Document Your Experiences

Now you may go back to your chakra exercises and begin to identify your psychic gifts. First, let yourself come into balance with all your energy centers. It is always good to center yourself when starting a psychic exercise. Do this by connecting to your Belief and your internal and external guidance systems. Feel the peace and love of the Universe and believe that any intuitive image is given to you for a special purpose.

Once you have done this, start with your lower chakras and open up to connections from the Other Side. You may feel the power of the kundalini as it combines with the Universal Flow. You may open to spontaneous psychic intuition that is given you by the golden light and energy of the Universe.

When you are ready, open your heart chakra to healing energies and positive feelings. Next open your throat chakra to the communication of your guides and angels. Look for the clear visions through your third eye, and finally let yourself float to other planes of psychic experiences guided by the golden thread along the white beam of your crown chakra. When you are ready, slowly bring yourself back to consciousness, filled with the love and peace of the Universe and in tune with your psychic experience through your chakras.

Remember, the way you work through your energy centers is different from anyone else. You may experiment with all the material in this chapter and develop a technique that is best for you. As you work with your chakras, you may find yourself opening more and more to your psychic gifts.

Chapter 7

Relying on Your Guides

As you go on to practice one or many of the different forms of psychic work, you can count on spiritual guides to help you along the way. Whatever these forces may be—Edgar Cayce called them "the invisible empire"—you can count on them to guide you along your life map and protect you from harm. This chapter will give you the opportunity to meet and identify your team of spiritual advisers.

Your Spiritual Companions

Does everything in your life happen by chance or fate, or is there some sort of a force that exists around you to help you through life? Men have been trying to answer that question since ancient times.

There are many terms to describe the spirit forces that exist beyond our current accepted reality. Spirits, guides, angels, power animals, and gatekeepers are just a few of the names that have been used by those who experience a connection to the unknown world around them.

ALERT!

The guides and other spirits that are described in this book are there for good. If you feel that you are getting negative advice or communication, you should stop contact with them and seek a qualified counselor in your area.

There are many published books that tell you how to meet and connect to your guides or angels. The premise of this book is that you are already connected, even though you may not realize it yet. It is hoped that by the time you finish this chapter, you will be more aware of the unknown forces that are already with you, and that you will begin to develop a communication technique that will help guide you throughout your life map.

Do you believe that you have an unseen helper around you? Are you already aware of this force? And if not, do you trust that you will come to learn more about it? Regardless of how you believe, if you focus on good and positive feelings, you may be amazed at the incredible results.

Do You Have Miracles in Your Life?

Do you believe that there are miracles that happen in your life? If so, when and how often do they take place? Are your miracles generally large events that happen periodically, or are they part of your everyday existence? Do you know who works these wondrous acts? Is it God, an angel, a deceased relative or friend, a spirit guide, or something or someone else?

FACT

A miracle is something that happens beyond the scope of reality. Miracles are usually attributed to a supernatural power that intervenes in the normal course of events and changes their expected or predictable outcome. Examples include miraculous healing and changes in negative weather patterns that the forecaster had failed to identify.

Miracles come in all forms. There are the big events that are just too unbelievable to reject as evidence that things happen that are beyond the abilities of man to achieve. There are also little day-to-day events that are often overlooked because they happen so naturally that you begin to take them for granted. Do you keep a record of the miracles that you recognize? Here are some suggestions that may help you keep track:

1. Pick a time each day to be aware of miracles.
2. Keep a record of what you ask your Belief.
3. Review the day to see if you received any of the miracles you asked for.
4. Review the day to see what miracles, large or small, took place that you didn't ask for.
5. Be aware of what you received. Sometimes a miracle is granted in a different way than you requested.
6. Acknowledge a resistance as something that might be leading to a miracle.
7. Give thanks to your Belief for all miracles large and small, known and unknown.

The more you become aware of the events in your life that take place without your noticing, the more you will begin to see the miracles that have been around you all along. Keeping a record of daily events will help you get in tune with your guides.

Be Careful of What You Ask For

If you focus on wanting something, you may get what you wanted, but it might not be what you really needed. If you get what you need, you might not realize it because you are so focused on what you wanted.

Let's say, for example, that you need a new car. You ask for and expect to receive a new car. You might even try to manifest it. Then, you receive an opportunity to get a used car; it isn't new, but it's just right for what you need. If you are still focused on the new car, you will not celebrate the miracle of getting the car you needed.

When you ask for help, consider specifying that you are asking for the right solution for all concerned at the time of the request. Believe, in the case of our new car example, in the gift of the right vehicle that will help you with your life work. Ask for the right words to come out of your mouth and the right thoughts to come through your mind. Ask for the right psychic information to come at the right time, and ask that you might use this information in the best way for the greater good.

Acknowledging Resistance

When things aren't going exactly the way you had planned, a miracle might be working behind the scenes. Many of you focus so strongly on what you think should happen that you misunderstand what *is* happening.

If you pay attention and work with the resistances in your life, rather than fighting them, you will become aware of the miracle that may be behind the resistances. If you force your way through a resistance, you may find yourself where you really don't want to be.

Guides in the Form of Angels

The word "angel" comes from the Greek, and it means "messenger." Angels are usually depicted as human-like beings in long flowing robes with halos over their heads and a pair of wings to help them travel between heaven and earth. In early Christian times, angels were called demons and could be either good or bad. Later, the term was expanded to refer to the evil angels who are disciples of Lucifer. This book is about connecting to positive angels who are here to help you help others and yourself.

Rudolf Steiner, a philosopher and spiritualist, believed that there exists an ascending order of spirits that includes angels, archangels, archai, Exusiai, Dynameis, Kyriotetes, Thrones, Cherubim, and Seraphim. Each level had more responsibility in the role that they played with the human race. Angels are close to our level of consciousness and are therefore the most recognizable form of spirit messenger. Steiner claimed that he was shown this system of order through psychic visions.

FACT

The Christian church teaches that there were seven archangels: Gabriel, Raphael, Michael, Uriel, Jophiel, Zadkiel, and Samael. Lucifer was the eighth archangel. He was cast out of heaven and became the leader of the dark angels, or demons.

It is possible that mankind was much more open to the spirit world before religious movements, such as early Christianity, tried to eliminate views that were not part of their doctrine. Many early pagan beliefs were absorbed by the more organized religions, and these early beliefs then changed as time went by. As an example, early pagan celebration dates were adapted to Christian celebrations, including Christmas and Easter. It was in this manner that the good demons (*diamons*) of the Greeks became the evil demons of the Bible. At the same time, the Christian religion embraced the concept of angels as the good messengers of God.

It is possible that the early paintings, which influence our view of what an angel looks like, came from an actual encounter with a spirit by the artist. The halo and/or golden glow may first have been seen as an aura. The energy about a spirit could very well shimmer, creating that effect. Because the spirit may have been seen in a suspended state above the ground, wings may have been added to make a more realistic picture. It is possible for a spirit or angel to appear to each of you in a manner that is acceptable to you. Your angels or spirits may or may not look like anything that is described in this book.

Do You Have a Guardian Angel?

Do you have a guardian angel or angels? If so, how do you know? Have you ever seen your angels? If so, what do they look like? Can you hear your angels speaking to you? If so, what are they saying? How often do your angels visit you—daily, weekly, or only occasionally?

Can you feel your angels around you? If so, when do you feel them? Do your angels produce certain smells or tastes for you to experience? Can you hear their wings or other sounds that let you know they are with you?

You do not need to see an angel to recognize that one is there with you. Validation can happen in many ways. Keeping a record of your miracles also reminds you that your team of angels is at work, whether you see them or not. If you feel that you have angels watching over you, then give them credit for the good job they are doing.

Relatives and Friends on the Other Side

Your guides may be people you already know. It is possible that a friend or relative who is now on the Other Side could act as a guide for you in this lifetime and is looking out for you. Have you been paying attention to the clues that might tell you whether you have such a guide? If you haven't, that's not uncommon—most people don't keep track of the number of miracles that take place in their lives.

Do you have a feeling that there is someone who has passed over who still keeps watch over you on this side? If so, who could it be? Perhaps you know or suspect you know who is there, but you can't see for yourself. You may get validation from almost anywhere. It could be a sudden reminder of something special when the person was alive.

ESSENTIAL

If you are having trouble defining who you currently have watching over you from the Other Side, you may want to go for a psychic reading with a competent and ethical psychic. She may have the ability to recognize who is with you from the Other Side.

Once you learn who is traveling with you, you can begin to develop confidence that there really is someone there to help you handle both minor and major problems. You can actually have a conversation with your guides, even though it seems to be a one-way conversation. Just believing that someone hears you can give you confidence that a miracle is in the making.

The Other Side may not appear to you while you are in a waking state. Many times your guides will visit you in your dream state. This is especially true if you have an active conscious mind that is constantly cluttered with your thoughts. Your psychic communication usually rises to the surface when your active mind stops to relax. The only time you relax may be when you sleep.

The World of Spirits

In addition to angels and the souls of those who have passed on to the Other Side, there are other nonphysical entities that exist in the spirit world. A spirit may be a fairy, ghost, power animal, or another entity. Some people believe that spirits are evil and the idea of communication with a spirit may bring an image to your mind of working with the devil. Others are afraid that evil spirits would take control of their body, mind, and spirit.

FACT

An exorcism is a rite that is performed by a priest of the Catholic Church to rid a victim of the evil spirits that possess him. The rite has been used since the early 1600s. Other religions perform their own type of exorcisms. For example, Pentecostal Christians use the laying-on of hands.

The fear of spirit possession is very real to many people. The ones who are most vulnerable to this concept are those who are not grounded in a strong belief. Their self-doubt can leave them open to the idea and fear of being possessed. You need to banish your fears and accept the goodness of the Universe with the help of its golden light.

On the other hand, you may consider a spirit to be something that can be your guide and help you through life. You may have an image in your mind of what a spirit looks like. You may already be working with your spirit. A spirit who is there to help you is called a spirit guide.

You may consider your positive spirit guides as you identify what may journey through your life with you. As you consider that possibility, think back on your life, and you may find you already have a good idea. The following questions are designed to help you remember clues that you may have dismissed in the past.

Who's Been Guiding You?

For a brief moment, take a relaxing breath, exhale, and think back to your childhood. When you were very little, did you have a fantasy world where you could play and talk with spirits? If so, how old were you when you first met them, and how old were you when you stopped communicating with them?

How did you experience your childhood fantasies? Did you see, hear, feel, smell, or get a taste of whom or what they were? Did you ever tell anyone about them? If so, what was their response? Did other people's advice affect the way you accepted or rejected your fantasy experiences?

If you have had a form of spirit with you, is that being still there? If so, how do you communicate with them? In which of the five senses do you experience them? If you don't, when was the last time you were aware of them? If they are not there now, can you imagine what it was like when they were with you?

The spirits you may have communicated with could have had particular shapes and roles, such as any of the following:

- **Fairies:** Spirits that resemble tiny people, fairies live in the woods and are known for their magical powers. They are a part of Celtic lore and especially popular with children, probably due to their small size. A fairyland is a magical place where children live in a fantasy world full of enchanting wonderment.
- **Gatekeepers:** In the psychic world, these are spirit guards who watch out for you as you travel about in other realms. A gatekeeper is your

strong and powerful guide and protector. You can count on this being to help keep your energy centers in balance as he controls what enters and leaves.

- **Power animals:** Animals have been connected to mysticism since time immemorial. If you have a power animal, it could be one from nature, such as a wolf or a bear; a domestic pet, perhaps one that crossed over but still lingers with you to watch over and comfort you. You may have a favorite animal that you think of often that may already be a guide for you.

Whatever your spirits are, they may visit you in your dreams. Do you have dreams that include forms of spirit guides or animals? If so, how often do you dream about them? Do they come for specific reasons that relate to your life situation at that time? Do they have messages for you from beyond?

Meet Your Team

Let's take some time and begin to meet your spiritual guides. Remember, each of you has a different relationship and connection with them. You may or may not see them, feel them, hear them, smell them, or otherwise sense them. On the other hand, you may get a clear view and understanding of who they are and why they are with you. If you're ready, find a relaxing place and get comfortable.

E ALERT!

Remember, you can always bring yourself out of a light image trance. All you have to do is take a deep breath, exhale, open your eyes, and come back to your conscious mind, feeling positive and safe.

Take a deep breath, exhale, close your eyes, and begin to feel the connection to your third-eye chakra. Allow yourself to feel the loving and peaceful energy of the Universe as it flows downward into your body. Feel the golden bubble of protective light that is forming around your total being. Feel the golden tether of the Universe that keeps you in balance and leaves you free to be open to the Universe's guides that have been assigned to you. Let yourself enjoy a brief moment of total universal freedom filled with peace and love.

Ask your Belief permission to meet one or more of your guides in any positive form they may take. Allow yourself to relax, breathe in and out, and wait for a feeling of affirmation. This affirmation may come as a direct image, a voice, a pleasant sound, a feeling, or even a smell. You may experience nothing at first, so just wait patiently and believe that the right images will come to you. It is possible that this is not the right time to meet your guides.

You may get a faint image, or a lot of images swirling together. You may see colors, or you may hear a whole group of voices. If everything is going too fast, ask your Belief for help in slowing down your images. If you can, focus on just one image and concentrate on defining to yourself what you are sensing. Allow your guides to become comfortable in revealing themselves to you.

FACT

Some people become frustrated because they don't get the opportunity to meet their guides, at least in the same manner as other people describe meeting theirs. Just being in the flow of positive peace and love is good for you. Just imagining your guides will bring you closer to them.

Make the Connection

If you are able to sense your guides, can you communicate with them? If so, which sense do you feel most comfortable using? Even if you see nothing, you may still ask questions. You may receive your answers in pictures, by voice or other sounds, by feelings that you can translate into words, or through positive and negative tastes and smells. You may have feelings in certain places in your body or some other sensation or image. You may ask if there is a name that you can call your guide(s).

The first step is to get an understanding of what you may be telling yourself through your guides. You may ask for guidance in many different aspects of your life, from health to your life's work. Don't expect an answer right away. It might come then, or it might come in the near future. Always keep the feeling of universal peace and love flowing through you when you are making the connection to your guides. It is possible that you may know that they are there but that you may never really see them. That's okay, for the important thing is that they are with you.

Channeling Spirits for Yourself and Others

Another form of psychic communication and guidance is channeling. A channel is a conduit for something to pass through. A psychic channel is a person who has another entity or spirit communicate through them. This may be a voluntary or involuntary action on the part of the host body—the channel isn't always aware of what is taking place. Channeling can happen when you are in trance or asleep.

When you act as a channel, your voice and mannerisms may change to reflect the personality of the entity that is coming through. During this time, the spirit may convey information by speech, by automatic writing, or even in different artistic forms. Many channels bring a message of universal peace from a higher source of knowledge.

Experiencing Channeling

If you'd like to try your hand at channeling, it's a good idea to begin with someone experienced with the concept, like a hypnotherapist. She can help facilitate you into a deep channeling trance.

ESSENTIAL

It is also possible to channel when you are fully awake. Ask your Belief to let the right words come through your mouth. Believing that this will happen will actually help you to channel universal truths that are good for both you and the people you are speaking with.

You can also try automatic writing or typing by allowing yourself to enter a relaxed trance state and leave your fingers free to be used by the spirit. Just ask your Belief that the right messages for that moment come through your hands and fingers. Like all other forms of psychic development, practice and patience will help your technique to improve. (Chapter 16 covers psychic artistic development.)

Visit the Akashic Book of Records

Another source of information, especially on your soul's development, is the Akashic Book of Records. It is believed that every detail of every soul's existence is recorded there.

To visit the Akashic Book of Records, get comfortable, take a deep breath, exhale, and relax. You may focus on your third eye and bring your whole body into tune and balance. Feel the Universal Energy of peace and love fill your body, and the golden bubble of the Universe protecting you. When you are ready, use your own astral projection technique and allow yourself to follow the golden tether upward into the Universe.

Let yourself float upward until you come to the great Hall of Records. You may ask that you be able to see and read the sections on your soul that would be most helpful to you at this moment. If permission is granted, let yourself be guided to the proper place in the records and experience the information with all your five senses. You may want to follow a specific theme through several of your past lives, or you may want to focus on one life.

FACT

It is to these records that Edgar Cayce traveled for information on the past lives of the individual for whom he was doing a reading. By understanding his past lives, that person was given the opportunity to get back in tune with current opportunities for soul growth.

When looking into a past life, always look to see who in that life might also be in your current life. Compare the roles you each have had, and look for unresolved karma. Also ask to understand the theme of that lifetime so that you may apply the knowledge to help you improve in this lifetime. When you're ready, bring yourself back to earth and back to consciousness.

Chapter 8

Clairvoyance, or Psychic Sight

...ost common psychic ...rvoyance, or psychic sight... you will have the op- ...ne different types of ...plore your own visual ...it is important to re- ...many people are visual, this may not be true for you. If you are not a visual person, remember that the visual sense is only one of five senses, and all of your senses provide you with vivid feedback.

Your Sense of Sight

You see with your conscious mind as well as with your unconscious and your Universal Mind. Your conscious images are experienced live—what you are seeing is happening at that moment. Conscious sight is the reality, as it is shared with other people. When you experience a conscious visual image, it is then stored in your unconscious memory.

The unconscious mind is capable of replaying a stored conscious visual image at a later time. Your unconscious mind will replay the image in the way that your conscious mind processed it. Five people might all share the exact same experience and then recall it, through their unconscious minds, differently. Each one may get part of the experience correct and part of it wrong. Each person is replaying what he recalled from the experience when it actually happened.

FACT

Clairvoyance literally means "clear seeing." A psychic who is clairvoyant has the ability to see what is generally acknowledged to be unseen or not real. A psychic who understands her power of clairvoyance accepts it as part of her reality.

Second Sight

In addition to your external visual reality experiences, you may also have the gift of clairvoyance, or second sight. Some of you may already be aware of and using this gift; others may have chosen to try to ignore or block it. Second sight may appear to you at any time, usually when you are least expecting it.

Second sight can combine with your other senses and may be experienced in all three phases of time—past, present, and future. The past images may come from your present lifetime or from a time period back in history. They may relate to your life or they may have nothing to do with it.

Second sight into the future means seeing something that has not yet happened. These images may just "pop" into your head and cannot be related to anything that is currently taking place in the reality of the moment. If your third-eye chakra is open and unbalanced, you may receive second-sight images relating to any place in the world. In other words, you may be overrun with psychic garbage.

Manifest reality is all that you experience that is real and observable by others. Unmanifest reality manifests itself in second sight but may not be able to be perceived by others as a reality experience.

Realistic and Symbolic Visual Images

There are two different ways that you may experience clairvoyance. The most common way is to see a realistic visual image. It can come to you either when you are awake or when you are asleep and may relate to the past or the future. It can also be triggered by what you are experiencing at a particular moment in time.

The other form of second sight is symbolic. Symbolic imagery often involves the kinesthetic sense. The images may provide you with a "gut feeling" of their meaning. All psychics must learn to develop their own interpretations of the symbols they visualize.

Different Types of Clairvoyance

There are several different types of clairvoyance, including the ability to see through objects, over long distances, into the past (an ability known as retrocognition), or into the future (known as precognition). Clairvoyance may involve being able to see health conditions of people and/or animals, having psychic dreams, visualizing other worlds and beings, and seeing divine images.

You may be able to have psychic experiences in all of the different ways, or in some, or in none. Your mental makeup will help determine whether you have the potential to experience and develop the psychic abilities of second sight.

FACT

Mental telepathy is mind-to-mind communication and is part of your range of psychic abilities. Visual telepathy is the communication of a visual image from one person to another. It is different from second sight or clairvoyance because only your mind is involved. For more information on telepathy, read on to Chapter 11.

Many people with the gift of second sight can see into the future or the past, whether through dreaming or contact with spirits, angels, or guides. The more you become aware of and understand what you are already seeing in your mind's eye, the more confidence you will have in trusting and using your psychic gifts in the future.

Contact with Spiritual Beings

One aspect of clairvoyance is seeing spiritual beings like angels or spirit guides. Note that this isn't the same as seeing ghosts, who contact you on a physical plane. A spirit usually contacts you from your inner mind—either your unconscious or your Universal Mind—and its vision materializes in your mind's eye.

Spirit guides can help you navigate successfully through your life map. They have the ability to communicate with your Universal Mind and to gather wisdom that will help you make positive decisions. Although they most often appear in human form, they may be experienced in other shapes as well.

Power Animals

Spiritual communication may come in the form of a power animal that is there to guide and protect you. If you feel that you have a power animal, it can be a strong element in guiding you through life. Just the image of strength that goes with a power animal can give you courage to take positive risks. These risks can be incorporated into your Belief System, and it becomes easier to overcome the fear of failure. If you believe that something, including a power animal, goes with you to guide you, you will be more open to being in tune with your life map.

Learn from your dreams—they may be of symbolic nature, especially if they involve a specific animal or other spirits. If you can see spirits in your dreams, you have an even greater opportunity to develop an understanding of how they are here to work with you.

Angelic Communication

Your spirit guide may take on the form of an angel—and you may have more than one angelic being guiding you. These guides may appear as someone you recognize who has passed over to the Other Side, or they may take on shapes of those you have never met. They may visit you on a regular basis or only at times when you need a little help. If you can see your angels, you have been given a special gift from your psychic side.

Visions of the Past and Future

Precognition is a more unmediated form of psychic ability. This gift is more direct because it can allow you to see an event as it will happen in the future, rather than having a spirit guide who will share information with you regarding what is going to happen. Most often, precognition works as a realistic image, but it can also be viewed in symbolic form. The event can be recognizable and related to you or someone you know, or it can be something that you know nothing about. You may see it only once, or it can occur over and over. It can come to you in a dream or a vision.

Scrying is a form of divination that uses certain visual aids (like crystal balls, tea leaves, clouds, mirrors, or even the swirl of cream in coffee) to help produce the proper visual trance for seeing into the future. When you look at these objects, your eyes will go out of focus, and you will engage your second sight.

The earliest psychic images a young person may receive are often precognitions. They appear out of nowhere, and, more often than not, they predict an event that is related to an impending tragedy—the death of a loved one or an accident. Once a young person has seen signs of the future event in his mind and sees it actually happen, he may feel responsible for the event and believe that he caused it to happen.

Looking Back at the Past

The opposite of precognition is postcognition—seeing into the past to events that have already occurred. The images could be related to the individual's own lifetime or to something not closely connected to her. A location or an object may help induce a postcognition trance. The event seen could even be from a distant lifetime or time period.

One form of postcognition is time bending. There are those who believe that they can merge different time periods for the purpose of healing the past. They project themselves back into events from the past so that they may release the negative aura that may have been trapped in that time period. It is believed that if mankind can heal history by resolving the mistakes of the past, the future will not be caught in the same unresolved karma.

Trusting Your Imagination

Have you ever experienced any of the visual images discussed so far and dismissed them as just your imagination? If so, you are not alone. Many people never give their psychic ability of second sight a chance to help guide them through life. Perhaps you have dismissed psychic images that you have experienced in the past as just "your vivid imagination." But was that really all it was?

If you have a good visual imagination, it is all right to let it take you on an imaginary adventure. You don't have to worry about what you imagine just yet—it doesn't necessarily have to be psychic information. If you spend a lot of time imagining negative possibilities, maybe that is happening because you are not spiritually grounded. When you are worried about an unknown result, ask your Belief or spiritual guide to help you. And if you begin to feel uncomfortable, you may always discontinue the session by taking a deep breath and returning to your conscious mind.

As you let your imagination run wild, make note of your thoughts and compare them to events in the real world. These notes may record events that have already happened—that is, from the past—but you should also note events that happen in accordance with the way you envisioned them. It is okay for you not to fully understand the process that is taking place as you imagine. All you really need to understand is that imagination is an ability that you have. Just accept it and allow yourself to take a very large step in your psychic development. The more you work with it, the more you will learn to trust your psychic gift of second sight.

ALERT!

When you let your imagination flow, always make sure you are grounded. By connecting yourself to your Belief and the Golden Light of the Universe, you are taking steps to protect yourself from any negative images that you may experience.

Focusing on the Psychic Image

The unseen is with you all the time, as it is with everyone. It is a reality that is waiting to manifest itself. When you focus on it, you have brought it to a different form of reality, one that has been manifested. It is good to remember that others may not see what you see. The unseen is there to help guide and teach you.

When you want to focus on the second-sight image, you need to first relax and focus on nothing in particular—just as you do when you are looking at a hologram and want to see both pictures. When you have identified the second-sight image, you can begin to focus on it.

Your psychic image may begin as a vague picture that superimposes itself over your reality image. If you are in a convenient location and situation, you may find that closing your eyes and focusing on your third eye will help you to sharpen your second psychic image. Remember to keep yourself grounded in your Belief and let yourself be protected by the Golden Light of the Universe.

It is possible to become so focused on the psychic image that you forget how to refocus on your reality image. If you feel this happening to you, take a deep breath, exhale, and release your focus on the psychic image.

Discerning Auras

As you have already learned, an aura is an energy field that surrounds all living things as well as places, events, and objects. Although the feeling of the aura is important, so is its visual form. Auras may be seen in colors or simply in wavy colorless lines. If you can see an aura, you have been given an opportunity to gain a wealth of knowledge about many different situations and conditions that others may not have access to.

It is also possible for some of you to see auras of objects. You may be able to see negative or positive energies coming from particular places or personal belongings. If you can see this type of aura, you are sensing the energies of people that have been absorbed by inanimate objects. Some of you may even be able to change a negative aura into a positive one.

Working with Your Gift

Psychic visual experiences differ from person to person. Your particular vision may come from either inside yourself or from an outside source. The goal here is to encourage you to identify, develop, and work with your visual psychic abilities. And the first step is to identify how you see.

It is very possible that you may have a gift of second sight that is different from those addressed in this chapter. Your mind is special and unique. It does have psychic abilities, but they may or may not be visual. If you do have the gift of clairvoyance, it is likely connected to one or more of your other four senses.

Second-Sight Exercises

The following exercises will help you identify and begin working with your visual psychic abilities. Although you can do these exercises on your own, it can be both fun and educational to do them in a group setting. When you compare your second sight to that of others, you may be amazed at how different or similar they are. You can always record the scripts and play them back, or have another person read them out loud. You can also experience them as you read them to yourself.

ALERT!

When you begin to practice psychic development exercises, it is very important for you to be in tune with your physical, mental, and spiritual self. This includes being spiritually grounded, in the proper frame of mind, and having a full stomach.

What's Under Your Eyelids?

You may begin this exercise by finding a place that is comfortable and relaxing for you. You can either sit or lie down. When you're ready, take a deep breath, exhale slowly, and let your eyes go out of focus as you concentrate for a moment on your third-eye chakra. You may take a few moments and experience the rest of your energy centers coming into balance. As you continue to breathe slowly in and out, you may feel the loving and peaceful energy of the Universe entering your body. You may feel a protective bubble of universal golden light surrounding you as you examine your psychic gifts of second sight.

When you are comfortable and ready, focus your mind's eye on the images that are behind your eyelids. You may see an image clearly, or it may be out of focus. It is possible that the images you see are moving so fast that it is hard to focus on any one of them. If that is the case, allow yourself to relax even more and begin to slow down the speed of your images. This may be hard to do at first, but as you continue to practice, you should be able to bring your images into sync with your focus.

If you are able to see images under your eyelids, what are they? How do they compare to the different types of second sight that were discussed earlier in this chapter? Are they similar or different? Are your images comfortable or uncomfortable? If an image is uncomfortable, can you change it to another image?

Can you interpret your images to understand their meanings? You might ask your Universal Mind to help provide you with answers to any questions you may have. The answer may not come right away. Be patient, and remain alert to your insights. The answers may come from within or without.

You may not have any images at all, and if so, that's okay. Clairvoyance may not be your psychic strength. It is possible that you could see colors behind your eyelids. It might be one color, or different colors that appear in various shapes or forms.

Can you get images about the past or the future? Can you see your guides, or angels? Do you have images that relate to health or to your Higher Power? Are there any other images that you can see under your eyelids, and can their meanings be understood? When you are ready, take a deep breath, exhale, and return to consciousness in a positive relaxed mood.

Dream Imagery

Another exercise is to explore your dreams. As you relax and concentrate on your third eye, think about the dreams you've recently had. Do you dream in pictures? If so, are your dreams symbolic, realistic, or do you experience both types? Do you travel to and explore places in your dreams? Do you dream of past lives or future events? Do you see guides, angels, or loved ones who have passed over in your dreams?

Another great way to work with your psychic intuition is simply to close your eyes and imagine. You might imagine a story with a theme that relates to your current life or from any point in time. Through this exercise, you may find insights that relate to your life. Imagination is often a great method for finding the truth.

See the Second Image with Your Eyes Open

Have you ever had a second-sight experience when your eyes were wide open? If so, it may seem natural to you. If you rarely do or have not had the opportunity to experience it, however, here is a suggestion for an exercise to try. Allow yourself to enter a relaxed state as you focus for a moment on your breathing.

Focus on your third-eye chakra. Your eyes will go slightly out of focus as you put yourself into a light hypnotic trance. You may suggest to yourself that you are comfortable and open to the psychic images that are waiting to help you grow in your intuitive development. Let your mind drift as you enjoy your connection to your visual energy center.

You may begin to be aware of a second image in your visual screen. Wait patiently and let this image slowly become clearer and clearer as it comes into focus. Let yourself see it clearly as you watch from the safety of your protective bubble of golden light. Allow yourself to watch and process this image, and know that you can end it anytime you want and return relaxed and positive to your conscious mind.

Keep a record of what you see and when you see it. Does your second sight relate to the past or the future? Are there times and places where it is easier to get these images? Can you look at a person and see energy or auras around her? Do the auras change?

Can you look into a person's body and see a medical problem? Can you create a healing image? Can you project your mind's eye to a remote location and see what is happening at that very time there?

Keep a Record of Your Experiences

As you begin to develop your psychic abilities, keep a record of what you experience. Just like learning or honing any skill, the more you practice, the sharper and stronger your second sight will become.

At first, you may not receive many images—or you may get so many that they confuse you. Remember, patience is the key word. After all, what you are doing is getting back in touch with natural psychic gifts that have been with you for a very long time. Ⓔ

Chapter 9

Clairaudience, or Psychic Hearing

Experiences of clairaudience, or psychic hearing, vary almost as much as incidents of second sight. Your particular auditory experience may come from inside yourself or it may be external. Some people hear voices, while others are attuned to particular sounds or even music. In this chapter, you will learn how to identify and develop your psychic gift of clairaudience.

The Gift of Clear Hearing

Clairaudience literally means "clear hearing," and in psychic terms it is the ability to hear voices, sounds, or music that doesn't exist on the "normal" plane. These sounds may be internal, or they may exist on a different plane, in a different lifetime or location. If you have the gift of clairaudience, you can hear more than most other people.

Man has been guided by his internal voice since the beginning of time. The Bible makes reference to the Voice of God speaking to the prophets. The ancient Greeks received guidance from *diamons*. The shamans of many cultures used the voices in their heads for divine advice.

QUESTION?

What are diamons?
Diamons are divine spirits that offer wisdom, usually through internal voices. Communication with a diamon was an accepted form of psychic guidance until the Christian church classified diamons as demons, servants of the devil.

A Voice in Your Head

Today clairaudience is identified in many different forms. You may hear your own voice or one or more other voices. These voices may be heard as spirit guides, angels, deceased relatives or other spirits, symbolic figures, divine wisdom, or even animal guides. These voices may come when you are awake or in your dreams.

You may only hear a voice when you have a specific need, or you may receive regular guidance from it—and there may be several different voices that you can perceive at different times. You may be able to project yourself out into the Universe and have a conference with brilliant minds on the Other Side.

You may be able to channel the voice of your spirit guide or let the voice of a departed spirit speak through you. You may hear the spirit's message and be able to repeat it word for word. You may actually become the other personality and lose your style of speaking or even your thought process. This is usually done while one of you (yourself or the medium) is in an altered state of consciousness, as during a séance.

ALERT!

The voices in your head should be ones that offer you positive guidance and encouragement. If for any reason you constantly hear negative voices, you should immediately seek professional help to understand what you are hearing.

Sounds and Music

Besides voices, certain sounds may provide you with psychic insights. Some people hear ringing in both or one of their ears as a warning from the Universe. You may already be receiving such a communication without even realizing it. If you have sounds in your head, pay attention to their possible meanings.

Do you hear music in your mind? Have you ever had a song pop into your head and a short time later hear it being played on the radio or television? If so, what does that mean? It could be your spirit guides telling you to pay attention to other messages that may give you psychic insight. There is always a meaning to the messages, sounds, or music, and sometimes when you hear them you are merely receiving a confirmation of your intuitive gifts.

External Voices, Sounds, and Music

Besides the voices, sounds, and music in your mind, you may be able to hear real voices, sounds, and music that most others cannot hear. This may be due to very sensitive hearing, much like an animal that hears an arrival long before most humans can. For example, you may hear music being performed from a different time period if you are in the place where it was played before.

You may be able to hear spirits who exist around the area where you hear them. They may try to communicate with you, or they may just go on about their business, re-enacting a scene from their life as if you were not there. You may eavesdrop on a celebration, a dance, an argument, or a battle. All of these activities run their own course with or without you.

Some of you may be able to hear the sounds of another time period. The sound may be one that has left an impression on the location or on an object. It may also be possible for you to project yourself into the future and hear the sounds of future events.

You may externally hear the voices of your guides, angels, or those who have passed over. They may be a direct communication to and for you. It may be hard to determine if the voice, sound, or music is in your mind or if it is external and heard by your ears. It really doesn't make a difference as long as you accept it as a positive reality. The more you become aware of and trust your external voices, the more you will develop your psychic intuition.

Hearing Someone Else's Thoughts

You may be able to tune into what someone else is thinking. Betty has the gift—she thinks it's a curse—of hearing negative thoughts from other people. She can be in a crowded room and all of a sudden hear an angry voice in her head just as if it had been spoken out loud. She tries to tune the voices out, but if she drops her protection, they filter back into her mind. Communicating with someone else's thoughts is a form of mental telepathy that will be covered in Chapter 11.

Many psychics have trouble dealing with the sensitivity of their gifts. They often turn to bad habits to help them escape the burden of their talents. The bad habit itself may create an altered state that can open a chakra and cause more mental anguish.

Ruled by the Throat Chakra

The energy center for clairaudience is in the throat area. When it is open, you may be able to receive communications from your psychic sources. If you inadvertently open your throat chakra when it is not in balance, you may open yourself to more than you want to hear. On the other hand, if you block your throat chakra, you may find yourself frustrated, as this blockage may result in your not being able to receive your internal guidance.

As with other types of psychic abilities, effective use of clairaudience depends on the receiver. You are the mechanism through which the voices, sounds, and music are received. If you are not in total alignment with the signal, you may miss or hear incorrectly the messages from beyond. It is important to take proper care of your gift of hearing.

If you haven't read Chapter 6, you might want to go back and review the functions of your chakras. Before you work on your psychic abilities in clairaudience, it is a good idea to be familiar with how to protect and ground yourself. You may also open and balance your body's energy system to feel the love and peace of the Universe. As you become comfortable and more efficient with the exercises in this book, you will find yourself easily maintaining your psychic energy balance.

Is What You Hear Real or Imaginary?

As with other psychic functions, you may at first question any clairaudient gifts that you may have. It is easy to excuse a psychic event as an accident in synchronicity. Rational thinkers will always have a manifest-reality reason for everything. It is hard for them to accept a reality other than the one they are used to seeing, hearing, and feeling. At the same time, there are those who look at every event as a psychic happening. Your ability to step back and see both views is very important to the success of your psychic development.

When you try the clairaudient exercises, you may hear all your different voices, sounds, and music without worrying for now about whether they are real. The goal is for you to gather the information first. Once you have done that, you can compile your experiences to see what feels right for you. It is possible that some people will not understand or believe your psychic experiences. Don't worry about it. They need to come to terms with their own psychic abilities, and it may happen sooner or later, whether in this lifetime or at a later date.

It's okay not to be able to explain your clairaudience. You may have many clairaudient talents, or you may have one or even none. If the hearing sense is not your strength, another one will be.

Internal Clairaudience Exercise

If you would like to begin this exercise, find a comfortable place to relax, either sitting or lying down. It is good if you are in a place where you will not be interrupted for at least half an hour. If you are worried about falling asleep, set an alarm or have someone check on you at the time you wish to end your exercise. You may have someone read the exercise to you. You may also record it in advance and play it back for yourself, or you may read it as you progress, taking as much time as you want.

You may begin by focusing on your breathing. Inhale and exhale slowly, and allow yourself to feel the peace and love of the Universe as you do so. With each breath, you may feel your muscles relax more and more. When you feel any particular muscle stiffen, just let it relax. Let your eyes go out of focus and slowly close as you begin to concentrate on your third eye.

Now you may feel the energy of your third eye begin to flow as it opens to the Golden Light of the Universe. You may feel the peace and love in total balance with your third-eye chakra. You may hear the tone of the energy as it finds its balance. Continue to breathe in and out slowly, and spend a few moments with the love and peace of your third eye as the Golden Light of the Universe gently encloses you in its protective cloak.

Balance Your Chakras

Now you may begin to work your way down through the rest of your chakras, focusing on your throat chakra next. You may feel the love and peace of the Universe flowing downward to and through your throat energy center. When you feel that this center is balanced, focus on your heart. Continue to repeat the opening and balancing exercise, on each chakra until you have opened and balanced your root chakra. After you have completed your balancing exercise, you may turn your focus back to your throat chakra, the source of your clairaudient abilities.

Listen to Your Mind

When you are ready, you may focus on your throat chakra and let your energy center open to any voice, sound, or music that flows through. At first there may be a lot of interference from outside sound stimuli or internal static from your conscious mind. All you need to do is relax and feel the love and peace of the Universe flow through your throat center. Just breathe in and out and let your mind wander. You may become aware of a distant voice, sound, or music. Just let it continue and focus on hearing it clearer and turning up the volume if needed.

Many composers hear their compositions in their head before they put them on paper. A composer might wake up in the middle of the night and write down what he just dreamed. Sometimes the music can flow so quickly, it is impossible to capture all the notes.

Identify Your Guides, Spirits, or Angels

You may ask that you hear the voice or voices of your guides, angels, or other spirits. There may be more than one guide, each of whom has a specific purpose in communicating with you. You may get an answer through your own internal voice, or you might hear other voices. You may hear the voice of a loved one who has passed over to the Other Side.

You can ask the name of the voice on the other end. It may be revealed to you, or you may come up with your own name. Do your voices have an agenda for you? If you have a question for the Universal Mind, your guides, or the angels, you may ask and turn it over for an appropriate answer. You may or may not get an answer right away. You may receive insights on world conditions, advice on health issues for others as well as for yourself, or spiritual messages that can help you grow in your knowledge of the Universe.

Dreams You Hear

Do you hear voices in your dreams? Is the voice from your guides, angels, or other spirits? Are the voices from deceased loved ones? Do you hear the Voice of God or other divine figures when you dream? Do you receive universal insights when you are asleep?

Do you hear conversations in your dreams? If so, are you listening to others, or are you participating in the dialogue? Have you ever dreamed a conversation and then experienced it when you were awake? Do you have dreams of conversations from a different time in history, as if you were hearing an event that has already taken place?

Do you hear sounds when you dream? If so, what are they, and what do they mean? Do you dream the same sounds over and over, or do you get different sounds such as water flowing, wind blowing, or natural or mechanical sounds? Can you determine a pattern of events in relationship to sounds that you dream? Are the sounds pleasant or unpleasant?

Do you hear music in your dreams? Is it something you have heard before, or are the melodies entirely new? Do you dream music and then hear it played somewhere at a later time? If you write music, have you ever dreamed the main idea of any of your compositions?

Keep a Record of Your Experiences

While you are in a relaxed state, ask yourself if there are any other kinds of internal clairaudience that you may receive. You may hear intuitive voices that may or may not make sense to you. Remember, you are the information gatherer at this point in your life map. Even though you may not understand it at the time you receive it, its purpose may become apparent in the future.

ALERT!

Be prepared! Keep writing material close to your bed for insights that come in the night. You may even need a flashlight so you can see to make notes. When you travel, carry a small notepad or diary with you. If you choose to use a recording device to make your notes on, always carry a fresh set of batteries and extra tape.

You may hear the information more than once from both your internal and external sources. As you become more aware of your clairaudience, it is a good idea to keep notes of what you hear internally.

You can write down an event after it happens—as soon as you can—making note of the time, date, and your mental, physical, and spiritual condition at the time. Also make note of each situation, including associations with other people, needs that you may have, and even locations and the regularity of your clairaudience.

You may find a special place, time, and technique that will provide you with the best and clearest psychic clairaudient experience. Once you have identified your best signal, anchor the state so that you can also use it in different locations. Give yourself a key word, phrase, or touch to help you connect with your psychic intuition. The more you practice, the easier it will be to enter your clairaudient state.

External Clairaudience Development

Now it's time to check your external clairaudience. When you actually hear voices, sounds, or music that others may not, it is often difficult to get anyone else to believe you really heard something that they didn't. It is always nice to have someone else verify what you have heard, but it is not necessary. The important thing is for you to feel comfortable with your psychic ability to hear more than most others do. For example, you may be able to hear different tone frequencies or much weaker signals than most other people can.

Because the external clairaudience experience can happen without warning, it is possible that sometimes it might catch you off guard. However, you should always remember that you can take your Belief, the Golden Light of the Universe, and your guides, angels, or other spirits with you wherever you go. You may always feel grounded and safe regardless of any voices, sounds, or music that you hear without warning.

> Every day, especially the first thing in the morning, take the time to find a few moments to center yourself. If you allow yourself to feel in balance with your mind, body, and soul, you will be prepared for external clairaudience.

Do you hear any external voices, sounds, or music? If so, do you hear the same thing over and over, or do you hear different sounds, voices, or music? Are there any specific places where you hear these sounds? If so, how well do you hear them? Can you focus on these sounds so that they can become clearer?

Can you remember external clairaudience and recall it later in your mind? If so, can you replay the sounds? Can you turn the volume up or down, or slow down or speed up the sounds you first heard externally. Can you remember what you have heard long enough to write it down?

Do you hear sounds from plants? Some people can actually hear a plant make a sound when it needs watering. If you can hear other sounds, what are they? You may hear the sound of energy as it moves through the air. You may hear sounds that relate to emotions emitted by other people or even animals.

Sounds from the Past and Future

Can you visit a location and hear sounds that may have been made there some time before? If so, can you determine when the sounds were made and what was taking place at that time? Do you hear the same sounds at the same location at different times? Can you tell the mood of the sounds? Can you remember these sounds so that you can recall them at a later time?

Do you hear external voices, sounds, or music that relates to the future? If so, do you receive warnings, good news, or even sweepstake numbers? Can you identify the voices, sounds, or music you hear externally? Do they come to you at specific times, places, or locations? Does a voice ever speak to you "out of nowhere" to warn you of impending danger?

Psychic Hearing and Vision Combined

Now it's time to combine your clairvoyant and clairaudient abilities to examine how they work together. If you're ready, you will experience your internal psychic seeing and hearing abilities first.

Find a comfortable place, and prepare yourself to experience your universal golden light trance. Take a deep breath and slowly exhale. Close your eyes, and focus on your third-eye chakra. You may allow yourself to open and balance your chakras, taking time to feel the positive, peaceful, and loving energy of the Universe.

Wrap yourself in a bubble of golden light from the Universe, and then focus on the psychic energy flow of your third-eye and throat energy centers. When you feel very comfortable and peaceful, you may ask your Belief to experience either a visual image or a sound in your mind that may help you in your psychic development. Be patient. At first the images may come slowly.

> If for any reason you become uncomfortable, you may always stop, take a deep breath, exhale, open your eyes, and come back to your conscious mind relaxed and feeling positive and filled with the peace and love of the Universe.

As you learn to "tune in" to your psychic flow, it will become easier and easier to connect. You may have a lot of conscious clutter that needs to be filtered out. You can accomplish this by just letting it come and go without trying to control it. If you resist or try to redirect your conscious clutter, you will wind up fighting it rather than stepping aside and letting it flow off into space.

Let any images you have become clearer and clearer with each breath you take. Can you see and hear your image at the same time? Can you change views or raise and lower the volume of the sounds you hear? Can you watch your images as if you were watching a movie or video? Can you replay or slow down or speed up your images?

Moving Through Time

Can you receive images in pictures and sound that relate to the future? If so, do they relate to you, to someone you know, or to a larger area? Can you be shown and told things that will be helpful to you and/or others in the future? Can you see and hear warnings through your internal images?

Can you experience images and sounds together that are from a different time in history? Perhaps the images are from a past-life memory. Can you project your mind back to a period of history and see and hear what it was like to be there? Can you remember these experiences and replay them later in your mind?

> Also consider your dreams. Can you remember dreams when you were able to see an image and hear the sounds? If so, can you interpret what your dreams mean? Can you see and hear a deceased relative or another person from the Other Side? Do these dreams relate to the past, present, or future?

Switching to External Mode

Now it's time to combine external vision and hearing. Have you ever found yourself drifting off in your mind and experiencing a visual scene that is accompanied by sounds? Have you ever been in a specific location and flashed back to a different time period and heard and saw it as a reality? Are you able to see and hear spirits, angels, or other entities? If so, can any of these beings communicate with you?

Are there any other ways that you are intuitively able to hear and see images? If so, have you learned what these images mean? Are you afraid of them, or have you learned to rely on them for guidance? Can you remember the images after you have experienced them? Do you enjoy your contact with your psychic pictures and sounds?

As you learn how to balance and use your clairvoyant and clairaudient abilities, you will begin to rely on these abilities for insights and guidance in your work, relationships, and spiritual development, as well as in other aspects of your life. Be patient, and remember to stay grounded and protected. Like any other skill or talent, the more you use it, the more it is ready to work for you.

Chapter 10

Clairsentience, or Psychic Feeling

Clairsentience is the psychic use of your sense of feeling, whether it's physical (touch) or emotional (concerning your sentiments). As you progress through this chapter, you will have an opportunity to examine your clairsentient abilities and develop strategies to use your psychic ability without becoming bogged down with too much information.

A Certain Kind of Feeling

Clairsentience means "clear feeling." Many people argue that "feeling" is the most important of the five senses, perhaps because it is most often combined with one or more of the other senses. Even by itself, it can provide a wealth of psychic information.

FACT

Gavin DeBecker has written a great book entitled *The Gift of Fear: Survivor Signals That Protect Us from Violence.* If you are interested in intuitive feelings, this might be a good book for you to read.

There are two different types of feelings—those experienced through touch and those experienced as emotion—and each type can be processed internally and externally. Both types of feelings may relate to the past, present, or future. They may come to you in dreams, during trances, through your mind, or through external touch. It can be very difficult for some people to differentiate clairsentience from their other senses.

You may be able to feel the emotions of others or the temperature of the weather in a past life. Edgar Cayce was able to project himself to a location he had never been before and report back on weather conditions. Sensing psychic feelings can often be problematic for those who absorb the feelings of others.

Intuitive Touch

Touch is a very powerful sense. When you touch something, it can unleash a flow of psychic images. You may feel repelled or drawn by people or items that you touch. You may be able to feel an aura or energy field around a person, a location, a plant, or an animal. A touch can create a peaceful and secure feeling or evoke anger.

Many intuitive healers get much of their information through touch. Just as you may be able to feel the pull of an underwater current, they can feel the current of energy as it flows through a body and can direct its movements with their hands.

There are many different ways that the sense of touch provides you with psychic information. It may be as simple as feeling an energy field around someone. It may be through the use of a dowsing rod or a pendulum when you feel the answer to a question you have asked the Universe. It may be that you can feel a tingle in your hands or a hum in your third eye when you are experiencing a psychic connection. As you are collecting information, you might feel a pain, an itch, a tickle, or a pulsating sensation.

You may have a psychic defense system that issues warnings or validations through certain feelings. Even though many originate in your mind, you still may actually feel them externally or physically. Learning how your body produces certain physical feelings that relate to psychic messages can be very helpful to you as you develop and become comfortable with your intuitive abilities.

The feeling of certain textures can produce psychic images as well. For instance, a certain food texture could trigger a past-life memory. The same thing is true for the texture of something you touch or wear. Textures can suddenly change your focus to the second image of a psychic hologram.

QUESTION?

Do you find yourself emotionally drained because of the knowing feeling you get from your psychic gifts?
If so, you're not alone. If this is happening to you, review the early chapters on connecting to your inner guidance system and on the protective Golden Light of the Universe.

Feelings Evoked by Objects, Places, or People

Have you ever held or touched an object and gotten a feeling about its past? You may have been able to feel a mood through the object or something else about the people who have held it before. There is a belief that your energy is absorbed by anything you come in contact with. If you were affected by a strong mood during a time when you connected to an object, your mood or feelings would have been integrated into the object's energy. When you are open to this stored energy, you will receive an impression of its ownership history.

Have you ever been someplace and all of a sudden felt a very strong emotional feeling that was not related to your mood at the time? Have you ever had the feeling in certain locations that ghosts or spirits or something else was watching you? If so, what type of feelings did you have? Were they feelings of happiness, sadness, fear, peace, or something else? When you visit places where you have never been before, do you ever have the feeling that you are "home" again?

Can you think of someone and sense his mood or state of well-being at that time? Can you look into a person's eyes and feel the essence of her soul? Can you feel if the person is sincere or a potential threat? Have you ever met someone for the first time and felt as though the two of you have known each other for your whole lives? All of these feelings come through your psychic abilities of clairsentience.

Have you ever felt that your guides, angels, or something else was protecting you? If so, how do you get this feeling? Can you create a feeling that you are being protected when you need or want that feeling? Do you have a technique that you use everyday to surround yourself with Universal Protection? If so, how does your feeling help you?

Absorbing the Feelings of Others

Do you absorb feelings and/or emotions from other people, places, or objects? If you do, how do you respond to what you feel? The intuitive ability to feel is a wonderful gift. But it can also be a terrible curse. For those who are extremely open to clairsentience, it's as if feelings have the power to penetrate the very essence of their souls. This statement is true of many artists and healers.

ESSENTIAL

Many first-time students of massage, Reiki, or nursing have a great deal of trouble in dealing with the physical, mental, and spiritual pain of their clients and patients. The students are absorbers, suddenly thrust into the unbalanced energy of those they are trying to heal. If you are learning hands-on healing arts such as massage or Reiki, it is a good idea to ground yourself often.

If You Have the Gift

Your psychic gift may be the ability to experience the mental, physical, and spiritual makeup of other people, locations, time periods, and all other things living now or in the past. Once you have absorbed any of these feelings, they become part of your energy. The feelings will continue to stay with you unless you are able to release them.

Any energy you absorb, positive or negative, can impact your own energy as long as it remains with you in the form it was received. If the energy is positive, it can have a positive effect on your total energy. But if the energy is negative, it can have a negative effect on your total energy.

If you are an energy absorber, you are not alone. Many other people do the same thing. You always look for the good, and it seems as if all you receive is the bad. Yet your natural ability is to care and to absorb. It's okay to care and absorb, and it's also okay—in fact, it's even better— to turn the concerns and negative energy over to your Universal Team to help resolve and purify.

If you are an absorber, you may allow yourself to let the negative energy pass through you and out into the Universe for cleansing and healing. You need not be affected by the energy that is going through you. In Chapter 17, you can learn how to use your psychic healing gifts without being overwhelmed by them.

Emotions That Become Physical Feelings

Do you ever get an emotional feeling that changes into a physical feeling? Perhaps the hair stands up on the back of your neck or you feel a pain in your neck. Your head might buzz, or you may feel a sudden heaviness in your stomach. Your knees might get weak, or perhaps you get a pain someplace in your body. Perhaps you experience some other kind of cue that lets you know that something is not right.

Sadness can cause you to feel heaviness in your heart center. Your third-eye chakra may respond to your aura being invaded by someone else's energy. If you are grounded, you may be able to actually feel your protective shield or the bubble of golden light deflecting off the unwanted attempt to take over your space.

Not all transferences of emotional feelings are to warn you of bad news. You may get a body feeling that validates to you that something psychic is taking place at that moment. You may feel a buzz of psychic energy in one or more or your chakras. You may get a special feeling when someone is thinking positive thoughts about you. There are many ways in which you can transfer an emotional image into a physical feeling.

ALERT!

If you take in the emotional baggage of someone else, living or dead, you have become "responsible" for that person. Over a long period of time, the responsibility can affect your health. You can ask your spirit guides for help in getting released from this burden.

Manipulation of Energies

Part of clairsentience is being able to manipulate the energy of the Universe. Can you receive Universal Energy and then project it into someone else's aura or body for the purpose of healing? Some of you may be able to bring the strength of the Universe through you rather than absorbing the negative energy from someone or something else. Do others find that you have a calming or healing effect when you touch them? Can you smooth out the energy in the auras of other people? If so, you may be a natural healer.

Is your energy so strong that it affects others without your even realizing it? Do you have trouble keeping wristwatches running? Do you have trouble with your electric appliances, computers, or other electronic items? If so, you may be emitting a very strong psychic energy field with the power to affect sensitive equipment.

Can you produce extra strength to move objects when you need to? Do you have the ability to move objects with your mind or by sending an energy field through your fingers? Many of you may have special strengths that are part of your psychic energy. If you have that gift, you have an opportunity to do a lot of good with your "power" from the Universe.

An Open, Balanced Heart Chakra

The energy connected to your clairsentient powers is located in the heart chakra. When the heart chakra is open, you are open to the emotional energy of many different sources. You may receive clairsentience from other people, animals, plants, objects, locations, time periods, ghosts, those on the Other Side, and forms of energy.

If your heart chakra is out of balance, you can receive too much feeling energy, or you might even absorb negative auras into your own aura. If your heart center is blocked, you will receive or be aware of very little emotion.

Protection for your clairsentience is extremely important. When your heart chakra is open and unbalanced, you could be overwhelmed with external emotional and internal feelings. They can come from people, locations, dreams, past lives, future events, ghosts, or deceased spirits.

Creative abilities are often the most powerful when the chakra centers are open. At those times, artists, writers, musicians, or dancers produce and/or perform their greatest work. When they are caught up in the energy flow, they are in a state in which their conscious minds are not fully aware of what is taking place. They can only focus on the creative flow until it has run its course. These trance states may last a short time or may go on for days, placing the artist at risk of losing touch with reality.

When the centers close up again, the creative effort may or may not be complete. If the results are unfinished, there is always the possibility that the centers will not open again. If the work is complete, there may be a chance that the chakras will remain closed and that there will be no more works of that kind produced again. It is the ego mind that causes the doubt, not the intuitive trance. If you are balanced, the flow is natural. The creative energy will always be there in its own way, which will always be the correct way for that moment in time.

A Chakra-Balancing Exercise

You may open and balance your heart chakra with the chakra-balancing exercise. Find a comfortable place to relax and focus on your breathing. Begin by connecting to your third-eye chakra, and ask your Universal Power to bring down its loving and peaceful positive energy. Include the protective bubble of universal golden light and let it flow over and around you.

When you are ready, let yourself open and balance each chakra, beginning with your third eye and on downward until you release the kundalini energy to mix with the peace and love of the Universe. Now let yourself be aware that your crown chakra is open and balanced and ready to receive the proper clairsentience that is right for you at this time. Allow yourself to focus on your heart chakra.

Investigate Your Clairsentience

From your relaxed state, with your focus on your heart chakra, you may begin to investigate the particular manner in which you receive your intuitive feelings and how you can develop and use them. Do you feel emotions? If so, what kind of emotions do you feel? Can you feel the moods of other people or animals? Can you feel the moods of specific locations or from objects?

Can you feel the moods of spirits of beings who may have died and left unresolved issues on the earth plane? Do you feel emotions about certain events in a different period of history or about the future? Are you overwhelmed with emotions at certain times and don't know why? Do you feel the emotions of family or friends with whom you do not have daily contact? Do you ever get a "gut feeling" that you should contact someone immediately?

Feeling Connected

Do you feel that you are in tune with your life work? That does not mean that you are necessarily sure of the absolute direction you are going. Being in tune means more that you feel you are being guided in the direction you should be going. Do you have a deep feeling inside that you are a part of a much larger movement and that many more people are involved? Do you feel that even a resistance is something that may be placed there for a reason that you do not yet understand?

Do you feel out of place with the rest of the world? Do you feel as if you are living in the wrong time? Do you resist your gut feelings and take actions that you do not feel are the right ones? Do you take actions that seem to be compelled by some energy that is not your own? If so, you may be an old soul who is more in tune with a past life than the one you're currently living.

FACT

An old soul is a person who has been through many reincarnations. That person's soul contains a lot of psychic memories that can come through an open chakra. If the person is not aware of what is happening, he or she may find this psychic information to be extremely painful.

The feeling of being disconnected is not uncommon for an old soul. You may be aware that you spend a lot of time fighting your emotions rather than trying to communicate with them. Once you understand the psychic abilities you have in this lifetime, you can understand and develop them to help you get back in tune and connected to your life map and life work.

Combining Your Psychic Senses

Once you gain some understanding of your clairsentient abilities, you can then work to merge them with your other senses. First, let's combine your feeling sense with vision and hearing. As you do so, you will become aware of how these three senses work for you and how they can be used in your psychic development.

When you are ready, you may get comfortable and focus on your breathing. Next focus on your third-eye chakra and feel yourself connecting to a loving and peaceful flow of Universal Energy. Now you may open and balance your chakras as you feel the protective bubble of golden universal light totally covering you.

Continue to focus on your third eye, and then add in your throat and your heart chakras. When you are ready, ask your Universal Power that you may see, hear, and feel the psychic information that is right for you at this moment in time. If you have a specific question for the Universe, your guides, or your angels, you may ask it at this time and give permission for the answer to come when it is ready to be received. You may give yourself a few moments to let the images form in your mind.

QUESTION?

What's your best form of communication?
If you communicate with your guides, angels, or other spirits, can you see, hear, and feel them? Is one of the senses stronger than the others? Or do all three of your senses help develop a stronger connection to your guides, angels, or other spirits?

Add the Senses of Taste and Smell

In addition to sight, hearing, and feeling, you may also use your senses of taste and smell to help produce your psychic images. It is now time to add them to your intuitive assessment exercise. Some of you will get powerful images through smell. The smells you sense may come to you as a communication from the Other Side, or you may experience a smell from a different period of time when you visit certain locations. Whenever you are receiving psychic information, pay attention to which one or more of your senses are gathering the information.

As you remain in the trance, ask yourself the following questions. Do certain tastes or smells evoke psychic images? Do these images relate to past lives or future events? Or can you experience something that is taking place in present time, simultaneously though in a different location? Do you ever have visions? If so, in which one or more of the five senses do you experience them?

Can you visit a location and experience it in a different period of time, using all five of your senses? Can you see, hear, feel, taste, or smell what took place there before or what will take place there in the future? Can you project to a different location and experience with all your five senses what is happening at the same moment? Can you communicate using your mind with someone who is not with you physically?

Can you see, feel, hear, or smell other spirits? Do your guides, angels, or other spirits have a particular scent? Which one or more of your senses are the strongest and most reliable at experiencing psychic external images? Which sense is the weakest? Are there any other types of psychic images that you experience that could be developed for positive use and to help guide you along your life map?

Create a Psychic Anchor

You have now engaged your five different senses in imagery designed to help you identify your psychic gifts. The more you can identify your strengths, the more useful they will be in the rest of this book as you examine specific psychic functions. You may be strong in all of them or strong in some of them.

When you are in your relaxed state, with your chakras in balance, give yourself a key word or touch that will help you bring back your intuitive state. The more you can enter a safe and protected intuitive trance, the more you will maintain your balance. It is okay to carry your bubble with you.

ALERT!

If you feel overwhelmed emotionally and are having trouble finding a balance in your life, you should seek out a qualified counselor in your area. Sometimes a person forgets how to close an open channel once it is open, and in that case it is advisable to get some help.

Beware of Misusing Your Gifts

The goal as you develop your psychic gifts is to understand what your ability is and to become comfortable in engaging it. Remember, no one on earth is just like you. No one has your special psychic abilities.

However, there are people who use their psychic gifts for their own selfish gain. They are very good at identifying absorbers, for instance, and taking full advantage of them to satisfy their egos. They have a need to control with their psychic powers. But what they don't realize is that the power they wield is not their own but the power of the Universe. They may possess what seems to others great power and control in their current lifetime, but they may be out of tune with their life purpose. It is inevitable that they will have to settle the score with their karmas sometime in the future. Beware of these psychic predators who feed on the unsuspecting, leaving a wake of confusion and self-doubt in those whom they successfully dominate. Ⓔ

Chapter 11

Astral Projection and Telekinetic Powers

In this chapter you will have the opportunity to learn about and experience astral projection through physical or mental out-of-body experiences. Then, you will practice mental telepathy and psychokinesis, a fancy word for feats like spoon bending or moving a solid object with your mind.

Out-of-Body Experiences

Chances are that at some time in your life, you experienced the sensation that a part of you was leaving your body and that you were flying through space. It could have happened when you were asleep, or it may have happened when you were awake. If this is true, then you have had an out-of-body experience, otherwise known as astral projection.

There are many theories about what takes place during an out-of-body experience. Some believe that there is some form of energy that leaves the body and goes someplace else. The destination could be somewhere on the earth plane or in some other dimension. It could be a time long past or it could be the future. It may be far away—even in distant galaxies—or it may be heaven.

Edgar Cayce practiced astral projection in many of his readings. He would go out into the Universe to the Akashic Book of Records and review the history of the soul that he was doing a reading on. He also traveled to the location of many of the subjects who would request readings through the mail. He even seemed to be able to travel through the subject's body and see the medical problems the person had.

FACT

Once, while Cayce was in his trance state, someone passed an object over his body, through his energy field, and it severed his connection to the Akashic Book of Records. When it happened, he suddenly sat up. His body acted as if something had been disconnected.

An Ancient Memory

It is possible that your soul knows the ancient skill of astral projection. It may be that something was deposited deep inside your unconscious mind at a time when your soul had no physical form, when you were free to ride the waves of energy through the different dimensions of the Universe.

As your soul reincarnated, it eventually evolved into a human form. Now, do you feel as if the weight of your physical body holds you back from the enjoyment of travel that you had so many lifetimes ago? Or are you worried that you might fly again, only to become separated from your physical body with the possibility that you might not be able to return?

Many adults can remember when as children they had an unsettling experience of finding themselves suspended in air, separated from their physical bodies. The first time it happened to Pam, she got up after a nap and noticed that her body was still lying down. In a state of panic, she quickly laid back down and carefully reconnected with her physical body. You may have had a similar experience, and like her, you may not want to have another one.

Shamans from many different cultures have traveled to other dimensions through their out-of-body experiences. In an altered state of consciousness, a shaman can travel through the earth, sky, and the underworld. To help them perform the journey, shamans use guides, animal helpers, or even psychedelic drugs. Perhaps you have a memory in your unconscious or Universal Mind of being a shaman in a past life.

Alien Abductions

Another form of out-of-body experience is alien abduction. There are several different types of encounters, including sleep abductions. Sleep abductions can take place at night, when the victim is sound asleep. The aliens may transport the whole body up to a waiting spaceship. In other cases the physical body is not taken—only the person's essence is removed.

Once they have been transported, the abductees are examined and experimented on by the extraterrestrials. They are then returned to their beds. Victims cannot consciously remember the experience, but they often have a sense that something is wrong. Hypnosis can be used to regress the person back to the event and relive the experience. Many subjects who have no way of knowing each other's experiences still relate stories that are very similar.

Near-Death Experiences

Another form of out-of-body experience is the near-death experience. Have you ever had a near-death experience? Many who are revived from a state near death relate similar experiences of floating free of their bodies and observing their deaths from above. Then, they feel as if they are being pulled toward the light, but for some reason instead of joining the light, they return to their bodies.

Survivors of a near-death experience are never quite the same afterward. Their five senses are often changed and are much more sensitive than they were before. This change results in sort of a state of hyperawareness that causes them to respond differently to sensory input, even though they may not realize what has taken place.

ALERT!

If you would like to read more about near-death experiences, one of the first books on the subject is *Life after Life* by Dr. Raymond Moody. The book relates similar stories by patients of what happened between the time they were declared clinically dead and the time they came back to life.

It is not known exactly what transpires in a near-death experience, anymore than we know what happens during other out-of-body experiences. Even though there is no scientific proof, many nurses claim to see the soul leave a body after it physically dies.

Astral Projection in Four Parts

Experiences of astral projection may be physical or mental, and they may occur spontaneously or be consciously evoked. Let's look at the physical out-of-body experiences first. These experiences involve transportation of your physical form so that you have actual physical experiences through all your senses. A physical out-of-body experience can be very powerful. However, it can also cause much more stress if you are not balanced and grounded.

It is also possible for your mental body to separate from your physical body. With this type of out-of-body experience, you would not feel your body traveling with you. You would be more of an observer than a participant. When you come back, you might remember your out-of-body experience in the form of new wisdoms, insights, or visions.

Spontaneous Astral Projection

Some of your out-of-body experiences may occur spontaneously, without warning. In such cases you are not aware of what is going to happen until it happens, and suddenly you are on some type of astral plane. You may be transported out of your physical body, or you may feel your physical body itself lifting up. You may find yourself suspended in midair or in a specific location, which you may or may not recognize.

The spontaneous out-of-body experience is usually the one that causes a great deal of concern to the traveler. It can first happen at any time, and when you have no knowledge of what astral projection is, you will have no choice but to be totally unprepared. You may have had such an experience and now live in fear that it may happen again. These spontaneous experiences often happen when you are ungrounded and in a state of some sort of confusion. It is during this unbalanced state that you are open to the energies that enter your chakras and cause an out-of-body experience.

If you have experienced spontaneous out-of-body experiences before, and you worry about them happening again, develop a technique to keep yourself grounded and always connected to the golden thread of the Universe. Give yourself a key word (or an anchor) that can bring you instantly back.

Learn to recognize the conditions that help produce your spontaneous out-of-body experiences. If you are aware of what takes place just before you leave, you can interrupt the astral projection and bring yourself back to consciousness.

Planned Out-of-Body Experiences

A planned out-of-body experience is one that you specifically strive to achieve. This is done through properly preparing yourself physically, mentally, and spiritually. The better you take care of your physical body with proper diet and exercise, the better prepared you will be to handle the exertion that astral travelers sometimes feel. Otherwise, you run the risk of facing health issues.

Being in the proper mental and spiritual frame of mind is also very important for an out-of-body experience. If you are out of balance, confused, or focused on anything but peace and love, your trip may not be a positive and productive one. If you are in tune with your Belief and ask that you receive the proper experience, you will be much more prepared. You may go where you want to go, or you may wind up in a place where you are supposed to be.

ALERT!

Before you try astral projection, make sure you are very comfortable with the technique and that you trust it for safe use for out-of-body experiences. And always remember that you may always come back to consciousness at any time.

Psychic Invasions

Have you ever seen a physical image of someone who is in the same place as you, but you know that it is impossible for him or her to really be there? Sometimes it's a very strong feeling that someone is there, or you may hear a voice or experience a smell. Perhaps they have come to visit you on an astral plane. Their presence is so powerful that you actually see an impression of them. This visit may be wanted, but that isn't always the case.

Some of you are more at risk from psychic invaders than others. You may already have a natural psychic defense system, like your golden bubble, guides, angels, or other beings that fend off unwanted visitors. But if you are vulnerable or unbalanced, and let your protective guard down, you could be open to psychic invaders. These visitors might not mean harm, but they have no sense of someone's privacy. They can rob you of your sense of self.

Safeguarding Yourself

If this is a problem for you (and up until this time you may not even have known it), there are some basic steps to take that will help you deal with unwanted visitors:

1. Always stay grounded and connected to your Belief safeguarded by the Golden Light of the Universe.
2. Keep yourself balanced physically, mentally, and spiritually.
3. Stay in constant communication with your guides, angels, or other spirits.
4. Listen to your inner guidance system.
5. Pay attention to what is taking place around and inside you.
6. Learn to trust and rely on your helpers. If you sense an invasion, ask them to intervene.

There may be times when you want to have a visitor. If that's the case, set up a time and ask them to join you.

Many of you travel in your dreams. You may be more successful lifting off when you're sleeping than when you're awake. Some of you may go places in your dreams that you actually plan to visit in the future.

It is also possible for you to have visitors while you are in your dream state. If you go to sleep unbalanced, you may be opening yourself to unwanted invaders who project into your open chakras. The best protection is to use the same technique that you use for psychic invaders when you are not asleep.

Go Places with Your Mind

It's time to try a little space travel. Before you begin, you need to know that each person experiences astral projection differently. That's a result of our differing mental makeup and sense perception abilities. (For a good review of your sensory abilities, refer to Chapter 5.) When you have an out-of-body experience, you may not be able to process your experience in all five senses—and that's okay. Your mind will make up for it in other ways.

Knowing how your senses can work for you may help give you more control in astral projection. You can tune them up or down, step back and observe, experience emotions, or control many other aspects of your out-of-body experience.

You May Begin

If you're ready, find a comfortable place to sit or lie down. You may want to try placing your body in a position that feels as though at any time you could be floating on your back. Lying on your back with your arms and legs spread apart may help produce the feeling of flying or floating on water. You may begin by breathing in and out slowly.

You may continue to take nice deep breaths as you feel yourself relaxing more and more. You may experience muscles that are stiff and muscles that are relaxed. Every time you feel a muscle stiffen up, you may relax it, as your entire body relaxes more and more.

You may now let your eyes close and focus on your third eye. As you connect, allow the peace and love of the Universe to flow through your third-eye chakra.

Take a moment, and enjoy this special feeling of peace and love as you continue to breathe in and out slowly. You may allow yourself to feel the Golden Light of the Universe begin to flow down through your body. As it works its way downward, you may feel the golden light opening and balancing the energy flow through each of your centers: the throat, the heart, the solar plexus, the navel, and the root. When you are ready, let the loving energy flow in and out of your body as your crown chakra opens to universal guidance.

Now, let yourself feel the golden bubble of the Universe totally surrounding your earthly body. Focus on your third eye, and feel the golden thread of the Universe grounding you and providing a secure tether to your earthly ties. You may feel safe and secure and fully protected by your universal beam of golden light. Let all of your five senses become aware as you experience peace and love and prepare to float up into the Universe.

Physical Astral Projection

When you are ready, allow yourself to focus on the beam of golden light. Let yourself feel its gentle pull as it slowly lifts you upward. You may feel the strength of the Universe as it begins to lift you up and up. You may experience this with all your senses: seeing, hearing, feeling, tasting, and smelling. Feel your body lifting upward.

ESSENTIAL

You may not feel your entire body lifting up. You may feel only your mental body as it leaves your physical body. In other words, you may feel a physical out-of-body experience or a mental out-of-body experience. One type of travel may work better for you than the other.

Let yourself float up a little at first, and feel both the lightness of your body and the positive tether that connects you to the ground and to the Universe. Look around and experience your new surroundings in all your five senses. Now let yourself float upward in the atmosphere. You may be aware that you are traveling through a tunnel or following a beam of light. You may ask that you go where you will be shown new insights that relate to your life map.

When you arrive, take some time to get acclimated. Let your five senses come into focus as you prepare to investigate. When you are ready to follow the golden tether back home again, take a deep breath, exhale, and return to your conscious mind filled with the peace and love of the Universe.

ALERT!

Always give yourself a suggestion when you are in your relaxed state of consciousness that all you have to do to stop the experience is follow your tether back to earth, take a deep breath, exhale, and open your eyes to be once again in a positive, peaceful, and loving state of consciousness.

Mental Astral Projection

To try mental astral projection, follow the same technique of relaxing, breathing, connecting to the Universal Flow, and opening and balancing your chakras. Once you feel centered and in tune, focus on your third eye and the golden tether that both grounds and guides you through your out-of-body experiences. Let yourself feel a part of your mental awareness that begins to float out of your body and upward into the atmosphere. You will feel complete freedom as you let yourself go higher and higher.

You may go along the golden tether out to the Akashic Book of Records or to other spiritual realms. You may go to a specific destination and observe the events that are taking place. You may visit time periods from the past or the future. You may meet with the masters of the collective unconsciousness in order to ask them for guidance in your life. When you're ready, you may return along the golden tether and back to your conscious world filled with the peace and love of the Universe.

Practice with a Friend

You might want to arrange to visit a friend through astral projection. Pick a time, and then try out your technique. You might not get a clear image at first, but be patient. Experience the visit in all of your five senses. When you have finished, make notes of what you experienced and check with your friend to see how close you were.

You can try both physical and mental astral projection. You can reverse roles and let your friend visit you. You may want to pick a place to meet and project yourselves there. You might try meeting in a past life or in the future. As you do, be sure to remember that you always keep yourself connected to the golden tether.

Mental Telepathy

Mental telepathy is communication on a mental level between two or more people or between people and animals. Mental telepathy is a form of clairsentience, or psychic perception of feelings. You might pick up on the emotions of a close friend or family member and suddenly know you need to contact them. Some of you may be able to hear what someone else is thinking. Some of you may be able to step into someone else's mind and see what they are seeing.

Law enforcement agencies have profilers who attempt to put themselves in the mind of the criminal so that they may gain valuable insights that will help police solve the crime. They work with known clues to help them fill in the blanks. On the other end of the spectrum, there are others with incredible gifts in telepathy that they choose to use for their own gain. These people attempt to control others—strangers or people they know—by using their psychic abilities.

Try reading minds with a friend or relative. One of you should go somewhere separate from the other, like into another room, and concentrate on an object, a word, or a symbol, while the other tries to learn what it is. Try up to five different items, one at a time, and then see how you did. You may be able to picture, hear, or feel what the correct answer is. Use your focus technique to prepare for the experiment.

FACT

In the 1980s, the U.S. Army created a special group of psychic remote viewers to help keep an eye on the country's enemies. The participants received map coordinates and were asked to project themselves to certain locations and report their observations. Unfortunately, once Congress discovered that the military was using psychics, the funding ended, and the program was terminated.

Practice Psychokinesis

Psychokinesis is the ability to levitate, to move objects (an ability known as teleportation), or to create healing. It is possible in the right mental frame of mind to summon incredible power from the Universe. The power is usually manifested while the individual is in some type of altered state of consciousness.

QUESTION?

What is teleportation?
Teleportation allows the mental movement of objects over a distance. The goal is to send a powerful mental energy that will actually shift a solid object. The energy could manifest itself as heat, as power, as an electrical current, or as a healing energy.

You can practice with a small object, perhaps one that will roll easily, like a compass that has a floating needle. After you have gotten yourself into a relaxed state and are in balance, allow yourself to feel the power of the Universe begin to flow down from your crown or third-eye chakra. Choose whichever is the most comfortable to use and provides the greatest strength. Now focus on an object that is within two feet of you. Relax and begin to feel the power of the Universe building up energy in your third eye. Let yourself visualize a solid wall of Universal Energy begin to push the object.

Be patient. It may take some time to adjust the power and refine the imagery that you use. Try changing your focus from your third eye to your fingers. Now let the Universal Power flow down over your shoulders, upper arms, elbows, lower arms, wrists, and finally to your fingers. They may tingle with the energy or fill with heat. You can use that energy to shift the object in front of you.

Always be patient, and remember that you have a gift that is as strong and maybe stronger than any of these. It may work for this type of psychic use, or it may be more useful for another type. When you have finished, release the psychic energy and come back to consciousness, full of the peace and love of the Universe.

A Spoon-Bending Exercise

Here is another fun psychokinetic exercise for you to try. Find a metal spoon that is not of value and okay to bend. Prepare yourself physically, mentally, and spiritually. Hold the end of the handle in one hand and the bowl of the spoon with the thumb and first finger of the other hand. Now imagine a wave of Universal Energy or heat coming down over your shoulders and all the way to your fingertips. Feel the power build to a point where the energy will literally melt the thin handle where it is connected onto the bowl of the spoon so that the spoon bends.

Yes, you can bend spoons—and do so much more. If you are in tune with your natural psychic gifts, the power of the Universe is ready and waiting to help you in your life work.

The Universe has incredible power, and this power is there for you to use. It is your choice whether to use it for yourself or the good of others. If you misuse it, you will face the consequences of your actions again, in a future karma. It is a wonderful opportunity and responsibility at the same time.

Chapter 12

Psychic Work in Your Sleep

Everyone dreams—even though each person's experience is different—but not everyone can remember his or her dreams. After you wake up, as you make an effort to remember your dreams, you will begin to recognize various types of dreams and their meanings. Then, you will be able to work with the psychic information that you receive in your dream state.

Psychic Dreams

Dreams are a great medium for receiving psychic information. They come at a time when your conscious mind is at rest and open to the messages of your unconscious and your Universal Mind. Because your conscious mind is so active, many of you do not relax enough while you are awake to receive the information that is there for you. At night, you may have many dreams, but most of them go unnoticed. Even if you are aware of having dreamt when you wake up, you may quickly forget the contents of those dreams.

ALERT!

If you dream of something more than once, pay attention. Many psychic dreams are given to you for a specific reason. They may concern your health, safety, or even career choice.

Dream Recall

When you prepare for bed, make an entry into your dream journal—you can also use a tape recorder. Make sure the listing includes the time, what you last ate, and when and how you feel mentally, physically, and spiritually. If you have a request for your guides, angels, higher power, or just for the Universe, ask that an answer may come in your dreams.

Then, when you awake, make sure that you record your dreams as you remember them. Include as many details about your dream as you can remember—the type of dream, theme, people, places, time period, and whether you have had this or similar dreams before.

Just as with any other type of memory recall, you may remember more of a dream over time. There are many pieces of information that the conscious mind doesn't notice, but they are taken in and stored in the unconscious mind. Your post-dream notes can help prime your unconscious memory pump. Once the memory is activated, it is possible to recall a lot more of the dream experience than was first noted.

I'm trying so hard to remember my dreams, but it seems that I'm not making a lot of progress. Should I keep trying?
When you first begin to work with your dreams, you may not feel as if you are making a lot of progress. The more patience you have, and the more willing you are to experiment with your dreams, the more your potential for growth will expand.

Dream Patterns

Even if you wake with no conscious memory of a dream, make a note in your journal about how you feel. Over a period of time, the data you collect will help you establish your sleep and dream patterns. Do your dreams occur regularly or sporadically? Do you remember dreams daily, weekly, monthly, or less often than that? Do you have specific dreams for specific moments in your life? Do you dream more when you eat certain foods before you go to bed?

The following sections will help you distinguish between various types of psychic dreams, including dreams that have to do with your past lives, dreams concerning the future, symbolic dreams, dreams of healing and creativity, and dreams that you share with others.

Looking Back to Previous Lives

One type of dream that often starts in childhood and may or may not continue into adulthood are dreams that deal with a past life. Children may not recognize that what they are dreaming is from a past life, but they may notice that in their dream, they and their family members appear in different roles.

A past-life dream is set during a different time period. The dream may be repetitious and have a theme that was imprinted in the soul of the past life. It's not unusual for the past-life dream to be traumatic—many of these dreams are nightmares. For example, a past-life dream may be an event that led up to a death scene, with the dream ending before the actual event. Upon waking, the feeling of terror lingers.

Past-life dreams are often karmic in nature. In other words, your dream may relate to unfinished business from a previous lifetime. The dream may give you a clue as to how you can resolve the karma in your current lifetime. It is possible to use a past-life dream as the catalyst to go deeper into the past life through the technique of hypnosis.

Look for Clues

Here is how you can figure out whether a particular dream is giving you clues or revealing episodes concerning your past life. Often, these dreams have visual images that you recognize. Does the dream's location seem familiar and yet as though it doesn't belong to your lifetime? Sometimes that distinction is easy to make, and sometimes it is not. A child may not recognize the difference of a few years, whereas an adult would. Also, if the turnaround time between incarnations is short, the child may blend his or her current life with the one that he or she experiences just previously.

If there are people in the dream, how are they dressed? Are they wearing modern clothes? Can you see yourself in the dream, or are you only experiencing it? If you cannot see yourself, hypnosis may help you get more information about who the characters in your dream may have been.

Is there anything else that may give you a clue about the possibility of a past-life dream? You may awake from a past-life dream with an emotion that connects to another lifetime. What other clues would you collect from a dream to imply that it may have been about your past lives?

Dreams of Flight

A subset of past-life dreams are flying dreams. Have you ever dreamed that you are able to soar in the sky, as free as a bird? Some people believe that dreams of flying date back to the earliest reincarnations of your soul because they go back to a time when you had no physical form. At that time you were able to travel using the pure energy of thought as your power. Dreams give your soul a chance to fly again without the constraints of your physical, human body.

Do you fly in any of your dreams? If so, where do you go? Do you travel to other worlds or to heavenly realms? Do you fly backward or forward in time? Where else do you fly? Do you fly alone or with others? Can you choose a destination before you go to sleep and fly there during a dream? Do you ever dream about falling or floating? Is there a pattern to these dreams?

Some people actually dream so deeply that when they leave their body, another entity comes in to occupy it. Before you go to sleep, remind yourself to stay grounded at all times.

Seeing into the Future

Do you have dreams about events that have not happened yet? Many of the great prophets throughout history have relied on their dreams to provide the insights that helped rulers make their decisions about the future. These predictions included floods, famines, and other weather changes. They also included predictions of wars and threats to the people, the land, and even to the rulers themselves.

When you are out of balance and your energy centers are open, you are susceptible to receiving psychic images from the Universe. These images include events that have not yet happened. When you go to sleep in a state of confusion and out of balance, your dreams become a conduit for images of the future. Unfortunately many of these types of dreams are not happy, but tragic.

Jenny, an early-childhood schoolteacher, had a very unsettling dream of a teenage boy being beaten and then a large building blowing up. The images were so strong that she could barely concentrate the next day in school. At home after work, she turned on the television, and there on the screen was the building she had seen in her dreams the night before. It was the Oklahoma City bombing.

Good and Bad

Is there a pattern to your prophetic dreams? Do you dream of winning numbers in the lottery before they are drawn? Do you dream about questions and answers on tests before you take them? Do you dream of meeting people and then actually meet them?

Do you dream of future events? If so, are these related to your life and the lives of others you know? Are your dreams about events that may take place on a worldwide scale? Do you dream of disasters before they happen, such as plane crashes, assassinations of famous people, or wars? How often do you have this type of dream?

FACT

Prophetic dreams may be messages from your guides, angels, or other forms of higher power. They are often given to you as a warning for the future. Listen to yourself after you have a prophetic dream. Your psychic intuition will indicate how you should respond.

How do you feel during and after you have a prophetic dream? Do you feel helpless, or are you compelled to take action as a result of your dream? Where do you think your prophetic dreams are coming from? Do you wish that you could block out this type of dream? What else do you experience when you have a dream about the future?

Lucid Dreams

It's possible to change a dream's outcome if you enter into a state known as lucid dreaming. You have a lucid dream when you move from dreaming into a waking state while the dream still continues. As you become fully conscious that you are experiencing the dream, you have the opportunity to control the dream events and change the dream's outcome. Try entering your dream state again, and consciously change the outcome of the dream. If it is a bad dream, run your positive feelings of peace and love over the negative image and sleep in peace.

Your Dream's Symbolic Meaning

Once in a while, you will experience a dream that feels like a riddle. It may involve snippets and pieces of events in your life, usually close in time to when the dream is experienced. These snippets may be from news accounts, or they may come from some memory in your unconscious mind. These pieces are woven into the dream theme but are out of character with the actual events.

Symbolic dreams may come in sequences or segments. They may be experienced over several different nights or weeks. The dreams can relate to you or to events that are taking place in the world. Dream themes can deal with events that have happened or with events that have yet to happen.

Symbolic dreams are easily dismissed as nonsense dreams. These are dreams that are often attributed to too much rich food or experiences you might have lived through earlier in the day. Even when a dream seems to make no sense, make a note of it in your dream journal, and you may find a pattern developing in your symbolic dreams.

Make Attempts at Interpretation

To help you identify a dream that has symbolic content, note the apparent theme of the dream. Is it repeated in the dream? Do you have the same dream or a series of different dreams with the same recurring theme? Are there people, animals, or other beings in your symbolic dreams?

Do you have houses or rooms of a house in your dreams? How do the dreams make you feel? Can you hear voices or other sounds? Do the actions in the dreams make any sense to you at first review? What else can you note from your dreams that may be considered symbolic?

ESSENTIAL

Analysis of a symbolic dream can be complicated due to the subject material and how it relates to you. Try to record as much information as soon as possible in your dream journal. Someone else, or a book on dreams, may provide a clue as to what and why you dreamed it.

Healing Dreams

Healing dreams are not as common as other types of dreams, but they can occur when they are needed. Healing dreams may originate from either the unconscious or Universal Mind. You may be too consciously involved with the medical condition of loved ones or yourself to look at the situation rationally. In other words, you may not be hearing what you are unconsciously telling yourself.

Dreams are a good way for your unconscious mind to get the message up to your conscious mind. While you are asleep, you are not analyzing the images sent up to you. Valuable clues to your medical condition, and possibly even your treatment, can come from your unconscious mind. The same may be true for information given to you about others, including friends and family, that may provide you with a different perspective.

A healing dream could also be meant for resolving old conflicts that have torn lives apart. These dream images may come to you with information that will give you a way to help say or write the right words to someone. They may include new insights that will help you resolve, either in your own mind or in communication with others, a situation that needs to be resolved and healed. A healing dream may come in the form of inspiration to compose or create a work of art or a poem that will bring about healing.

Identifying Healing Dreams

Do you have healing dreams? If so, how often? Are they dreams about yourself, members of your family, or other people? How do you receive your information—in symbols, actual pictures, voices, feelings, or in some other way? Do you wake up with a feeling of knowing that there is healing, rather than dreaming a picture image?

Do you ask for healing information to come through for you or others before you go to sleep? If so, how often do you get answers? Do you get healing messages to pass on to others? Do you receive healing poems, music, or artistic ideas in your dreams? If so, can you complete the idea into something that helps heal yourself and/or others?

FACT

Australian Aborigines, whose culture dates back as far as 65,000 years, can relate to their Creator through Dreamtime. Dreamtime is an altered state that helps them get back in touch with their ancient beginnings.

Simultaneous Dreaming

A dream experienced simultaneously between two or more people is known as a shared dream. Some shared dreams are also prophetic, and they signal a world event to come. These dreams may happen within a short time span, often only a few days before the event actually happens. Other shared dreams are simpler—they may be something that you share with a friend. Later, both of you realize that you had the same dream.

Past-life dreams may be shared as well, often by members of the same family. These dreams can go unnoted for years, unless someone brings up the subject for discussion. One couple found they both had the same recurring dream of drowning. They eventually discovered that their son had been having the same dream.

Compare Your Dreams

Have you ever discussed your dreams with other family members or friends? If so, have you found any similarities between your dreams and theirs? If you have not brought up the subject of dreams, you may want to try it. Suggest that you and a friend keep dream journals and compare them. You might like to form a dream group and meet at specific times to discuss your dreams.

The Internet is an excellent way to share your dream experiences. There are many Web sites dedicated to dream sharing. You may be surprised when you begin to talk about dreams with friends or family members to discover that you may have been dreaming the same thing for quite a while.

Inspiration and Creativity

Some of the world's great inventions have come from the dream state. Ideas for great books, music, and poetry can come through your dreams. They can come from your unconscious mind, usually when you have been thinking about a particular topic or problem. The unconscious mind simply put together all the information it had and sent it up to you while you were in your dream state.

FACT

There is a story that the sewing machine was invented with the help of a dream. In the dream, a native was throwing a spear that had rope attached to the point. When the inventor woke up, he had an idea. Changing the thread placement in the needle made it possible for the sewing machine to work.

The Universal Mind may send you information that you can use for a specific purpose. This information is given to you in the area that you are creative. If you are a musician, you will receive music; if you are a poet, you will receive the idea or words for a poem.

There is a difference between the information that comes from the unconscious and the Universal Mind. The latter information is about something you have not been working on, but something that you can do for the good of many. Use the same methods as mentioned earlier to identify and use your creative dreams.

Reviewing Your Dreams

You can use relaxation exercises to help you review your dreams. Before you let yourself go into a trance, reread or listen to your notes on the dream sequence that you want to review. Keep these handy so that you can refer to them again when you are in a relaxed state. When you're ready, get comfortable. Focus on your breathing and begin to relax your body.

Let your eyes close, and focus on your third eye. Feel the Universal Flow of peaceful and loving energy enter your body as you feel all your chakras opening and balancing. You may suggest to yourself that when you want to refer to your notes, you may open your eyes and still feel very relaxed and able to recall the memories of your dream. When you're ready, let the images of a part of your dream come into focus. You may experience your images in all five senses: seeing, hearing, feeling, tasting, and smelling.

Work with Your Sensory Images

If you are visual, focus on one picture image and see if you can change your view, bringing images closer or moving them back. Try to stop the action so that you can look for things you missed before. Now try to imagine the sounds that go with the images. If you can, change the volume or move around in the image and hear sounds as you move. Next, add feeling to your images.

Can you experience emotions connected to your dream? Can you place yourself in the dream and experience textures, temperatures, tastes, and smells? Can you experience your dream in all the five different senses? Can you discover things in your dream that you had not noticed before? Can you back up the dream to a point earlier than you can remember, or can you move forward to continue the dream beyond where it had stopped?

ESSENTIAL

The Everything® Dreams Book by Trish and Rob MacGregor is an excellent resource to help you study your dreams. The work covers everything from fantasies to nightmares, and it provides lots of help in interpreting dreams.

When you first begin to work with your dreams, be patient. It may take awhile for you to develop your dream recall technique. The way you recall is different from anyone else's, and so is the psychic information you receive in your dreams. It's like learning any other skill; the more you practice, the more you will learn to recall and interpret what you are experiencing through your dreams. Your dreams are truly the mirror image of your soul.

Improving Your Psychic Dreaming

If you are an active dreamer, or if you feel that your dreams can be a good resource for providing you with information from either your unconscious or your Universal Mind, here is an exercise to help you tune in to your dreams even better.

One of the most important things to do before going to sleep is to make sure you are grounded in your protective universal bubble, in balance with your energy centers, and in tune with your Belief and your internal and external guidance systems. If you create an anchor to put yourself in touch with your guidance systems, you will be able to enter that state before you fall asleep.

Once you've done this, take a deep breath, focus on your third eye, and feel universal peace and love flowing through you. Even though you may not want to, or if you have trouble experiencing these feelings, remember that they are not related to whatever else is taking place in your life. They are just simple relaxing waves of energy provided by the Universe.

At this time, ask your Belief, your guides, angels, or other beings for help with your worries and anxieties. Ask that the information you receive from your dreams be the right information for what is needed at this particular moment.

ALERT!

It is not uncommon for you to have a visit from a deceased friend or relative in your dreams. They may come to you to comfort or warn you. The same thing may happen with your angels or guides. Your inner guidance system continues to work when you are asleep.

Chapter 13

It's in the Cards and the Stars

Psychic powers may be used in divining the future. In this chapter, you will get an introduction to two of the most common forms of divination—the Tarot and astrology. Try your hand at these two methods, and see if either one feels right for you. The knowledge and wisdom you can get by relying on Tarot and astrology can help you as you progress through your life map.

The Origins of Tarot

Even though symbols used in tarot cards may have come to us from the ancient cultures of Egypt, Greece, Rome, and China, the origins of the Tarot deck and its use in divination are much more recent. According to the International Tarot Society, Tarot comes from northern Italy, where it was introduced sometime between 1420 and 1440. At first, the Tarot was just a new type of card game, similar to bridge, which was played by the upper class in Italy and France.

The tarot cards were handcrafted and elaborately illustrated. As the game became more popular and spread, each artist would add to or change the illustrations according to his cultural interests. Today, early tarot decks are highly prized by collectors because these works of art are windows through which you can view the history of the time period when the cards were made.

Tarot and the Occult

Although a witchcraft trial in Venice in 1589 may be seen as an indication that Tarot was used in divination, it wasn't until the 1700s that these cards generally became associated with occultism. Antoine Court de Gébelin (1725–1784), a Swiss pastor who became involved in matters of the occult, came to believe that the roots of Tarot extended all the way back to ancient Egypt and that the tarot symbols contained secret knowledge that had long since been forgotten. Gébelin's ideas were embraced by Jean-Baptiste Alliette (1738–1791), who maintained that the cards were somehow connected to mystical ideas found in the Book of Thoth.

QUESTION?

What is the Book of Thoth?
The Book of Thoth is a mystical book attributed to the Egyptian god Thoth, the inventor of writing, who was believed to have known the secrets of the Universe. It is said that forty-two of his books are still buried in the Hall of Records, physically located somewhere under the Sphinx.

Another hundred years passed, and in the 1850s French occultist Alphouse Louis Constant, writing under the name of Eliphas Levi, linked tarot cards to the teachings of Jewish mysticism, or the Kaballah. Constant, who was a priest and a Rosicrucian, believed that Tarot was also related to the Bible.

Then in 1909, the Order of the Golden Dawn, a hermetic society that studied divination and magic, commissioned A. E. Waite to create a tarot deck using Golden Dawn's special symbolism. That deck, now known as the Waite-Smith set, has continued to be the most widely used in the United States, although there are many different styles on the market as well. (This chapter will refer to the Waite-Smith set. If you would like to use an alternate set, the interpretations for each card may not apply.)

A. E. Waite standardized the tarot deck to include seventy-eight cards, divided into the Major Arcana and Minor Arcana. The Major Arcana is comprised of twenty-two thematic trump cards that represent archetypal forces in your life. With the exception of the Fool, each card in the Major Arcana is assigned a number. The Minor Arcana includes fifty-six cards subdivided into four suits: cups, swords, wands, and pentacles (originally, wands were polo sticks and pentacles were coins). Each of the suits contains ace through ten, plus page, knight, queen, and king. The cards of the Minor Arcana can help you focus on your direction in your life journey.

Using Tarot in Divination

Tarot is no longer played like a game of cards. The deck is now mainly used as a tool to forecast the future. At first, learning to read the Tarot may seem like an insurmountable task. That's why there are professional readers who can interpret the cards for you. The reader's job is really to help you become aware of your life's direction and of the positive and negative outcomes as you continue your journey.

If you decide that you want to use the Tarot to enhance your psychic abilities, you should try different decks to see which one feels right for you. It may be that you relate to particular images, or perhaps you'll get certain psychic sensory clues that are evoked by a certain sense. Consider your other spiritual interests—you may relate to nature, to particular symbols, or to Native American imagery. What you are looking for is a set that will resonate with your psyche.

FACT

When you receive a Tarot reading from a psychic, the cards themselves act as tools to help the reader create intuitive images that relate to your life. The psychic may get internal information from his or her guidance system in one or more of the five senses.

The next section will give you one method of reading the Major Arcana cards in a divination exercise. For a more detailed look at the Tarot, check out *The Everything® Tarot Book* by M. J. Abadie.

The Cards of the Major Arcana

As you read these brief descriptions of the cards that compose the Major Arcana, do not try to memorize every detail. Your unconscious mind will absorb the information that is right for you. This information will come back to the surface of your conscious mind at the moment you need to know it. Your biggest task is to stay in tune so that you will be open and able to recognize the psychic information when it appears.

The Fool

This card has no number and may represent you and your life journey. There are many different symbols within the card's illustrations that may lead you to look back over your life or forward into the future. As you look at the Fool, you may connect with the great Superconscious and the life energy that flows through the symbols. The Fool is your ticket to the journey of life through the Sacred Circle of Tarot. The rest of the cards help shape the journey of the Fool.

The Magician (1)

The Magician is assigned the number "1" in the Major Arcana. This card signifies your conscious mind and the material world. The Magician can help you set your goals and develop an action plan, and this card may serve as a reminder for you to examine the direction in which you are headed.

The High Priestess (2)

The High Priestess is assigned the number "2" in the Major Arcana. This card represents your unconscious mind. It can provide a balance to the Magician. Together, the Magician and the High Priestess can help manifest your unconscious abilities and bring them to reality.

The Empress (3)

The Empress is assigned the number "3" in the Major Arcana. This card represents your memory, which is also a part of your unconscious mind. The Empress can help manifest realities as it combines with the High Priestess and Magician cards.

The Emperor (4)

The Emperor is assigned the number "4" in the Major Arcana. This card is similar to the Magician, except that it represents older and wiser knowledge. It helps balance the conscious mind and its material goals.

The Hierophant (5)

The Hierophant is assigned the number "5" in the Major Arcana. In the ancient Greek Eleusian mysteries, the Hierophant was the chief priest. Today, someone who is an advocate or who makes a case for somebody else is called a hierophant. This card represents your inner self, in particular your intuition. The Hierophant represents the process that your unconscious mind goes through when it evaluates the information sent down from your conscious mind.

Whenever you use a tool such as a tarot card deck to help you get psychic insights, make sure that you are in tune and in balance with both your internal and external guidance systems. If you are not, you may be startled by unexpected intuitive information.

The Lovers (6)

The Lovers card is assigned the number "6" in the Major Arcana. The Lovers represents your relationships. This card indicates the differences between you and others and yet offers an opportunity for compatibility.

The Chariot (7)

The Chariot is assigned the number "7" in the Major Arcana. This card represents both your positive and your negative efforts to control your journey. The Chariot provides you with the opportunity to balance your free will and soul purposes.

Strength (8)

The Strength card is assigned the number "8" in the Major Arcana. This card is your control over your ego or materialistic goals. The Strength card represents the kundalini energy that is coiled and ready to surge at the base of your spine.

The Hermit (9)

The Hermit is assigned the number "9" in the Major Arcana. This card represents your inner wisdom, which sets you apart from others. The Hermit reminds you that you have the opportunity to share your knowledge and help others in their journey.

Wheel of Fortune (10)

The Wheel of Fortune is assigned the number "10" in the Major Arcana. This card represents your knowledge of who you are. Regardless of what you may own, the true essence of yourself is your true wealth.

Justice (11)

The Justice card is assigned the number "11" in the Major Arcana. This card represents the process of resolving the issues and wrongs in your past. The past is not only this lifetime, but also the unresolved karma of your past lives.

The Hanged Man (12)

The Hanged Man is assigned the number "12" in the Major Arcana. This card depicts a man who is suspended upside down. The Hanged Man represents your ability to understand the second view of a situation. It's a hologram of two different focuses, the ability to see from two perspectives, as discussed throughout this book.

E ALERT!

You may notice that some of the Major Arcana tarot cards, such as Death or the Hanged Man, seem to have negative images. This is not the case, as you will understand when you read the card explanations more closely.

Death (13)

The Death card is assigned the number "13" in the Major Arcana. This card represents your rebirth into a higher level of consciousness. It is your opportunity to realize that you only take beyond the physical world what you have accumulated in your inner self on your life journey.

Temperance (14)

The Temperance card is assigned the number "14" in the Major Arcana. This card represents how you balance your positive and negative qualities. The Temperance card provides you with the opportunity to balance your conscious and unconscious minds.

The Devil (15)

The Devil is assigned the number "15" in the Major Arcana. This card represents the areas of your life that blind you to negative thoughts and deeds. Through the Devil card, you are given the opportunity to be aware of those of your actions that are contrary to the purpose of your life journey.

The Tower (16)

The Tower is assigned the number "16" in the Major Arcana. This card represents how you may suddenly become enlightened. The Tower is the psychic intuition that often comes exploding through your chakras when they are not balanced.

The Star (17)

The Star is assigned the number "17" in the Major Arcana. This card represents how you connect your unconscious mind to the Universal Mind. The Star reminds you of your opportunity to share with others the universal knowledge that comes to the surface of your conscious mind.

The Moon (18)

The Moon is assigned the number "18" in the Major Arcana. This card represents how you develop as you progress along your life journey. This card reminds you that you always have the opportunity to bring yourself back in tune with your soul's purpose.

The Sun (19)

The Sun is assigned the number "19" in the Major Arcana. This card represents symbolically your ability to offer life to all things in the same way as the light of the sun does. It gives you the opportunity, through nurturing love, to help others grow and flourish on their life journeys.

Judgment (20)

The Judgment card is assigned the number "20" in the Major Arcana. This card represents your spirituality and how you work with the Universal Mind. It offers you the opportunity to find a balance with your conscious, unconscious, and Universal Mind.

The World (21)

The World card is assigned the number "21" in the Major Arcana. The last card in the Major Arcana, the World card reminds you that your life is a never-ending cycle. It encourages you always to be aware of the Universal Mind and the journey of your soul and also gives you the opportunity to be in tune with your soul's psychic gifts which have been with you since the beginning of your journey.

Follow Your Inner Wisdom

Did you notice the similarity between the explanations of the cards of the Major Arcana and other forms of psychic development discussed earlier in this book? You may want to start working with the Major Arcana cards when you begin to use the Tarot.

To do a reading, separate the Major Arcana cards from the rest of the deck and shuffle them. Before you begin, ground yourself in a bubble of universal love and peace, and ask your psychic guides to provide information through the cards that can give you positive insights in your life.

> It is not necessary for you to follow any particular order in choosing the cards for your reading. The simplest way is to randomly draw a card out of the deck and examine it. Your intuitive mind will help you understand the reason you selected this particular card.

You can shuffle the deck and lay out the top three cards face-down from left to right in front of you. These three cards can represent your past, present, and future. Turn them over in the order you dealt them out, giving yourself time to reflect on each card. What intuitive images do the cards create in your mind? You may find that tarot cards can be an excellent tool to help you develop your psychic ability for both yourself and others.

The Roots of Astrology

Man has been fascinated with the world beyond from the first time he looked up to the heavens. We know that astronomers charted the stars of the night sky some 4,000 years before Christ was born. The Great Pyramids and the Sphinx of Giza in Egypt line up with three stars in

Orion's Belt, as it appeared more than 12,000 years ago. The Mayans of Central America also developed astrological charts to help them predict the future.

Many now believe that the three wise men who followed the stars to Bethlehem on the night of Jesus Christ's birth were in fact astrologers. The Greek scientist Ptolemy believed that the sun, moon, and planets affect human beings and events as they move through the heavens. However, in A.D. 333, Emperor Constantine declared astrology to be the work of demons and condemned the practice.

Nostradamus used astrology when he made predictions that are still being studied today. Carl Jung consulted astrological charts to help him understand his patients. His writing on the subject helped bring it back into the public spotlight in the twentieth century. More than one psychic predicted the assassination of John F. Kennedy using astrological charts. And there was much public uproar when people heard that Nancy Reagan had consulted an astrologer to help advise her husband, President Ronald Reagan.

What Is Astrology?

Astrology is a form of divination. It is based on the belief that the movement of celestial bodies affects human potential and other events on earth just as the moon directly influences the rise and fall of the ocean tides. Over the years, elaborate systems have been developed to correlate predictions of future events through the movement of these heavenly bodies. More than one system of astrology has developed. For instance, Chinese astrology is based on the phases of the moon.

One of astrology's central concepts is that because the soul is reborn at a specific time in relationship to the positions of the planets, its destiny as it journeys through its life plane is in direct relationship to the movements of celestial bodies. If you are aware of your position on earth in relationship to the stars, you have a better opportunity to be aware of your potential karmic gains and losses as you progress through your life map.

ALERT!

Astrology is a complex science and can require time and study to master, and there are many resources you can rely on if you choose. The objective of this chapter is to relate how astrology may be used as a part of your psychic development. You will be given a brief explanation of some of the symbolism that is a part of astrology.

Twelve Houses of Destiny

The most popular type of astrology today relies on the position of the sun at the time of birth to predict events in each person's future as well. Through the course of the year, the sun travels through twelve houses of the zodiac:

- *Aries*: March 21–April 19
- *Taurus*: April 20–May 20
- *Gemini*: May 21–June 20
- *Cancer*: June 21–July 22
- *Leo*: July 23–August 22
- *Virgo*: August 23–September 22
- *Libra*: September 23–October 22
- *Scorpio*: October 23–November 21
- *Sagittarius*: November 22–December 21
- *Capricorn*: December 22–January 19
- *Aquarius*: January 20–February 18
- *Pisces*: February 19–March 20

Each of the twelve signs has its own personality traits. Since you were born under a specific sign, you are expected to exhibit the personality traits of that sign. As you delve into the science of astrology, you will read about personality profiles and compatibility of the different birth signs. If you have a strong relationship with someone who has an incompatible birth sign, remember that you can help make the relationship better. Don't just abandon it.

Each of the astrological signs contains one of four elements. These elements are fire (Aries, Leo, and Sagittarius), air (Gemini, Libra, and Aquarius), water (Cancer, Scorpio, and Pisces), and earth (Taurus, Virgo, and Capricorn).

Your Horoscope

The daily positions of the planets affect each sun sign. To learn what to expect on a daily basis, many people rely on their horoscopes. Horoscopes are posted daily and are available online, in newspapers, and even on radio programs. These are general, and they apply to people according to their sun sign. Some people won't make a move until they find out what the stars say that day.

A more detailed horoscope, also known as a birth chart, is a map of the heavenly bodies as it appeared at the time of your birth. Usually, it appears in the shape of a wheel and is filled with symbols, or glyphs, for your sun and moon signs. A good astrologer has the ability to interpret the symbols to help you understand the potential meaning of your birth chart. With the astrologer's help, you can begin to use your horoscope as a guide to the future.

When an astrologer prepares your personal horoscope, he is relying on information that is based on hundreds of years of data that has been refined over time. Once you have acquired your own chart, you are free to use the information as you wish. I hope it will help you move positively through your life journey.

Learning of future possibilities with the help of your horoscope can offer you the opportunity to avoid possible hazards as you progress along your life map. If you want to investigate the science of astrology further, refer to *The Everything® Astrology Book* by Trish McGregor.

Astrology and Psychic Interpretation

Now that you've had a brief introduction to astrology, you might ask how it fits into your psychic development. Your intuition can play a big part in the way you interpret your birth chart. So the first step is to find a competent astrologer who will provide you with your personal horoscope and who will help you understand what it means. If your astrologer is also a psychic, she will be able to use her astrological knowledge in conjunction with psychic powers, such as clairvoyance, to see into your future and identify potential problems and potential opportunities.

With today's technology, it is possible to make yourself an astro-logical chart on your computer—all you need to do is purchase the software. The Internet is also a major source for information on astrology. Visit ✍ *www.astrology.com*, one of many sites that offers horoscopes, quizzes, free readings, and more.

A Reading of Your Birth Chart

You can use your own psychic ability to help you interpret your own birth chart. The proper way to prepare yourself is to balance and ground yourself in the peaceful and loving light of the Universe before you begin. You may ask your internal and external guides to help you.

Just as you have learned to access your intuitive mind, prepare yourself to do the same when you examine the information in your birth chart. Using your five senses, ask your Belief to receive the right images in your mind to help you understand your positive potentials. Now as you consider what you read or are told about yourself and your future, let your internal and external guidance systems provide you with the correct responses to help guide you.

The science of astrology, combined with psychic interpretations of your horoscope, can be a powerful tool to help you through your life journey. You are the one who can best understand how to work with your birth chart. Your psychic intuition is good, and it will help you as you travel along your journey. Ⓔ

Chapter 14

A Plethora of Psychic Tools

This chapter will introduce you to several more tools that psychics use to help them access their intuitive abilities. There are a lot of options to choose from—like using a crystal ball, casting runes, or reading brewed tea leaves, just to name a few. You will need to find the tools that can help raise your intuitive vibrational level, so try them all out, and keep yourself open to receiving psychic information.

Scrying and Divination

Scrying is a form of divination. Its name comes from the word "to descry"—to make out dimly. Scrying is usually done for the specific purpose of peering into the future. This may be done through a number of different tools. Reading a crystal ball, the smoke of a candle, or oil poured on water are all forms of visual scrying; however, any of the five senses may be used.

Scyring is actually a way of entering into a trance state. As you stare at an object and let your eyes go out of focus, a second image (a hologram) begins to appear. As you focus on the hologram, you step into a different time zone. Usually, scrying is used to see the future, but it is also possible to use scrying methods for visiting the past. As long as you focus on the second image, you will stay in your psychic trance, and when you shift back to the reality of the moment, you will return to your normal state.

Other forms of divination require that you manipulate a physical object and then enter your trance state to interpret the patterns formed by your actions. Examples of this include the casting of runes or I Ching coins. Once these items are cast, the psychic uses the unconscious mind to make interpretations of the patterns they make, seeing what possibilities the future may hold in store.

When you select a tool that can potentially enhance your psychic ability, make sure that it is in tune with your energy. Sometimes people try to use an aid that is not right for them, which can result in loss of confidence in their psychic power.

Identify and Use Your Psychic Tools

Before you begin to work with a tool, always let your energy balance and become in tune with universal love and peace. Take a few moments and center yourself. Use your self-hypnosis anchors to help you feel the protection of a golden bubble of universal light surrounding and filling you with peace and love. Ask your Universal Power that you may experience something positive from the tool you are experimenting with to help you become more in tune with your life map and soul's purpose.

While you are in a relaxed and connected intuitive state, let yourself open up to both your internal and external guidance systems. Internally, ask that the images may come through in one or more of your senses that work best for you. Ask that your external team reaffirm what your internal guidance already knows. Then let yourself be aware of the affirmations that may come to you.

A psychic tool should have the right feel. Just like rediscovering a soul mate, a psychic tool may be one that you are also finding again for the first time in this life. You may come across an implement that feels as comfortable as an old shoe. The next step is learning to trust it once more. Once you have found your old friend again, keep it with you as you continue your psychic development.

Crystal Balls

When you think of a gypsy fortuneteller, chances are you imagine a woman in mystic clothing peering into a crystal ball in a dimly lit room. As she gazes into the sphere, she begins to see a glimpse of your future. She seems to go into some sort of a spell as she continues her monologue in her monotonous voice. You may wonder how it is that this magical crystal ball holds the information of your soul.

ALERT!

As you have learned earlier in this book, every psychic you visit will read differently. Always be aware of the ones who are not true readers and use their skills for their own gain. Always compare what the psychic tells you with your own psychic knowledge of your guidance systems.

The truth is that the crystal ball is only a tool that helps induce a self-hypnotic trance in the gypsy. The sphere becomes the window through which the gypsy sees, hears, feels, tastes, or smells the vibrational level of the client's soul. Just as Edgar Cayce read the soul's history in the Akashic Records, the fortuneteller uses her trance state to access essentially the same information. All readers will gather different images through their own special techniques, which they have developed over time.

The crystal ball helps you go into your psychic trance. To try it, center on the ball, letting your eyes go out of focus, and ask your guidance system to provide you with the proper images for the information that you are asking from your Universal Mind. The more you practice and pay attention to your natural psychic intuition, the more you will be able to define the type of crystal ball that may be right for you.

Choose Your Crystal

Crystal balls come in various sizes and in a wide range of prices. Some can cost over a thousand dollars or even more, depending on the material they are made of. For some of you, the energy in rock crystals—those made of natural stone—corresponds with your psychic vibrational frequencies. In other words, the crystal may help open your psychic energy centers and make your intuitive connection stronger. If, on the other hand, your frequency and that of the crystal ball are out of sync, it may interfere with your natural psychic ability.

FACT

A natural rock crystal is generally composed of a clear piece of quartz or beryl. It is believed that these substances contain magnetic properties that can help amplify your body's own energy field. The combination of the two energies is thought to help your connection to your soul and your ability to use your psychic gifts.

Different kinds of rock crystal have different vibrational levels. The best way to find out which is right for you is to go to a store that sells several kinds of rock crystal balls so that you can compare how they resonate with your vibrational level. If you are not affected by the energy in rock crystals, you may want to look at other types of crystal balls, such as those made of glass or Lucite.

Other Types of Crystals

A crystal does not have to come in the shape of a ball or a sphere. It could be a natural shape or one that has been cut or faceted. You may find a crystal with the right vibration for you that you will want to keep with you all of the time. You might have it set into a piece of jewelry, to be used as a pendant, earrings, or ring. You may find that when you wear, touch, or hold a special crystal, you are much more in tune with your psychic ability.

Your perfect crystal might not be a crystal at all. You might find a different type of stone that contains the right energy. You could even use a piece of metal, wood, or coral to help you get into your psychic trance zone. If you are sensitive to energy, the more you learn to work with it, the more in balance your psychic vibrations will be.

Rocks and Runes

Some of you might enjoy collecting special stones that you can cast in patterns that may help produce psychic images. These stones could be from the ocean or the mountains. They may come from the same place or from many different locations. The more compatible the stones' energies are with yours, the more productive the readings will become.

You may want to begin collecting stones that have special meaning to you. Look for the right stones by placing your hands over them to see if you get a special feeling; you can also sit nearby and feel the energies emanating from them.

Once you've got a set of stones, you can begin developing a pattern in casting your stones. You could read them on the first throw or the second or the third. If you are not sure how many times you should cast the stones before reading their patterns, ask your unconscious mind for some guidance.

Once you have determined your course of action for casting, you can read your stones as often as you want. The more you do, the stronger your psychic images will begin to appear.

The Energy of the Stones

Feeling the energy of a stone or a group of stones may help induce a psychic trance. To try this, select some stones that have positive vibrations for you. You can hold them in your hands as you let your eyes go out of focus and enter your intuitive trance state. Now focus on the positive energy of the stones and ask that the right images be given you to provide answers to your questions.

You can also look for a large boulder and use its powerful energy to go into a trance. Find one that you can sit on, and try communicating with it. As you do, remember to always allow yourself to be grounded and protected in your golden bubble of light of the Universal Mind.

Casting Runes

Runes are ancient Norse symbols carved on small rocks or tiles. When a diviner casts runes, she can use the symbols to interpret the results in order to get answers to questions about the future. Make sure that the set of runes you select has an accompanying booklet that explains the meanings of the symbols and helps guide you on how to find the answers to your questions. Casting methods vary. You can select a single rune tile from a bag, cast them in lots, or place them in patterns as some people do with tarot cards.

I Ching

Another form of casting similar to rocks and runes is I Ching, an ancient Chinese method of divination. To cast I Ching, you would use three coins. After throwing the coins six times, you get a hexagram. There are sixty-four possibilities, all of which are interpreted in I Ching, or *The Book of Changes*. I Ching doesn't exactly foretell the future—it is intended to guide the searcher to find his own answers.

Tea Leaves and Other Tools

Another psychic tool that is associated with gypsy fortunetelling is tea leaves. If you would like to try reading tea leaves, brew yourself a pot using loose-leaf tea. Pour a cup, and let the tea leaves settle. As you drink the tea, communicate with your Belief. Consider your goals for the reading, and prepare to read the patterns in the leaves after you finish.

FACT

Gazing into a bowl of dark liquid is one of the oldest forms of psychic foretelling. Early rituals included the use of blood and even the entrails of freshly sacrificed animals to help create an intuitive trance state.

Here is a routine that you may want to try. After you finish your cup of tea, slowly turn the cup upside down and let any remaining liquid drain out into the saucer. Then, twirl the cup around three times, and turn it right-side up again. Now, you can gaze into the tea leaves left in the bottom of the cup and intuitively read the patterns they formed.

If you try this, be sure to use a kind of tea that you enjoy and that is also relaxing. Let your eyes go out of focus, and let the information flow up to the surface of your conscious mind. If you find this method potentially helpful, you will want to develop your own ritual for focusing.

Coffee and Water

If you are a coffee drinker, you can use the movement of the cream as it mixes with the brown liquid to help you enter your trance state. As you gaze into the cup, let your eyes go out of focus and become aware of your holographic psychic image as it emerges from the mixture. Once you have done this, you can contemplate the information you received as you sip your coffee. It is always a good idea to keep a notepad handy to help you remember your psychic information.

If you want to abstain from coffee or tea, you can also use a bowl of water and add some oil to float on the surface. As the oil forms swirls, gaze into the bowl and let your eyes go out of focus. Drift into your psychic trance and collect the information that is given to you. When you are finished, take a deep breath, feel the peace and love of the Universal Mind, and slowly come back to the surface of your conscious mind.

FACT

Nostradamus used a ritual of gazing into a bowl of water. Before he started his trance, he would dip a wand into the water and anoint himself. Then he would enter a trance that would let him see into the future.

Smoke and Steam

Smoke and steam can help induce psychic trances as well. Some psychics prefer to gaze into boiling water that has both steam and bubbles. Native Americans use sweat lodges to help them create trance visions. The dimness of the light and the feeling of the heat help create altered states in the participants.

Gazing into fog, mist, and clouds are also excellent ways to produce psychic images. Another benefit to using these elements is that you have the opportunity to go to a special place and experience the positive feelings and energy that are there to amplify your intuitive images. Once you have had a positive experience at a special location that may have had clouds, mist, or fog, develop an anchor that will help put you there in your mind anytime you want to connect to your psychic imagery. You can then use your special place as a tool and go there any time you want.

Mirror Images

A mirror is another tool that can help you enter into your psychic zone. You can certainly use a stationary mirror; another option is to find one that is rotated by a small motor. A black mirror is an excellent object to gaze into. To make one, find a picture frame that has a good piece of glass in it. Paint both the frame and the back side of the glass black. Assemble, and try using it as a psychic tool.

Gaze into the mirror and let your mind go out of focus. Reflect on the images that you are intuitively experiencing. As you define your imagery and practice going out of focus, it will be easier for you to enter your intuitive trance state.

QUESTION?

Have you ever looked out through a window that has old glass panes?
The view is very wavy and a natural way to help your eyes go out of focus. Try getting comfortable and staring out through the window. As you enter a trance, let yourself become open to a hologram of psychic knowing.

The Ouija Board

The Ouija board is one of the more controversial kinds of psychic tools. This is largely due to the belief that the players are contacting dead spirits or other entities from the Other Side who help guide the participants' hands over the board as a means of communication. Many Christians believe that those who use the Ouija board are communicating with the devil. Others believe that it is only the players' unconscious minds that are providing the answers.

The word "Ouija" is a combination of *oui* and *ja,* the words for "yes" in French and German. The game board includes all the letters of the alphabet and the numbers zero through nine, plus the words "yes," "no," and "goodbye." The roots of Ouija go back to ancient China, but it was Elijah Bond who created the current game in 1892. Ouija boards became very popular after World War I, when relatives of soldiers who died in the war would make an attempt to contact them through the Ouija board.

To use the Ouija board, two or more players place their fingertips on a heart-shaped planchette that has three felt-tipped legs. The planchette glides over the surface of the board and spells out the answers to the question asked. Sometimes the spirits have a mind of their own and take over the game.

ALERT!

If you use the Ouija board, always make sure that you are very grounded and protected by the Golden Light of the Universe. Many people have played the game for fun, only to find out that the Other Side is very serious.

The Art of Palmistry

The ancient art of telling your future by reading your palms is thought to have originated in China or India as early as 3000 B.C. In Europe, it was practiced by witches and gypsies, and its popularity rose in the late nineteenth century as the public became more interested in spiritualism and the occult.

According to palmistry, the shape of your hands carries information about your physical and artistic traits. Lines, creases, and bumps found on the palms contain information about the past events of your life as well as the future; there is also information about your life map and soul's purpose. Some readers compare palmistry with astrology. They look for a relationship formed in the patterns in your palms to the signs of the zodiac.

QUESTION?

Is there a difference between reading the right and the left palm?
If you are right-handed, your left hand indicates your life map while your right hand reveals how you have followed your soul's purpose. If you are left-handed, the roles of your hands are reversed.

Changing the Patterns

The lines and markings in your palms may actually change over time to reflect the changes in your life. However, you can also actively work to change your palm patterns—thus changing the potential of your future—

through the practice of Zen or yoga. Both of these practices, and yoga in particular, are spiritual belief systems that seek to liberate the spirit from physical matter for the purpose of becoming one with the Universal Mind.

Tools That Entrance Your Senses

It's fun to cast runes, look into coffee grounds, or try your hand at the crystal ball, but you don't need fancy paraphernalia to work with your psychic powers. Your senses can be effective tools as well—see if you can rely on sounds, smells, touching, or emotions to gather psychic information.

Playing by Ear

Sound can be a very important element in helping to create a psychic trance. Try playing soft music in the background, or get a small fountain, sit by a stream or the ocean, and listen! Another alternative is to use a recording of natural sounds. The sound of drums, bells, or chimes is also an effective way to put yourself in touch with your intuitive mind. Even a verbalized tone, such as chanting or humming "ohm," can help.

An Emotional Connection

You can also try to establish an emotional connection; for instance, you could visit a place that has certain meaning for you. If your emotion is deep, it can help you enter a trance state. Maybe you feel deep calm when you visit a special place in the woods, or when you come to the beach. You could have special associations with visiting a church, synagogue, or temple, especially if these places can put you closer in touch with your Belief System. For some people, the simple action of staring at the full moon will give them a feeling that they can use psychically.

FACT

Many cultures use sound to help induce trance states. Australian Aborigines use the didgeridoo to produce a constant drone. Native Americans and Africans use drumbeats. Tibetans use bells and horns to help establish connections to the Universal Mind.

Special Scents

Certain smells may also help induce a trance—it's common to use incense, a candle with a special fragrance, fragrant oils, or herbs. You might want to burn some sage as a way of clearing old energies out of your present location.

Even a memory of a particular smell may affect you deeply enough to induce the trance state. Whenever you want to connect, take a deep breath and experience the feeling of something special.

The Magic Touch

The touch or feel of an object, such as a stone or perhaps something old that already has the experience of ancient wisdom in its energy, can help produce a psychic trance. It could be the clothes you choose to wear, the temperature of the room, a baby's blanket, or a piece of soft fleece—any such object may create the right feel to help you enter a trance.

Create Your Own Method

Once you try out various sensory techniques described here, you can go ahead and create your own method. For a moment, let yourself go into your relaxed trance state and think back over your life to times, places, and/or events that induced you into a spontaneous trance. It might have been a time when you looked into a steamy mirror after stepping out of a bath or shower. You were already in a relaxed state, and as you looked into the unclear image in front of you, your eyes suddenly saw something entirely different. It might have been on a foggy night when something seemed to materialize out of the mist.

It might have been a sound that induced you into a state of trance, such as the monotonous drone of an engine or a machine. It could have been the sound of many voices talking at once. It could have been while you were listening to a certain piece of music. It could have been an emotion that suddenly took over your conscious mind. As you think back, let your unconscious mind release your memories to you.

You may get an idea that you had not considered before. Make a note to try it out for helping you enter and enhance your psychic trance state. Some ideas may come to you later on in either a waking or a dream state. Once you have opened yourself to the possibility that you already have used naturally psychic tools in the past, all you have to do is wait for your internal and external guidance systems to remind you of them. These reminders may come from outside of yourself, so be aware at all times.

ALERT!

Whenever you open your psychic abilities in order to receive information about the future, make sure you know what you are requesting. If you are not sure right from the very beginning, you may open yourself to knowledge that is not necessary for you to know at the current time.

You may even have knowledge of psychic tools that are waiting in your unconscious mind from a past life. Now is the time to let them be updated to your present lifetime so that they may be used again to help you become and stay in tune with your life map. If you believe that you are letting your intuitive gifts be used for the greater good of others, you will be amazed at how you will become confident in and learn to rely on your own special psychic gifts. They are already there, no matter what tools you decide to work with.

Chapter 15
The Art of Dowsing

In its strictest sense, dowsing is the act of searching for water or minerals hidden in the earth by relying on a dowsing rod. However, psychic dowsing may be used in many aspects of your life, as you will learn in this chapter. Various forms of psychic dowsing may be performed with a pendulum, Y-rods, L-rods, the bobber, and even your fingers.

What Is Dowsing?

Dowsing is an ancient art of gathering information with the use of dowsing tools. There are historical records that indicate that dowsers have been around since the times of ancient Egypt and China. The best-known tools are the pendulum, the forked stick, and the Y-rods, but there are several others as well. The Europeans used dowsers during the Middle Ages to locate underground supplies of coal. There is no scientific explanation as to why dowsing works. It is thought to be an extension of psychic ability.

Today most of us associate dowsing with hunting for water. The ancient name "water witch" or "water wizard" is often still applied to someone who has a talent for dowsing for water. However, there is a lot more to dowsing than just finding water. Many psychics use the art of dowsing to help them enhance their abilities. It can be used for locating oil, deposits of other rich minerals—even lost people!

Dowsing can involve the different senses, especially the "feeling" and visual senses. Most dowsers say that they simply "get a feeling" that helps them make decisions. Others allow their feelings to create a visual image, or an image using other senses. Learning the art of dowsing is like learning to play a musical instrument. The more you practice and learn your strengths, the more you will define your abilities.

Getting Started

Just as with other psychic modalities, it is advisable for you always to take the time to center yourself before beginning to dowse. Once you are comfortable getting yourself centered, anchor the feeling so that you may recall it whenever you want to dowse.

Take a deep breath and slowly exhale. You can do this anywhere you are, standing or sitting. Now focus for a moment on your third eye, and feel yourself connecting to your Universal Mind. With your next breath, inhale the love and peace of the Universe. Allow yourself to be open to the psychic flow that guides your ability to dowse.

Why do you need to focus and center yourself?
The object is to enter an altered state and clear your conscious mind so that the unconscious and the Universal Mind can get their message up to the surface of your conscious mind.

Now you are ready to start dowsing. You can practice by focusing on your third eye. Focus and release; repeat the process a couple of times. Once you get used to focusing on your third eye, you will find that this will actually help center you. When you are dowsing, you may not have the chance to focus anymore than centering on your third eye.

Pendulum Dowsing

The pendulum is the easiest method of dowsing to learn; the term itself is a fancy word for any object suspended from a string or chain so that you can swing it freely. It should have some weight to it, but you don't want a pendulum that's either too heavy or too light. The weight can be of any material, from a fine crystal to a metal washer. The length of the chain or string can measure anywhere up to a foot.

FACT

Anton Mesmer was one of the first to use the pendulum to induce a hypnotic trance. The subject's eyes would go out of focus when he stared at the swinging object, which established the first step of a light trance state. The term "to mesmerize" means to hypnotize.

You don't need to make your own pendulum from scratch—a necklace with a stone would do just fine, as long as it will dangle freely and comfortably from your fingers. An old-fashioned pocket watch, which happens to be a traditional induction device for a hypnotist, can also be used for dowsing.

Let the Session Begin

Many people make daily decisions with the help of their pendulums, through the responses they receive from how the pendulum swings. Using a dowsing pendulum is another way for keeping in touch with your inner guides and your unconscious and the Universal Mind.

When you have found the right implement and have centered yourself, take hold of the string with your thumb and first finger. (If holding it that way is a problem, you can try another position that is comfortable for you.) Let the pendulum swing freely at a length of anywhere from eight inches to a foot below your thumb and finger. Now hold the pendulum in front of you, with your thumb and finger at eye level, and at a comfortable distance away from your head, approximately eighteen inches.

ALERT!

If you have trouble holding your arm steady, you can brace it with your other hand by holding your forearm just below the elbow. You can also rest your pendulum arm on a support that still allows the pendulum to swing freely.

Show Me "Yes"

First, you'll want to figure out which movement of the pendulum will indicate a positive answer. Let the pendulum dangle freely for a moment. Keep your two eyes focused on the hanging part as you focus on your third eye. When you are ready, ask the pendulum, "Show me 'Yes.'" The pendulum will swing in one direction. Keep your arm as steady as possible and let the pendulum go to work. It may swing back and forth, sideways, or front to back, or it may rotate in a circle either clockwise or counterclockwise. Let it swing freely for a few moments until you can clearly see what direction the pendulum swings to indicate "yes."

Show Me "No"

Now that you have established the direction of "yes," ask the pendulum to show the direction of "no." Again, make sure that you are allowing the pendulum to swing freely, and pay attention to how it changes direction to indicate "no." Now ask it to reaffirm "yes" again, and watch as it changes direction again. You can practice changing between "yes" and "no" several times so that you will get used to the different ways the pendulum swings.

When you begin to work with your pendulum, you may find that it swings in very small movements. If that's the case, you may need a little more weight to help build up the momentum. Try different devices until you get one that works best for you.

Now ask the pendulum to stop, and wait until it comes to a standstill. Your pendulum should slowly stop its swinging. As you practice, this exercise will relax you while you keep yourself focused on your third eye with your mind and on the pendulum with your eyes.

Ask Permission to Dowse

Now you are ready to ask your pendulum questions. All questions need to be phrased so that the answers are either a "yes" or a "no." If the pendulum cannot answer the question—if, for instance, the answer is not available—it will come to a standstill.

First, ask your pendulum for permission to ask questions at this time. If it swings in the direction of "yes," you are free to ask questions directed to the source that controls the pendulum. If it is "no," you may not be totally centered or the subject matter may not be appropriate at this time.

What Questions Do I Ask?

You might start with something simple, like a question about the weather: Will the weather be fair tomorrow? Try something that is relatively unimportant and at the same time can be checked for accuracy. Here are a few other ideas:

- Will the stock market go up today?
- Will I hear from my friend today?
- Will I get a response for a question I've asked today?

Many pendulum users ask questions that they would pose to their guides, angels, or the Universal Mind. They are usually looking for some sort of direction to take when making a decision. These decisions can be as simple as where to eat or as complex as guidance in career moves and relationship situations. Some people involve dowsing in every decision-making aspect of their lives. It is their way of consulting their Belief System.

Who or What Controls the Pendulum?

So who or what is really controlling the pendulum? Is it you, your unconscious mind, or your Universal Mind? Maybe the communication comes from your guides or angels? Or is it purely by random or involuntary body movement related to your questions so that you are giving yourself the answer you want? No one knows for sure.

You will have to decide for yourself as you continue to experiment with dowsing. However, it does seem that there is a strong connection between dowsing and psychic ability. It may become a very important psychic tool for you. Don't get discouraged if your results aren't earth shattering at first. If you find it enjoyable and positive, you can always pick up a dowsing tool when you want to ask for a little more help from the Universe.

FACT

An old tale claims that if you hold a needle suspended on a thread over a pregnant woman's stomach, you will be able to determine the birth date and the sex of the baby. Ask where "yes" and "no" are; then ask permission. With those basics covered, you can then ask the month and day of birth and sex of the baby.

Forked Stick Dowsing

Using the forked stick, also called the Y-rod, is the most popular and best-known method for water dowsing. The material does not have to be made of wood, although many an old dowser uses a fresh twig cut from an apple or willow tree. The Y-rod can be made from a coat hanger or even plastic wire. The only requirement is that the tool be stiff enough to hold its shape and flexible enough to bend.

If you are cutting a branch, choose one that can be pruned to a Y shape. Leave two to three inches on the stock end before the Y forks. The length of the Y's branches should be between one and two feet in length. The size and flexibility of the branch may determine the length to which you cut it. Trim off all the "nubs" on the branch that may interfere with holding the stick.

Remember that other dowsing implements are meant as guidance tools for your decision-making process. For major changes, always make sure you have a system of checks and balances so that you are not relying entirely on your dowsing information. Work with your guides, your Belief, and your common sense.

To find your correct dowsing position, bring your upper arms and elbows in, close to the sides of your body, with your forearms bent slightly upward. The palms of your hands should face upward, with your fingers clasping the ends of the Y-rod and your thumbs pointing outward beyond the ends of the rod. Grip the ends tightly in the palms of your hands. The shorter the handles of the Y-rod, the closer your hands need to be together.

Pull the rod handles apart until the entire rod, including the point, is parallel to the ground. You are now ready to dowse. The Y-rod may not be as easy for you to work with as the pendulum, so remember to be patient. As you move closer or over a target, the tip of your dowsing rod will begin to pull downward. The closer you get, the more you will feel the pull.

Dowse for Water

The best way to test your ability in using a Y-rod is to look for water. Try it over a sink or a known water pipe. Don't hold the rod over the water at first. Make a slow swing until you are in the direction of the water. You should feel a pull. Now move over the source and see if the tip of the rod is pulled downward.

The feeling of the energy that the Y-rod picks up is like an underwater current. This current pulls and bends the rod. Practice dowsing different known water sites, both inside and outside your house or apartment. The more you work with your Y-rod, the more comfortable and confident you will be in your dowsing abilities.

Then, move on to places where the source of water remains unknown—in your backyard, a vacant lot, or out in the country. Ask your Y-rod to locate the best vein of water. Slowly turn in a circle until you feel a pull. Follow the direction of the pull until you are directly over the water supply.

Getting the Details

Ask the rod to tell you how deep the water is. Hold it in position and count slowly upward from one. Eventually, you will reach a number when the rod tip is pulled downward. You might want to start in increments of ten feet, such as, "Is the water ten, twenty, thirty, forty feet belowground?" Once you have determined the depth within a ten-foot range, you can go to single feet.

ESSENTIAL

To try a fun dowsing experiment, have someone hide a jar of water within a specified out-of-doors area. See if you can locate the water by dowsing for it. You can also try this experiment with other items.

Next, ask the rod how many gallons a minute the water flows. Again, count slowly from one to the number at which you get the greatest pull on your rod. This should give you the speed of the water flow. It is always fun to try this exercise with more than one person and then compare notes after you have finished.

Map Dowsing

Believe it or not, you don't have to go to a site in person. You can dowse for water from a map of the property. To try map dowsing, have someone draw a map of their property, leaving out the locations of their water and septic systems. Hold the rod over the map and ask where the water supply is located. Mark where the rod indicates it is.

Try the same for the septic system. If you have more than one person involved, you can compare the results of your dowsing. You can use this method for many other uses as well—for instance, to search for missing people or animals. You can also ask your Y-rod to locate lost items.

FACT

Over the years, map dowsers have been employed to locate oil, gold, and uranium deposits using geological maps. A good dowser can hone in on the goal from many miles away. Even Edgar Cayce tried his hand at hunting for oil.

Dowsing with L-Rods

Another method of dowsing uses L-rods. L-rods are usually made of metal, with the most popular being made from a bronze welding rod. The metal rod is cut in approximately two-foot lengths. The rod is bent at a right angle about four inches from one end. Often a cardboard or plastic tube is placed over the short end, and the tip is bent again to keep the tube in place.

When you grip the rods with your fingers, holding the tubes, the L-rod is able to swing freely. Hold the rods approximately chest high, with your hands at the width of your shoulders. Let the long ends of the L-rods point toward each other. They swing easily, and if you are not careful you could poke your eye. Sometimes, the rods are lightly tapped against each other before each dowsing experiment so that they can be cleared of the past energy.

L-rods have traditionally been used to locate underground water and sewer pipes. The dowser starts with the rod tips pointing away, and when the pipe is located, the rod tips cross. You can make L-rods from metal coat hangers. You can also ask "yes" or "no" questions of L-rods in the same way you would with Y-rods.

Measuring Auras

L-rods are great instruments to use for measuring auras. Your body has an energy field that extends a distance out from you. Some of you may have very small auras, which may mean you are open to having your space invaded. If that is the case, the L-rod won't open until it's very close to you. If you have a strong aura, you can spin the L-rod from several feet away from your body.

ALERT!

If you are very sensitive to the energies of other people, make sure you are sufficiently grounded and protected before you work with your L-rod. You are just measuring the energy and do not need to absorb the aura you are measuring.

To measure someone's aura, start from a distance of approximately ten feet, making sure that no one else is in your subject's energy field. Begin to walk slowly toward him, with the L-rod tips facing each other. As you get closer, note the point where the rods swing open. That is the point at which you have entered the person's aura field. Even ten feet may not be far enough away for some people, and if the rods are already open, you may have to step backward until you step outside of the aura.

It is educational and fun to work with several people when you practice your skills at measuring auras. You may also be able to see the auras you are measuring. They may look like colorless waves of energy, or you may see the auras in color. If the L-rod responds well to you, you may have the ability to measure changes in people relating to their attitudes, health, and their positive or negative spiritual growth. You may be able to help many others if you have the gift of working with and changing someone else's aura.

Dowsing with a Bobber

Another dowsing tool is the bobber. It can be made of different materials, including a wooden twig, a flexible metal rod, or even a piece of plastic.

The device can also be made from coiled wire. For the tool to work, there needs to be a weight at the end.

Whatever you use, the bobber must be flexible enough to respond easily to your questions. The length and size can vary from eighteen inches down to a very small device. A spring on the end ensures that there will be a lot of play in the bobber.

To grip a bobber dowsing rod, hold it in the palm of your hand with your thumb on top and pointing away from you. Your forearm should be level, which will mean the bobber rises slightly toward the tip. The bobber on the other end will either bob up and down or sideways. Ask it to show you which way "yes" is, and then where "no" is. Once you have determined "yes" and "no," you are ready to ask your questions.

FACT

Dowsers played a very important role in the Vietnam War. They were used to search for and find land mines. The ancient art of dowsing was regarded by some as more accurate than modern mine-detecting technology.

Finger Dowsing

If you find that you have a natural gift for dowsing, you may not need to have a tool other than your fingers. This ability is part of your mental makeup. Each of you will respond a little differently whether you dowse with a tool or with your fingers. Some of you may feel tingling or heat or cold or heaviness or even have a response through one of your other senses when you use your fingers to dowse.

It is always important to make sure you are centered, grounded, and protected before you begin to dowse with a part of your body. To use your fingers effectively for dowsing, the energy must flow and circulate freely through all of them. Rub your hands together to raise your temperature and get the blood moving. Next, shake your fingers to make sure that you have released any energy that has been absorbed by other fields. Ask your Universal Mind to show you how you will receive accurate information through your fingers that can be used positively to help yourself and others.

If you are dowsing an aura, hold your hand open, with the palms facing the person you are measuring. You may start about two feet away from her body and slowly move closer. As you move in, you should begin to have some sensation in your fingers. You are now feeling the other person's energy field. As you move slowly around her, you may feel differences in her energy.

As you develop and fine-tune your dowsing abilities, pay close attention to all the information you are receiving. Are you getting images in pictures, sounds in your head, tastes in your mouth, or the aroma of certain smells? If so, these may become very useful as you further develop your psychic gifts.

Remote Finger Dowsing

You can use your fingers in the same way as other dowsing tools to get information from maps or other items. Remember always to ask for specific information. The clearer you are about what it is you are asking for, the more accurate the information that comes back will be. Always start with a large area or general information and then begin to hone in on the target. Check from several different directions.

You can also dowse items such as clothes from a missing person. You can ask for "yes" and "no" sensations through your fingers or other parts of your body and get the same response that a dowsing tool would give you. Your entire body is a resource ready and waiting to assist you in reaching your psychic potential. The more you are aware of your feelings, the more you will begin to know your special gifts.

What Works Best for You

Now that you have had a chance to experiment in several different dowsing techniques, you can choose what's best for you. Once you have determined whether it's the pendulum, the Y-rods, the L-rods, the bobber rod, or your own fingers, you can search out your best tool.

One option is to find a family heirloom such as a special gold chain that means a lot to you and will be the most sensitive to use. You can also purchase or make dowsing tools; rely on your psychic intuition to pick out something that feels right. It is important for you to have something that is comfortable to you and also that gives a strong answer. At the same time, you want to remember that it is not the tool that provides the answers. Those come through your unconscious and your Universal Mind. It is also a good idea to find a small dowsing tool that you can easily carry with you at all times. A pendulum fits into your pocket or pocketbook, where another type of rod may not.

Once you've picked out a reliable dowsing tool that responds well to your questions and returns good information on things you are searching for, you can use it to look for other psychic tools. Use your dowsing tool to select a good crystal ball, rune set, or a tarot deck. Take your dowsing implement to a psychic store that sells some of these aids. Let your dowsing tool and your intuition help in the selection. For instance, you can ask your dowsing rod for a "yes" or "no" answer to the question of whether a specific psychic tool is right for you to use.

If you find that dowsing is one of your psychic gifts, the more you use it, the more it will work for you and others in your life. Ⓔ

Chapter 16

Creative Psychic Talents

Not all of us are accomplished artists, but each person does have unique creative talents that she may or may not have begun to develop. You can use your psychic gifts for creative purposes, whether you consider yourself to be artistic or not. In this chapter, you will examine the process of automatic writing, automatic musical creativity, and other artistic abilities.

Automatic Writing

There are two kinds of automatic writing. One is a channeling process in which the writer is serving as a medium for a spirit who guides the author's hand over paper (or the computer keyboard!), producing writing that ranges from letters and memoirs to poems and even entire novels. The other kind of automatic writing involves allowing the unconscious mind to take over and guide your hand, as it writes down things you were not consciously aware of, such as your soul's memories of previous lives.

As you might expect, the definition of exactly what takes place during the process of automatic writing is subject to debate. Some believe that you are stepping aside and letting your spirit guides speak for you in this process. Others think that other entities may be communicating through you. Whatever the process, the goal is for you to find a resolution of a situation or condition through your writing that you would not have found otherwise.

A hypnotic writing trance can be experienced at different levels. It is entirely possible that you could be in such a deep state that you were totally unaware of what your hands or fingers were doing. At the same time, you may be aware of the process, but you may not recognize the message until it is given to you to put down on paper or enter into your computer.

FACT

World-famous psychic Arthur Ford died January 4, 1971. Within a short period after his death, he began to communicate through automatic writing with author and close friend Ruth Montgomery. This correspondence resulted in the book *A World Beyond*.

Automatic writing doesn't even have to be *writing*. Some people can go into a trance and record what they are moved to say, or they may have someone else write down what they are saying. While some psychics accept this form as automatic writing, others argue that it's simply channeling. You will have to come to your own conclusion, but it may help you to compare this example with the case of a musician who can compose a beautiful piece of music and yet cannot write musical notation—someone else has to write it down so others may play it.

Therapeutic Automatic Writing

Therapeutic automatic writing can help you gain a different perspective on certain events or conditions in your life that need resolution. Just as with a pendulum, the goal is to access your unconscious mind and receive answers to your questions without the interference of your conscious mind. For instance, the words could tell a story that is symbolic of your situation as it could be seen through someone else's eyes. It is possible that you may not even be aware of what you are writing, and the information could be in complete sentences or fragments and short phrases.

Always make sure that you are grounded and have a clear understanding of what you are looking for before you attempt automatic writing. If at any time you become uncomfortable with the process, take a deep breath, exhale, open your eyes, and come back to the surface of your conscious mind.

Automatic Poetry

Perhaps you already enjoy writing poetry, but did you know that your hobby is therapeutic? That's because it offers you the opportunity to use verse and symbolism to work out and understand things that may be troubling you. It is possible that you have already been involved in some sort of an automatic trance state to help you, and you may not have been aware of what you were doing. If this is the case, it may be a good time to review your writing and look for the holographic second theme that relates to you.

Channeling Spirits

Channeled written works have been in and out of public favor for the past century. Madame Blavatsky had much to do with the rise in the interest of channeling in the latter part of the nineteenth century. Since that time, there has always been a small interest in the subject with periods of wider publicity, especially during the 1960s, when Jane Roberts published her channeled series of Seth books. Many successful writers are channeling and don't even know it. For those fortunate few, all they have to do is sit at their keyboard, or get a pencil and paper, and let the words come through.

FACT

Automatic writing is a manifestation of spontaneous creativity. During the process, the person doing the writing has no prior knowledge of the information that is brought up to the surface of his conscious mind. As long as the results are positive and can provide something for the good of mankind, it is okay to be open to the wisdoms that come through the automatic creative-writing trance state.

It is possible that you may become the voice for an entity from another world. You may start to write down messages from beings from other planets. These voices may serve as warnings for the peoples of the earth, with predictions of dire consequences if they do not change their negative and destructive ways. It is always your choice as to whether or not you want to write down these messages from beyond. Many times this type of automatic writing echoes the basic truths of universal consciousness.

If you are using automatic writing to channel other entities, you need to make sure that you are grounded—otherwise, you may get results similar to playing with the Ouija board. You might become a voice for a spirit that does not have your best interests in mind. Some spirits may be looking for a way to get their negative messages out. If you are not prepared, one of these spirits may take advantage of you. Always ask your Belief that the information going through you is from a source connected with universal love and peace, and is of the purest intent for all concerned.

Try It Out for Yourself

Now that you have considered the different types of automatic writing, perhaps you would like to give it a try. You can develop your own trance style. You don't have to understand exactly what is happening when you enter your automatic creative trance, but it's important for you to be comfortable and to give yourself permission to trust in what is taking place through you, just as with any other psychic gift.

ALERT!

Once you have learned to trust in the knowledge that is to be written through you, you will become more in tune and open to the positive information provided for you by your internal and external guidance systems. You can channel from a positive source, or you can reach into your soul's rich creative history for inspiration.

The Necessary Preparations

The first step is to prepare yourself. Is it easier for you to write with a pen or pencil on a pad of paper, or to type out the message on a keyboard? It may be easier for you to dictate to a tape recorder or to someone else. You may want to experiment to determine the best method for you.

Once you have made your choice, the next step is to prepare yourself physically, mentally, and spiritually before you begin to write. Pick a location that is positive and where you will not be interrupted. Make yourself as comfortable as possible, and wear loose-fitting clothes. You may want to use relaxing sounds or smells to help you enter your trance state.

You may want to set at a desk or table where your arm can rest on the surface. It's okay to recline and let yourself feel more physically relaxed. Make sure that you have eaten and that you are prepared to stay in your writing state for a specific period of time. The time period does not have to be long, especially at first. It could be fifteen minutes to half an hour, with a goal of eventually being able to remain in a trance state for at least an hour.

If you are using a keyboard, the right chair and the right position are important. If you are going to write in longhand, make sure you have a good pad of paper and several sharp pencils or extra pens. You may want to also have a tape recorder ready.

Setting Down Your Goals

Before you start, write down your goals for the session. You can put them at the top of your paper, or you can make notes on your keyboard screen. If you have questions you would like answered, include them as well. If you are looking for specific information from the Universe or from your soul, clearly define what it is that you are looking for. Start the session with as positive an attitude as possible.

When you have established an automatic writing goal, you may receive suggestions from your guidance systems at any time. You may want to ask your Belief for help with ideas on the subject that you want to write about. Once you have done this, be prepared. Always keep a notepad or a recorder close to you. You may get information in your dreams, in the shower, when you're exercising or driving, or at almost any other time. After you have noted the idea, it will develop further during your next writing trance.

Prepare Spiritually

You have defined your goals, and it is time to prepare yourself spiritually. That means getting yourself in tune with your internal and external guidance systems and feeling the protection of the Golden Light of the Universe. Use your regular relaxing trance induction, beginning with deep breathing and focusing on your third eye. Next, balance and open your chakras, letting your whole self become balanced. Now let the peaceful and loving Golden Light of the Universe begin to flow into and around your body.

Enclose yourself in the protective bubble of the Universe and ask that you receive only the right information for the greatest good of all. Now ask the Universe for help with your questions or other goals. Suggest to yourself that you will let your conscious mind focus on pleasant thoughts as your unconscious mind opens to the messages of your soul, your unconscious mind, or the Universe, whichever is the most appropriate for you at that time. Suggest to yourself that when you have finished, you will come back to the surface of your conscious mind, relaxed, positive, and in tune.

Now you are prepared and ready to experience automatic writing. Don't expect earth-shattering results at first. It may take some time to get your bearings. It is not necessary that you even look at your keyboard or the paper. At first it may seem as if all you're getting is gibberish, but be patient. Don't let yourself get discouraged.

Writing from Your Unconscious

If you choose to use automatic writing to tap into your unconscious, you have the option of dealing with the past or the future. In terms of writing about the past, you may want to tap into a soul memory. If this is the case, you probably already have a specific time period in mind that you want to write about. Remember your five different senses: seeing, hearing, feeling, tasting, and smelling. Use the images that are the strongest for you so that you can step into the image in your mind.

FACT

Jess Stearn, a biographer of Edgar Cayce, also worked on a biography of Taylor Caldwell and used hypnosis to take Caldwell back to visit some of the past lives that she would write about. *The Search for a Soul: Taylor Caldwell's Psychic Lives* was the result of this research.

You may begin to feel like you are observing a play. Make sure you let yourself describe as much of the action and surroundings in all your sense imagery possible. You may hear sound or voices. If so, write down what you are hearing. Listen for as many sounds as possible, and make sure you note them as you write.

You may find that you are actually experiencing the images you are recording while you are in your automatic writing trance. If this is the case, record the emotions, the temperature, tastes, sights, and smells that surround you. You may become a character in the story. Perhaps you are able to step into your writing and experience whenever you want, and at other times step back and watch the action. Some of you may be able to do just one or the other.

Where do these psychic experiences come from? Is it just your imagination, or did you tap into a source of knowledge of the past? Perhaps it is a memory of a past life or images given to you by the Universal Mind, or maybe you have tapped into another dimension of time. These questions are up to you to decide.

After you have finished your session, allow yourself some time to readjust to the present. As you look back over your experience, remember that you stepped into a hologram, whose purpose was to switch your focus from your reality into the reality of the images experienced through your unconscious mind. If you were unaware of what you were writing, it may not make any sense at first. Review your collected data and make notes to help establish your goals for your next session.

Looking into the Future

Writing about the future is not very different. If you'd like to write science fiction and would like to get a more realistic view of the future, you have the option of asking for guidance of the Universal Mind. Remember that if you are able to see into the future, it is a gift you were born with, and all you are doing is developing ways that you can use it to help others and yourself stay in tune with life potentials.

Your intuitive imagination can give you great future-tense stories. If you work with your guidance systems, all you will need to do is enter your automatic writing trance and let the writing begin. Once you get comfortable with the process, you may think of the process as being much the same as going to a play or the movies. All you have to do is let the story be written through you.

Give yourself the suggestion that as you write, you will experience what goes through you in all of your senses. You may also ask that when you end a session, you do not also come to the end of a segment. This suggestion will help your unconscious mind continue to work on the story while you are in your waking state. By the time you start your next automatic writing exercise, the material to be set down is ready and waiting. All you need to do is establish a consistent time when and where you can experience your automatic writing without interruptions.

Communication with Other Entities

You can use automatic writing to communicate with your guides, angels, or those from the Other Side. When this takes place, you become a channel for messages. It is very possible that your trance state may be deep enough that you are totally unaware of what is taking place during the writing process, and you will only know the contents of the messages transmitted through your pen or computer keyboard when you read them afterward.

When you attempt this method, start conservatively and slowly. It is important for you to become comfortable and to have complete confidence and trust in this method so that you can always remain in balance with your psychic abilities.

Pay attention to your guidance systems. When artist David Baker lost a son in an accident in the 1960s, he was visited sometime afterward by psychic Arthur Ford, who told him he would be taught a new method of painting from the Other Side. The result, called vitreous flux, made the cover of the *New Yorker* magazine.

Getting the Message

Your guides may have specific messages for you. They may help you resolve situations from the past, give you advice for the future, and help you in current decisions. Your guides may also have advice for members of your family or friends. It is up to you how to share them, but you might want to ask for ways to pass them on. Remember to ask that when you write, the material they give you will be useful for those around you as well as yourself.

Once you develop a communication pattern with the voices who want to write through you, keep a journal and specific notes on the subjects covered. You may find that what you write does not make sense at the present, but it may at some time in the future. You might think that what you are doing is like putting a puzzle together. It sometimes takes awhile to match different parts up.

You may want to use automatic writing to communicate with your Universal Mind or what many refer to as talking with God. You may write down the things you read in the Akashic Records. The universal truths that you write may be for yourself or others. The first step is to get them down, and then you can ask your guidance systems for help in what to do with the information you have collected. Something only becomes meaningful to others when it is presented in a manner that they can understand. In other words, part of your writing goal may be to interpret the hologram in a way that others may also experience it.

Although you may know who it is who is communicating through you, it may not come to you as an actual voice. It's possible to receive the information you write by just knowing. If you feel comfortable with this technique, just let yourself be open to the thoughts that enter your mind from your unconscious. Chances are that much of what is written will be validated by an experience that is yet to come, such as a conversation with someone in the near future.

Write While You Travel

You may use astral projection to help you visit other places and other times. You can use the type of induction that helps you travel in your mind and add the suggestion that you will be able to write down the experience as you go to your destination. You can use your senses of touch, smell, taste, hearing, and sight, or you can be an observer and report on what you observe. Always make sure you are grounded when you write and travel.

Music of the Soul

Another psychic creative ability in addition to automatic writing is the ability to get aural communications of music. It's possible that you have a musical talent, even if you haven't yet tapped into it. Perhaps you have always had a special interest in music, and you may even play or sing. Some of you may do it naturally, even if you don't have formal music education. It's also possible that at some time in the past, you wanted to learn how to play a musical instrument or to sing, but you got very frustrated with a particular aspect of the learning process and simply quit. If such is the case, remember that it's not too late to incorporate music into your life in some way that will be right for you.

Natural psychic creative talent is sometimes more of a curse than a gift. There is no way to teach that which you know intuitively. When you try to work with someone who teaches in a different way, the results are usually very discouraging for both pupil and mentor. Just because you can't learn the same way as others does not mean that you aren't creative in music. Natural ability cannot be taught; it is something that you are born with. It is a part of your mental makeup, just as your other talents and intuitive gifts.

FACT

When a musical performance reaches a trance level, it can be like having an out-of-body experience. You are just going along for the ride. It can have the same feeling as astral projection.

If you are already a musician, you can greatly benefit through automatic performance. Every single sound and note has the potential to allow Universal Energy to flow through it. It is the energy that provides natural intuitive performance. When the essence of the soul is allowed to flow through the energy, then the music comes from the Universe, and the performer is only the mechanism through which it is played. Your greatest responsibility is to keep the instrument of yourself in tune and to be prepared to amplify the music that is played through you.

Automatic Performance

This technique can apply not only to the performance of music but to anything that is creative. Before each performance, ask your internal and external guidance systems for you to be allowed to represent the Universe and perform at the best level that is possible. Always take a deep breath, exhale, and for a moment let yourself focus on your third eye and your guidance systems. Feel yourself becoming more and more in balance with the Universal Mind. Ask your Belief that you will be open to the sounds of the Universe to be played through you and that you become an amplifier for its beautiful music.

Suggest to yourself that you will let your unconscious mind open so that the musical images will flow out to be heard by those who are ready to hear the music. Let your mind, body, and soul become in tune with the universal peace and love that flows through the music. As you feel the energy begin to flow through and around your body, prepare to let yourself become totally absorbed in the music. Suggest to yourself that you are on automatic pilot, and what is coming through you is the pure music of the Universe. Now let yourself become immersed in your musical performance trance.

Spontaneous Creativity

Bob and Robin Orfant, musicians and composers, created three albums of music on the art of Maxfield Parrish. Neither one of them knew how to read music, except for guitar chords. To write the music, they took their instruments and a recorder and went to the deceased artist's old studio, where they became one with the remaining energy of his work. The music started to flow automatically, and with the recorder capturing the moment, the material for their albums was spontaneously composed and performed at the same time.

ESSENTIAL

You may have the psychic ability to become a music channel. This means that when you are in a state of trance, your talents are used by an entity who writes and/or performs through you. You may even become that personality for the period of time that you are in an altered state. If you try this, make sure you are well grounded and know how to return to your own reality.

The Art of the Universe

Excellent works of art are created while the artist is in a state of trance. Many artists do this so naturally that they don't even realize what is taking place. However, it may not happen every time an attempt is made to be creative. Usually the best trances happen when the artist's conscious mind is set aside and the unconscious takes over. If the artist does not know how to trigger his trance state, he can have a frustrating experience when he is unable to go into a trance.

Find Your Inspiration

To allow yourself to create automatically, it is necessary to enter an altered state of trance. When you do this, you are allowing the creative force of the Universe to take over for you. Set aside your ego and give credit for the process to your guidance systems.

ALERT!

Be patient! When you open up to the creative energy of the Universe, it is easy to become overwhelmed with the amount of psychic inspiration you suddenly receive. Ask that you receive knowledge of only that which you can develop into a physical reality.

Inspiration for your artistic creations may come from many different sources, as long as you are in tune and aware of possible communications. You may dream an idea that becomes a reality in the finished work. You may see, feel, hear, smell, or taste something that spontaneously develops into an artistic creation.

Importance of Preparation

Just as with other forms of automatic creativity, it is important for you to take the time to prepare yourself for the adventure. Give yourself permission to be open to the creative energies of the Universe so that what flows through you can be shared positively with others. It is okay if you are unsure of your creative psychic talent or whether or not you even have one. If you are open to the possibilities, you may be surprised at what you are shown by your guidance systems as they give you the opportunity to reflect the peace and the love of the Universe. Once you know that you are ready, let the creative energies flow through you, inspiring you to create great works of art! (E)

Chapter 17

Psychic Healing and Medical Intuition

In addition to using psychic powers to improve your creative abilities, you may be able to rely on your psychic awareness to heal. It's possible that you have natural psychic healing gifts, and this chapter will help you figure out if that's the case. You will also learn about different types of psychic healing and how a person's aura may be read and even manipulated for the purpose of better health.

Psychic Healing and Diagnosis

Faith healers have been a part of many cultures for millennia. Witch doctors, shamans, and medicine men, among others, played important roles in the societies they lived in. Jesus Christ was hailed as a great healer.

As late as the nineteenth century, magnetism and other methods of alternative healing enjoyed popularity, but many of the ancient healing arts eventually gave way to modern medicine. In fact, with the rise of modern medicine, the popularity of the old way of healing almost disappeared.

Edgar Cayce and the Healing Arts Revival

It was Edgar Cayce who unwittingly became the focal point of the New Age movement, which swept the country during the latter part of the twentieth century. Cayce's uncanny psychic ability to retrieve old healing remedies from the Akashic Records stored deep in the Universe changed the views of alternative medicine for many doubters.

While in a deep self-hypnotic trance, Cayce was able to scan a body with his mind and give a diagnosis based on what he saw. The subject did not even have to be in the same room for Cayce to be able to scan her body and give a diagnosis and recommend treatment for the affliction. The language that Cayce used in a trance was not the lingo or jargon of modern medicine. The treatments were given in terms that employed remedies long since forgotten. The diagnosis and treatments often focused on the body's energy system.

FACT

If you are interested in getting more information on Edgar Cayce, you can go to the ARE Web site at ✑ *www.edgarcayce.org*. ARE is the Association for Research and Enlightenment located in Virginia Beach, Virginia. It was founded in 1931 and is still growing in membership today.

Many of you have Edgar Cayce's potential to psychically read the health of others and help facilitate their healing. Each one of you will do it a little differently. You will have the opportunity to consider several concepts of psychic healing in this chapter.

Understanding Auras

As you have already learned, your body is an energy grid. You have many energy centers, including your seven major chakras. When the energy is flowing evenly and all your centers are in balance, you are in tune mentally, physically, and spiritually with yourself and the Universal Energy. Your three minds are all working together in harmony with your Belief System and your guidance team. You are always connected to your third eye and completely immersed in a golden bubble of universal peace and love.

Needless to say, to stay in this situation all the time is impossible. You are always being thrown off balance by life's resistances, both small and large. How soon you regain your balance and keep yourself in positive energy can have a direct outcome on your own wellness. When positive energy flow is blocked, negative energy can manifest itself through a weakness in your body, usually causing illness.

The flow of positive energy is what creates an energy field known as an aura. The more out of balance you are, the more your aura will be out of balance as well. That balance can be affected from moment to moment, and it is also influenced by the way you have taken care of yourself over a long period of time. The longer your aura remains unbalanced, the more susceptible you are to minor and major illnesses.

ESSENTIAL

Just about everyone has the ability to sense auras one way or another. If you are not aware of how you do it, you may not be paying attention to the clues you are giving yourself. Look for signals from your unconscious and your Universal Mind, and pay attention to your guidance systems.

Reading an Aura

Each of you will read auras a little differently. Your mental makeup will help indicate how you will best experience an aura reading. If you have a strong visual sense, you may be able to see it. If you have a strong hearing sense, you may hear—either by voice or by other sounds—the energy of the aura. If you are sensitive to touch, you may feel an aura. If you have a strong sense of smell, you may smell the aura, and if you have a strong sense of taste, you may actually taste it. Some people may be able to use all of their senses, while others rely on two or more that combine to provide them with the image. A feeling may create a picture, or a smell may produce a feeling.

ALERT!

When you begin to pay attention to auras, make sure you have a strong sense of being grounded and secure. This way you will not absorb the energy that you are attempting to read.

Your first step is to identify how you read an aura. Once you've figured that out, the next step is to collect the information you receive. What does it mean? When you read someone's aura, can you use the information to develop a model of his health? If so, can you compare what you read to how this person actually feels?

Ask yourself whether you can tell by the color of the aura, by white or golden energy, by sound, by feeling, by touch, by smell, or by taste? Can you dowse the individual's energy field? Can you feel negative or positive energy, and how can you apply what you feel to the actual health of the person? How about taste and smell? At first, you may want to keep a record of your observations to help validate the information you are receiving.

Identify Healthy and Unhealthy Auras

The next step is to apply your knowledge of how you read an aura to how you can develop an understanding of what you are reading. As you get experience, you will notice aura patterns that can give a sense of what the auras mean. These patterns will help you produce mind models of what is a good positive healthy aura and a negative unhealthy one.

Healing Negative Energies

Once you have an understanding of positive and negative auras, you can begin to locate the specific areas of a person's body that emit negative energy. You may even be able to determine through your five senses what the cause of the negative energy is and develop a healing model for the negative aura. In other words, you may be able to diagnose what someone's negative aura means and then develop a model for her to change it if she chooses to.

E

FACT

Many people do not want to know anything that makes them feel responsible for someone else. They put up a defensive mental shield to block any such knowledge. If you have knowledge, don't expect others to accept what you know. All you can do is drop hints and hope they discover them.

There are two specific ways that healing energy is transferred through you. It either comes in through you, or you let it flow out through you into the Universe. If you are a receiver, you are on the receiving end of someone else's energy. This ability is enhanced by your mental makeup. Receivers who do not find an outlet for the energy they take in can take on the characteristics of that energy.

If you do not understand your ability to receive energy, you can be overwhelmed by it when you begin to develop your psychic abilities of reading and working with auras. Massage students can suddenly manifest the pain that a client is feeling. A beginning Reiki student may feel the client's illness, whether mentally or physically. If you absorb the energy of the person you are trying to heal, that's because you haven't been able to work with your Belief System and have taken ownership of someone else's negative energy.

The other type of healer sends a strong Universal Energy through herself from an external source and into the client's body so that it flows over and removes the negative energy. The sender creates a stronger image of power, whereas the absorber is much more mellow. One potential problem for the projector is that the ego, and not the Universe, is responsible for the healing. If you take ownership of the power, you can totally change the healing energy into your own negative energy, which is not good for your clients or for you.

Develop a Model for Healing

What is going to be your strategy for healing? Can you develop a model in your mind of how you read someone's energy? Which of the senses or combination of senses will you use—vision, hearing, feeling, taste, or smell? Can you create a negative model and from that a positive model for a change? Can you imagine helping transform the negative aura into a positive aura? Your image would be based on the way you understand the difference between negative and positive auras.

Are you a sender or a receiver? Your conscious mind may not know yet, but your unconscious and your Universal Mind do. You may feel the Universal Power in your fingers, or you may have the ability to snatch away the negative aura and deposit it out in the vast Universe. You may want to take classes in alternative healing, such as Reiki, or in ways of understanding auras to help you find and develop your gifts.

ALERT!

Whenever you work on yourself or someone else with healing energy, remember you are only doing something that is complementary to Western medicine. You are not offering a substitute for what a medical doctor would do.

You can always practice on yourself. Try slowly smoothing out your own aura, especially on days when you feel out of balance. Can you create an image of any negative energy that might be in you? If so, can you bring a positive image over the negative and feel yourself being filled with universal peace and love from a healing energy at the same time? You may be amazed at the positive effect that healing energy can have on you or on someone else.

Harness the Power of Universal Force

Now it's time to focus on bringing the Universal Force through you as a healing energy. Try this with yourself first. When you work with others, you will not be able to put yourself in the same state of relaxation as you can when you are working with yourself. However, you will still be able to develop a strong connection to the Universal Power.

Take a deep breath and exhale slowly. Feel your body relaxing as you continue to breathe slowly in and out. When you are ready, focus on your third eye and let yourself feel the Universal Force of peaceful and loving healing energy begin to flow in through your third-eye chakra. You may feel this healing force as it starts to flow down through your body to your throat chakra. Let the healthy feeling of peace and love balance your throat center and continue on until all your energy centers are open and balanced with the peaceful and healing love of the Universal Force.

Feel your highest chakra, the crown center, open and balance, as you are aware of the total connection and protection of the Universal Force. You may ask your Belief that only the purest healing energy may flow through you to be passed on to the proper area of your or someone else's physical, mental, or spiritual body. You may ask that this loving healing energy allow the person for whom it is intended to find his or her balance and be tuned by this universal healing energy.

Let the Energy Flow

Now that you are centered, grounded, and protected by universal love, you may begin allowing the healing energy to flow through the areas that need healing. Remember, do it your way, the way that you have already identified as using your most powerful image senses. If you are clairvoyant, see. If you are clairaudient, hear. If you are clairsentient, feel.

If you are strong in taste and smell imagery, use those senses to help amplify the universal healing energy of peace and love that is flowing through you. If you are a receiver, ask for the negative energy to be collected by your loving hands so that it can be sent out into the Universe to be healed with peace and love. The more you practice these concepts, adding the special things that work only for you, you will find yourself more and more in tune with the healing, peaceful, and loving energy of the Universe.

Work with Someone Else

Once you are comfortable working with yourself, it is time to work with others. Use the knowledge that you have gained through your experiences, and work with someone you know who is receptive. Start slowly, and just read his aura so that you can develop a model of his health. Look for positive and negative energy and physical, mental, and spiritual balance.

It is very important to remember that you are not the healer—the Universe is. Your responsibility is to keep yourself in balance so that you are the best conduit possible for the universal healing energy.

When you have decided on a healing strategy, start to bring positive energy in and draw the negative energy out. This action is meant to help an individual connect to the universal healing energy. Always center yourself, and ask the Universal Mind to send its healing energy of love and peace either through you into the person or directly into the person. Next, you draw the negative energy out through you to flow back into the Universe to be healed with peace and love.

Reiki and Other Healing Modalities

Healing may also be performed through a practice such as Reiki, massage, body scanning, or magnetic healing—some of the many alternative-healing methods available to you today.

Reiki is the Universal Life Force. In Japanese, *rei* is the universal transcendental spirit and mysterious power, and *ki* is the vital life force. The energy in Reiki comes from the life force of the Universe.

The Art of Reiki

Reiki is an ancient healing practice that has undergone an impressive revival over the past few decades. After centuries of being forgotten, it was rediscovered in the 1800s by Dr. Mikao Usui, a Japanese scholar and physician who stumbled upon it while researching sacred texts on the healing methods of Jesus. Dr. Usui spent his life developing the method of Reiki and using it to heal the poor, as well as teaching the technique to a few of his disciples.

Reiki attunes the energy centers in the body with the Universal Life Force. Its practitioners have specific hand positions that connect the energy with the client. They spend about five minutes in each position before moving to the next. At the same time, the practitioner may use his or her intuitive ability to help certain areas of the body to heal using the Life Force energy.

There are three degree levels in Reiki. Levels I and II are taught in a relatively short time span and can usually be completed within a weekend. Level III is the master level. Learning and practicing the beginning levels of Reiki is not very expensive, and it a good way to begin experiencing alternative modalities. The fee for completing the third degree can run as high as $10,000.

Massage Therapy

Another healing technique is good old massage, because it uses hands-on techniques for comfort and healing. There are many different kinds of massage therapies, such as Swedish massage, which is very popular in health clubs and spas. Many massage therapists use their psychic ability to work the part of their client's body that has an energy block. A sensitive, in-tune, balanced massage therapist can also perform very effective healing practices by combining her knowledge of the human body with her intuitive abilities.

Each individual's healing modality is often developed around the specific abilities of the founder. You will hear terms such as *Universal Life Force*, which may mean the same as Universal Force, and even the religious concepts of God. You will know these truths in your own way.

Body Scanning

Some of you may actually be able to scan a human body in your mind and develop an image of the person's health by using your five different senses. A medical intuitive can psychically read your body and come up with a diagnosis in actual medical terms. Each intuitive will work differently, but they all have a common goal, namely, the wellness of their clients. If you have the ability to scan a human body in your mind, you may want to get some training in the medical field so that you can effectively communicate the images you psychically receive.

Magnetic Healing

The principle of magnetic healing has been used since Anton Mesmer worked with animal magnetism. He believed that he could rearrange invisible fluid in the body and bring about healing. Today there are magnets of different sizes that wearers believe can cure all kinds of ailments, such as lameness. There are magnetic bracelets and magnets to put in your shoes, and many people claim to be helped by wearing them.

Faith Healing

Another form of healing is practiced by religious communities and is known as faith healing or the laying-on of hands. Jesus Christ is believed to be the greatest faith healer of all time. His miraculous cures are documented in the Bible, and even today many turn to Christ in spirit and are healed. You may have the ability to imagine Christ while in a trance state, and to feel his healing hands as the Universal Energy of peace and love.

The Catholic Church also has many documented cases of spontaneous healing attributed to patron saints. The Cathedral of St. Anne de Beaupre, outside Quebec, in Canada, offers visual testimony to the many miraculous cures that have taken place there. Hundreds of crutches have been left after the afflicted walked away healed.

Members of the Pentecostal Church lay on hands in the name of God and Jesus, and the afflicted are healed by their faith—hence the term "faith healing"—and by the power of God, which helps them to be rid of the devil, the cause of the illness. Those belonging to the Spiritualist Church use mediums to interpret the individual's past lives so that the reason for their illness can be resolved, and they can become well again. Although there is no scientific proof that faith can actually heal, it would be hard to convince those who have seen it with their own eyes that it doesn't.

FACT

Faith healings are always suspect and disbelieved by the unfaithful, but there are "scientific" explanations. The mind may create psychosomatic illnesses. Even though they are experienced physically, there is no reason for them. In some cases, it is possible that faith healing cures illnesses that are a product of the mind.

Awareness of False Healers

Unfortunately, there are also people who claim to be psychic healers and yet have only a single true ability—the talent for scamming trusting and desperate people. These "psychic healers" have a bag of tricks, including incantations, to chase the illness out of the body and rituals to heal any affliction known. Of course, there is a hefty fee for their services.

To take it one step further, there are also "psychic surgeons." They do the surgery with their bare hands and are psychically able to plunge them into the body of their patient. They even pull out the bad body part and close the "wound" without a trace of a scar. They also have the ability to give "psychic injections" using their fingers as needles. Many of the body parts that have been analyzed after these so-called surgeries turned out to be organs from chickens.

However, there are many excellent psychics out there as well, and they may be exactly right for you. If you are looking for help from a psychic or from any other alternative healer, always ask what training they have had and how long they have been in practice. It is never a bad idea to ask for references from some of their colleagues. You may want to ask for a consultation first before deciding on the approach you want to take.

Your Own Healing Powers

Do you know or think that you have a psychic gift to be a medical intuitive? If you have this ability, it does not mean that you have to announce it to everyone you know. Once you become aware of your potential, you are free to use it in your own best interests and those of others, in a way that is comfortable and positive for you. Here are some questions to help you identify your healing strengths.

Do you have intuitive feelings about your or other people's health? If so, how do you get these feelings? Can you intuit other people's medical problems? If so, how? Is it through mental pictures, or colors, or just energy? Do you hear voices or other sounds that indicate a medical problem? Do you get a feeling of health problems? If so, where do you feel it, mentally or physically? Can you touch and feel auras? Can you dowse a body for health problems?

Do you experience smells that indicate health situations? It might be in the smell of someone's breath or body odor. Do you get a taste in your mouth that might give you a clue to a health condition? You may even get combinations of sense images that can give you a clearer indication of your own or another person's health condition.

Using Your Psychic Ability

If you have the psychic gift of knowing health conditions of others, you may want to develop it further. A medical intuitive is someone who has the ability to read others' health conditions and translate them into traditional medical terms. The diagnosis can then be treated medically. As with body scanning, you may want to seek the proper medical training to help you communicate what you already know psychically.

ESSENTIAL

If you want to develop your healing gifts, study as many alternative healing modalities as possible to help you decide which one works best for you and for those with whom you will work. The way you work with healing practices will be different from anyone else's way of working. The important thing is that whatever you do works best for yourself and others.

If you are already working in the medical field—whether as a doctor, a nurse, or in another professional capacity—and you have the psychic gift of reading health conditions, then you are ready to develop your intuitive side. The first step is to understand what you already know psychically. This includes understanding your mental makeup and learning how your mind processes sensory information. The next step is to create a plan to help you further sharpen your natural psychic talents. You are already in the health profession, so why not use all your tools and knowledge to help your patients heal?

Your Responsibility as a Healer

Not everyone is comfortable with the role of healer. It is a special gift, and it comes with a lot of responsibility. The first is to acknowledge that the real healer is the Universal Force of peace and love. The second is to understand that you are not a doctor or a nurse unless you are trained as one, and you are only assisting a person to use her mental and spiritual selves to work with those trained in medicine to bring about wellness. As a psychic healer, you are not a substitute for a trained medical professional.

ALERT!

It is very important to take care of yourself mentally, physically, and spiritually so that you will be in tune to work with the healing energy of the Universe. The opportunity you've been given is unique and different from anyone else's on earth. It is your choice to be in tune with it.

So many gifted psychics, whether they are healers or work in other modalities, do not live up to the responsibility of keeping themselves in balance. The result is the work they do may not be their best and they may not be able to use their intuitive healing gifts to the best of their potential.

Chapter 18

The Psychic Gifts of Children

You have already learned that you have had your psychic abilities through most of your life, but it's likely that as you grew up, the adults around you probably discouraged or ignored your special talents. Now, you have the opportunity to nurture and encourage the psychic abilities of your children. In this chapter, you will learn how to help a child identify and become comfortable with his natural intuitive gifts.

Listen to What Children Tell You

You may be a parent of young children, an aunt or uncle, or even a teacher. Or you may have young siblings, godchildren, or children of friends. Whether a child is your relative or whether you work with kids professionally, you are in a unique position to help them reach their psychic potential.

Through their early years, children accept the world around them without the same boundaries that they will have when they become adults. There are no limitations as far as a child is concerned. Their imagination is reality to them. They can see and comprehend dimensions that an adult is no longer able to do. Space, time, and other models of perception that they will inherit from adults as they grow older do not yet limit them.

E ALERT!

Many adults still carry the stigma that they received as a child from overprotective adults. Sometimes harm is caused by an overprotective adult who is afraid a child will not conform to the general thinking of society. They do not nourish the child's psychic gift, only stifle it.

A child has the ability to see both pictures in the hologram. They do it so naturally that both views are a reality to them. They can cross the line into a fantasy world that adults have long since forgotten. They can exist in an altered state of reality, and they can experience the world that Edgar Cayce called the unmanifest reality.

Children Are Teachers

Children are the true teachers. Many times their first assignment on earth is to teach an adult about a part of life that he has neglected. It may be as simple as unconditional love, or as complicated as resolving situations from the past. Unfortunately, many adults fail to grasp the opportunity to get themselves back in tune with their life purpose.

Many adults do not pay attention to what a child is really telling them. All they hear is idle chatter, and they may miss a wonderful opportunity to benefit from the experience. For a moment, imagine that a child is a visitor from someplace that had a different culture and language. Wouldn't you treat this special visitor with courtesy, like a guest? Think of that the next time you are in a hurry and the child wants to teach you something that is very important to her. Perhaps it's something that should be important to you, too.

Patience is the key to letting a child become your teacher. Remember that they are not yet used to communicating in the way that their minds know. They are still getting used to physical bodies that may not behave the way they expect them to.

Encourage Psychic Potential

You have a special opportunity to help children accept and become in tune with their rich psychic heritage. How you treat and nurture their intuitive gifts can impact their entire lives, either positively or negatively. If they feel threatened by their abilities, they may shut them off and never use them again.

Children may begin to indicate their psychic potential almost at birth. Study their eyes and how they look at you, others, and their surroundings. Observe how they hear and the natural movements of their bodies. As they grow, what characteristics do they develop that they could not have learned during their current lifetime? Keep accurate records. Here are a few suggestions:

1. Keep a daily record of your observations of behavior that may indicate psychic abilities.
2. Look for behavior patterns that indicate psychic abilities.
3. Videotape actions that indicate psychic abilities.
4. As the child grows, watch for responses to sensory input from all the five different senses.
5. When the child can talk, ask questions relating to how his mind works in the five different senses.
6. Determine how the child's mental makeup functions, and keep a record with follow-up questions.

As long as you allow children to feel confident that they can trust you with their knowledge, they will share it with you. If they think that you are not sincere, they will not tell you what they know. If you lose their trust, it may be hard to win it back again.

Some adults go so far as to threaten punishment for a child whose reality does not fit in the normal world. If you observe a behavior pattern that may not be accepted by others, you may want to discuss it with the child. Children can learn when to share what they know and when it is time to keep it to themselves. Remember each child is a special human being who is different from anyone else on earth. If you observe and identify the child's special intuitive abilities, you have helped them find a tool that they can use throughout their entire lives.

Begin Early

It is very important to establish the groundwork for psychic growth in the preschool years. Children in traumatic family situations develop their psychic ability rapidly, often as a defense and escape mechanism. You may observe a child of preschool age who has imaginary friends. If you tell this child that those friends are not real, the child may lose the ability to see them. On the other hand, if the child is comfortable with this gift, those friends may remain visible throughout the child's adult life, too.

Once children start school, they can become painfully aware that they are different from other children. If children are ridiculed, they will shut down their special intuitive gifts. The more you are aware of potential struggles, the more you can help them adjust to the differences in beliefs that exist in the world around them. They may develop the ability to see auras or other things. The more you let them feel free to discuss how they really feel and experience, the more self-confidence they will develop in their own special psychic gifts.

The Teen Years

Some children may not reach their psychic potential until their teenage years. As their bodies change, they seem to open even more to the energy of the Universe. The teen years can provide some of the greatest opportunities for psychic development and growth.

You can do a wonderful service to teenagers by giving them permission to explore and work with their natural-born psychic abilities. Imagine how it would benefit mankind if someone you encouraged to take the risk to grow psychically went on to use his or her gifts in a positive way.

ALERT!

In the following sections, you can examine different psychic abilities common to children, including astral projection (ability to fly psychically), memories of past lives, having prophetic dreams, and communication with imaginary friends (who may be their spiritual guides).

Memories of Flight

Can you remember what it was like to fly? Some adults still can. Children's minds accept a second reality of a nonphysical body. In that form, they are free to escape the gravitational restrictions of their earthly body. It is easy for them to move about in a weightless dimension because their minds have not yet been constrained to the limited views of the adult world.

Only when they become aware of their physical bodies do children start to pull back from this second reality. An adult's influence on a child during the transition years will make a great difference to the freedom of nonphysical travel he will have the rest of his life. Those who learn they cannot fly any more will more than likely never do it again during their current lifetime. Those who are encouraged to continue to fly in their minds will enjoy this freedom for as long as they want.

You can have a major impact on children who believe they can fly. If you start observing their mental processes at an early age, you will quite probably be able to detect when children leave their bodies for a short period of time. At that age, they do not separate their physical body from their mental body. In their reality they are flying with both mental and physical bodies, even though it is only their mental one that leaves. They can actually experience physical sensations as they travel about.

Encourage Astral Projection

If a child tells you he can fly, how would you respond to him? Would you tell him that flying was only his imagination, or would you ask him to tell you how he does it? Perhaps a good way would be to ask him to tell you what he knows in his own way. It may be that the experience he describes is astral projection. He may believe that he can instantly go to a different place, and he may view that experience as flying.

Children often have experiences that they tell you as a story. It makes no sense to you but makes absolute sense to them. Give them the benefit of their expertise. You may want to ask them when they first knew they could fly, what it feels like, and how often do they do it. What experiences do they have when they reach their destinations? Perhaps they go to other realms beyond the limitations of our earth.

A Few of the Benefits

Why encourage a child to fly? Of course, in the world of normal reality, no one can fly. So what good does it do to imagine? In the second view of reality, the world takes on a complete new dimension. If a child or an adult is able to enter that world, many wonderful things can result from the experience. Keeping the ability to fly in one's mind can keep the doorway open to unlimited experiences and resources.

FACT

When artist Kathleen Moore was a child, she was able to fly through her special enchanted woods filled with beautiful fairies, birds, and flowers. As an adult, she was able to bring this same enchantment into her beautiful paintings.

Knowing Where and How to Land

The hazard for a child who can fly is relating the experience to those who do not understand. If you encounter a child who has this ability, you can help her to understand that some people will not believe her. That way, she'll be prepared and protected from the possibility of ridicule. If she knows how to relate to the normal reality of the world around her, she can step into and return from her world of flight whenever she wants or needs to. Once children learn whom they can trust, they will have the freedom to explore and a place they can come back to with the confidence that their experiences will be accepted as a reality.

Stories from Before

Once children begin to talk, they may tell you stories from before. These stories can range from experiences before birth and between lifetimes, of past lives, or of things they know and experience from other worlds or dimensions. Their second reality is open to the Universe, and time has no parameters or boundaries for them.

If it is possible, you may want to set aside a period of time each day called Story Time. It may be during a period when the child is encouraged to rest, stay quiet, or read. It should be in a place they feel safe, comfortable, and free from interruptions. It is important to establish an activity that is fun and one that the child looks forward to. It should be an experience where the child feels free to let their imagination take both of you wherever it goes, as long as it is positive and beneficial.

Never force children to tell you more than they want to. If the experience of Story Time is unpleasant, they will not be as open and sharing of their stories from before. The more comfortable they are, the easier it will be.

It may take some time to establish a routine. Children tend to have a short attention span, and they may be reluctant to share at first. As long as they feel you are truly interested in what they know from the past, sooner or later they will become comfortable and learn to trust in your intentions. You may be amazed when they begin to confide in you about their experiences from before.

Collect the data from Story Time, and make notes on where you would like them to elaborate in the next session. Remember to keep in mind the five different image senses when you ask your questions.

Past-Life Abilities

It is very possible for children to be born with special psychic abilities that they acquired in a past life. A child who is given the opportunity will start to use those born gifts again as he or she grows and develops. Children may use their past-life talents at first as they remember how they used them from before. If current conditions are different, they could become frustrated and abandon them forever.

It is normal for a parent or other family member to want a child to do well with her natural abilities. However, please keep in mind that good intentions can sometime lead to pushing the child beyond her interests, and the result is that the child abandons special natural gifts.

Identify Abilities Related to Seeing

The first step is to identify the strengths of the child's use of the five senses. How well do they see? As they grow you may be able to watch their eyes looking at images that the normal human eye fails to detect. These images may come from their mind, or they may be an energy that they see. If it is their imagination, they will look up and to either the right or left. If it is something that is an energy form, they will focus on its location and follow it with their eyes.

A child may begin to see auras around other people. If they start when they are older, it is possible that they may think they need glasses to correct what they are seeing. They may be able to see spirits, ghosts, or angels. They may focus on another lifetime and become absorbed in this second reality. Many of these abilities are natural and are a part of a child's heritage from the past.

Identify Hearing Abilities

Some children may be born with the ability to hear at a level that would be considered a psychic gift. They may be able to hear the spirits, guides, angels, or even the Voice of God. They may be able to hear sounds from a different period of time. They may have the ear of a great musician in the past. The more you encourage them to develop this talent, the more they will be comfortable and confident in using it in the future.

Identify Feeling Abilities

Other children may be born with the ability to feel energy. They may bring forward a healing touch that can help many people in their lifetime. They may be able to feel moods and predict pending future events. They may have a great compassion for mankind that is a part of their soul's journey. If you know of a child with these healing and compassionate qualities, you may want to help guide them to gain confidence in these intuitive abilities.

Psychic Abilities Related to Taste and Smell

As in the other senses, some children may bring with them special psychic gifts in taste and smell. They may smell things in certain places that no one else is able to. They may have a reaction to the taste or smell of a food that is related to a past life. They may have a born ability to cook from recipes they have brought with them from the past. Their ability to smell may connect them to other images from the past, such as visual images or sounds or voices.

FACT

A child may be born with special artistic talents in music, drawing, writing, or painting. As soon as you spot the possibility of a natural talent, think about how you can encourage it to grow and flourish. The most important thing to remember is that their gift should be something they enjoy and not feel pushed into.

Memories of a Past Life

It's also possible for children to have such a strong memory from a past life that they have trouble separating its reality from their current life. They may treat you or others differently from the role they are currently experiencing. They may act like your parent or take on another family role.

Children can see someone as a threat in this lifetime in response to a situation is carried over from a past lifetime. They may react to a certain individual's presence with fear or other abnormal behavior. If you observe this, you may want to give the child a chance to tell you at an opportune time why they feel the way they do about that person. You may be able to help them adjust to this lifetime and help them use their intuitive ability as part of their guidance system in the future.

Working Through Unresolved Karma

A child may actually be part of an old unresolved karma from a past life. They may bring with them the opportunity for those close to them to begin to get back in tune with their soul's journey. It may be something between just you and a child, or it may involve even more players. Whatever the lesson is, the child is a part of it, and if it is not resolved, you may need to continue in another lifetime.

This old karma may include the carrying forward of psychic abilities from a past life. These abilities could have been developed for a special purpose, such as for survival. The problem is, this life is different, and the child may not know how to adjust their intuitive abilities from the past to their present life. The sooner you recognize that a child is struggling with an issue from the past, the sooner you can help them become in tune with their purpose in this life.

Imaginary Friends

You may notice children who carry on conversations with one or more other people who are invisible to the naked eye. These children may have what is commonly known as imaginary friends. These friends may have special names. Children may include their friends in many of the family's activities, or they may choose to play with them when they are alone. They may tell you about games they are taught to play by their friends from the Other Side. These friends may be connected to a specific location, but it is the child's natural gift for second sight that allows them to be aware of their presence.

So what do you say to a child who plays with imaginary friends? Do you encourage her, or do you tell her to stop? When Kate was a small child, she would play with the spirit of her brother, who had died before she was born. One day she and her brother were playing in the car, and her mother, who was driving, told Kate to behave. When Kate explained that it was her brother's fault, her mother reminded her that he was dead, and afterward Kate never saw him again.

Children walk a fragile line between their dual realities, and sometimes it is very easy to discourage them from being able to experience both views. Even when an adult takes an action that is intended to be positive for the child, it may in fact have a negative effect. It is a good idea to proceed with caution and a lot of sensitivity when you address the subject of imaginary friends with a child.

Guides and Angels

Many children have imaginary friends who are really their spiritual guides. You may want to ask a child if he has something or someone who does watch over them—it may look like a fairy, an angel, or even a deceased relative. Children may not see their invisible teams, but they may still hear voices, feel their presence, or smell a special odor when they need to have the feeling of support. You may be aware of something that is happening between a child and his or her team before the topic comes up for conversation.

Sometimes, when children see something that is watching over them, it can be an uncomfortable experience. They may not be happy about their abilities to be aware of the unseen. Not only can you help the child understand that she has a special gift that she shouldn't be afraid of, you may also be able to communicate with what the child is seeing and request that they do not scare the child. Sometimes even spirits need help in order to understand their effect on the real world.

The subject of angels or guides may be a good subject for discussion during Story Time. If children do have something that watches over them, ask them to describe or draw what it looks like. Find out how often they communicate with the spirits and ask them to share with you each time they have a new visit. You could be in for a great adventure that can teach you and help a child grow and develop their intuitive gifts.

Dreams and Nightmares

It is very possible that children's psychic abilities may manifest themselves in dreams and even nightmares. They may dream past-life memories that indicate possible psychic talents that can continue to develop in their current lifetime. In your Story Time, you may ask them to tell you about their dreams and nightmares. You can then explain to them the realities that apply to their life now and help them understand any others that are only a dream they do not need to continue.

E ALERT!

Nightmares may stem from unresolved past-life issues. A good way to help a child work through a nightmare is to help them connect with their Universal Protection. At an early age that may mean feeling a sense of something that is with them such as an angel that watches over and protects them from harm. Let them tell you what is the best for them, and then you can reinforce what they say.

A deceased relative may visit a child in a dream. They may be there to provide comfort when it is needed or to warn him to be aware of potential problems. If children learn to be comfortable and trust their dreams, they can incorporate the deceased relative as part of their guidance system. They can learn to believe that messages in their dreams are for the good if they use the information positively.

As they grow older, children may be able to perceive the future in a dream state. Usually the information they receive is of some pending unpleasantness, such as the death of a relative. They may blame themselves for the results of their dream. It is easy for them to become scared of this psychic ability, and they may try hard to make their gift disappear. If you know of a child who feels guilty for an intuitive gift, you can help explain to her that it is not her fault and that what she was born with is a gift that can be used for good throughout her lifetime.

Help Your Child Develop Her Gifts

Many adults develop their psychic abilities as children without the help of others. For most, these abilities came about as a direct result of the environment they were raised in. In many cases, psychic talents were developed under pressure to help them escape negative situations. That sensitivity has remained with them as adults, and now it may be out of balance with their environment. In other words, many adults developed psychic talents as children for a purpose that is no longer needed, but they do not know how to adjust this gift to their current life situation.

Imagine what it would be like for children to grow up in an environment that was filled with love and the freedom to understand. It would be a time when they could grow with the opportunity to reach into their rich heritage of abilities that they brought with them when they were born. Imagine a child who was allowed to understand his special gifts and learn to develop confidence in letting them be used for the good of others.

You have that opportunity to help children grow and develop their special psychic gifts. It may be the beginning of a special bond between you, the children, and the Universe. It is very possible that you may also learn and become confident in your own psychic abilities when you enter the world of unlimited opportunity of a child.

Chapter 19

Getting Help from the Pros

You have already begun work on getting in touch with your psychic powers. But you don't need to do it alone. In this chapter you will discover what it is like to go for a psychic reading and what you need to be aware of. Additionally, you will get an opportunity to learn how every psychic is different and how they came to receive their gifts.

Reasons to Get a Psychic Reading

Have you ever gone to a psychic? Many people go, either for a specific reason or just for fun. Some believe what they're told, while others are too skeptical to believe anything. They allow their skepticism to block them from being open to the messages in the reading. It's possible that you've never visited a psychic but that you have called a psychic phone line. If so, what was the experience like?

People have many questions about the future, particularly in regard to their finances, career, and relationships. Many visit psychics in order to get good advice and some insights—in terms of the past and present as well as the future. There is also a great deal of interest in visiting a psychic medium to contact loved ones who have died. Some want to know whether their loved ones are all right and whether they are still out there someplace. Others want to finish some unresolved communication from when their loved ones were still alive. It is also possible for the deceased to pass on some insight pertaining to the future of the living.

QUESTION?

What is the difference between a psychic and a medium?
A medium is a person who has the ability to communicate with the dead, and not all psychics have this ability. In other words, mediums are psychic, but not all psychics are mediums.

If you are planning to visit a psychic for a specific reason, you may want to do some homework before you make an appointment. Many psychics have a specialty and are much more accurate within their particular area of expertise, like past lives, health issues, or relationship situations.

If you decide to visit a psychic on a whim—for no apparent reason at all, and with no specific agenda—you may be more open to the messages that you are given during the session. It's also possible that your own psychic intuition will guide you to a particular psychic for a specific reason that you are not consciously aware of.

Being Skeptical

It's okay to be skeptical about visiting a psychic. If you are a pessimist, you will probably wonder if psychics can be relied on to tell the truth—after all, you may think, they are just giving the clients what they want to hear. If you feel uncomfortable about visiting a psychic, you are certainly under no obligation to do it. However, you can avoid quacks and charlatans and find a psychic who is right for you, as long as you keep your eyes open. Be wary of psychics who are concerned about money and suggest various services they insist you need. It's okay to look for ulterior motives when visiting a psychic you don't know.

You also need to be aware of the fact that every psychic will vary in accuracy. In fact, if you went to a single psychic over a period of time, you might get a difference in the quality and accuracy of your readings. On certain days your psychic may be out of balance and unable to give a true reading. Or, it may be that you aren't as open at one time as you are at another.

You won't always know where the interferences are coming from. For example, when the psychic Edgar Cayce went to Texas in search of oil, it seemed as though every step of the way something went wrong, and he failed to locate the "mother lode." Even though Cayce believed that he was doing it for the good of his work, it turned out that other partners in the company had other intentions for the profits. Because their intentions were not in keeping with Cayce's work, his energy was blocked and he was unable to gain the psychic balance and discover the oil.

Your First Psychic Visit

When you visit a psychic, it is good to remember that you have purchased a service. It is your right to receive your money's worth. It is always easy to become emotionally wrapped up. Your emotions, however, can distort your impartial view of the reading procedure. The following are some questions to ask yourself that may help you judge what is happening.

1. Is the psychic trying to intimidate or confuse you with her appearance or the surroundings for the reading?
2. Is there an opportunity or an attempt to gain information about you that could be used in your reading? Is there anything that the psychic does during the reading that indicates that she is looking for information to feed back to you?
3. Does the psychic seek to get confidential information from or about you, such as your financial situation or home address?
4. Will the psychic allow you to make a tape recording or video of your reading?
5. Does the psychic try to sell you other services or get you to come back for more appointments?
6. Is the psychic positive, and does she provide a potential for improvement in your life? Or is she negative, quick with warnings of doom and gloom?

Before your appointment to get a psychic reading, prepare by centering yourself. It is necessary for you to have positive intentions. If you go with a closed mind, it could prove to be frustrating for both you and the psychic.

A Cold Reading

The first time you visit a psychic, you will get what is known as a cold reading—a reading made for someone the psychic has never met. This type of reading is different from one in which there may have been previous contact or in which the psychic was privy to a certain amount of information about you. It is not uncommon for someone who has a favorite psychic to visit him periodically over a span of time. In such a case, the psychic becomes familiar with many aspects of that client's life.

A cold reading is a good way to see if the psychic knows his stuff. For you to have confidence in the reading, he will need to give you some information that proves to you that he is "right on." This material may not have anything to do with why you went for a reading, but at the same time it does validate certain information that you know that the psychic could not have known before you met.

Don't Give Any Clues

Be aware that some psychics are very skilled at eliciting information from you without your awareness. They are experts in observation. Every movement of your body, eyes, and facial muscles provides clues. The sound of your voice can verify whether the information they just gave you created an emotional reaction. Even the slightest hesitation can provide instant information.

ALERT!

When you visit a psychic for the first time, be aware of the clothes and jewelry you are wearing. If you bring someone with you and you have to wait for your reading, make sure you do not discuss the reason you are there.

To get information, a psychic may start off with general statements/ questions. As you agree or disagree, the psychic develops a general profile of you in her mind. For example, she may say something like, "I see that you have had some sadness in your life, wouldn't you agree?" When you answer that question, you are bound to give the psychic some information about yourself that will lead her to another question.

This technique is no different than what a good salesman would use when convincing you to buy his product. He'll first find out what you are looking for and then will describe his product with those same words. In this case, the psychic is looking for clues about you and your problem. Be sure you recognize this approach—this is not how psychic work should be done.

Psychic Validations

What the psychic may start out with is psychic validation—stepping into your energy information flow to retrieve information about you or others in your life, either current or past. This process serves two purposes. The psychic is validating to you that she is receiving accurate information that is already known to you but could not be known to the psychic. Additionally, this information acts as sort of a "pump primer" for the psychic.

During the validation process, the psychic is getting deeper into the "zone." Just as you practiced deepening exercises in earlier chapters, the psychic focuses on the source of knowledge that currently relates to you. It is impossible to hold that focus for a long period of time, so the psychic may drift in and out of the zone throughout the reading. You will get the best information when the psychic is in the zone.

Record the Session

If you are calling ahead to make an appointment for your reading, ask the psychic if recording the session is allowed. If you feel that the psychic is resisting or wants additional money for the recording, you may want to try another source for a reading.

The right type of recorder will make a great deal of difference in the sound quality. You want one that has a good microphone, either built in or plugged into the machine. Videocameras can also produce good voice reproduction.

There are several advantages to taping your reading. First of all, it is almost impossible to remember all the information the psychic gives you. You may be thinking about one specific piece of information and miss what comes afterward. It is also possible that you may not remember something that could help provide more facts later.

When you listen to the recording of the session, you can analyze the questioning method that the psychic used. You can also make note of the information you gave when you verbally responded. Did the psychic have a way to get you to provide vital facts in the reading? The recording will confirm or eliminate any suspicions you may have.

Participation in a Group Reading

Another popular type of reading is a group reading. The size of the group may vary from a few people to an audience in a theater. As the psychic makes his entrance, he begins to pull information from his Source about the people present at the reading. Some psychics use special effects, such as lighting, music, or meditation to help both themselves and the listeners enter the right state for the readings. They may also use certain rituals or routines to help induce a receptive trance state.

The group reading may have several different parts, including a message of wisdom from the guides or the Universe, a time for random readings focused on the audience, and a time for questions and answers. You may be selected, and you may not be. It's all up to the Universe—or is it?

Many of the same cautions for a private session are also true for a group session. Was there a possibility that presession chatter was overheard? Were there other opportunities in which information could have been extracted without the participants knowing? Did the guests reveal too much personal information? Can you observe how the psychic may be gathering material in a nonpsychic manner?

Go with the Flow

One of the best things you can do when you go to a group reading is to relax and go with the flow. If you are overanxious for information, you may telegraph that desire to the psychic, who in return may feed you back the same bits and pieces that you have already given him.

QUESTION?

What should I do with the material received during a reading?
It is natural to want to go out and take immediate action based on your new insights. It may be better, however, to let the dust settle. You might sleep on it and let your intuition digest it for you. Any immediate concerns can be given to your Belief System to help define an action.

Long-Distance Psychic Readings

It is not necessary to be in the presence of a psychic in order to receive a valid reading. As far back as the early 1900s, Edgar Cayce would respond to letters requesting readings. He traveled in his mind to the physical location of the subject and could give details such as the current weather. Toward the end of his life, his abilities to give readings over long distances were so well known that he was besieged with far more requests than he could fulfill.

When the use of the telephone became widespread, it became possible to give live psychic consultation from a great distance. Then came live call-in radio shows. Later, television shows allowed psychics to share their readings and advice with many listeners at the same time. (This also helped to popularize the leading psychics.)

Today, the Internet is a resource that enables you to contact psychics from all over the world. Many have books and other products for sale as well as online readings. It is possible to correspond with some of them before paying for anything. Let your own intuition be your guide if you decide to check out online psychics.

ALERT!

When a psychic gives you a warning, pay close attention. First, look at the reason the prediction was given. Would it benefit certain individuals or groups? Would this prediction require you to make a major lifestyle change?

Do Psychic Predictions Come True?

Are psychic predictions "cast in stone"? What do you think? If you are told something about an event that is going to happen, how will that affect your life? Is it possible to make changes that avoid predicted outcomes?

The concept of time is complicated enough to fill dozens of books. But what you need to understand when it comes to psychic readings is that a psychic prediction is based on images of the future as they are influenced by the events of yesterday and today. If nothing changes in the progression that leads into the future, the prediction has a good chance of coming true. However, if something happens to change the normal progression of events, the prediction will no longer be valid.

It is always good to watch out for potential agenda issues that a psychic may or may not have. Pay attention to your own psychic intuition. Remember, you can take steps to change the prediction. The event is still in the future. You might consider a lifestyle change, eating or other habit change, or change of travel dates.

Dealing with the Future

When you receive information about your future, whether it's good news or bad, the first step in dealing with it is to make sure that you are grounded in the present. Use your ability to connect to your third eye and your inner guidance system. Ask yourself what is the best way to work with the knowledge that you have been given in a good and positive way. You can even ask for the right words to come out of your mouth and for the right actions to be taken.

Next, ask your inner guidance system for some verification of the action that may be required. You may have already heard the message before. Ask for protection from the Golden Light of the Universe. Above all, listen to the messages that are coming through you internally and given to you externally. It's okay to use your own guidance system.

FACT

Fear of the future can paralyze you in the moment, keeping you captive and holding you from moving into the unknown. You don't need to take the risk by yourself. If you rely on your guide, you may have the courage to move forward, one step at a time.

You may want to use your ability to contact your inner guidance system regarding future potential events. The methods that you have had a chance to experience in earlier chapters can be very effective in helping you deal with possible anxieties concerning the future. The reality of life is what is happening at the moment, and each moment can have an impact on the future, either positively or negatively.

Every Psychic Is Different

As you have already discovered by examining your mental makeup, every person is different, and the same truth applies to psychics. Some psychics see their abilities as a service that should be paid for. Others refuse to charge money, believing that their gift is something to share freely. This is true not only in intuitive areas, but also in many other creative fields such as art, music, and writing.

You may be just as psychic as the psychic whom you visit to get a reading. The only difference is that you may not have identified your gifts yet. It does take courage to take the first step in giving yourself permission to understand that you are psychic. Now that you have almost finished this book, you may be starting to recognize and understand your intuitive gifts and ready to take that big step of beginning to help others.

As you examine how some of the gifted readers do it, you may discover a method or area that you can use as a model to develop your special type of psychic ability. In the previous chapters, you investigated different types of psychic abilities. You may have found some that work for you, and some that do not.

ALERT!

Many gifted psychics have not had easy lives. For many, the intuitive gift is also a curse. It's difficult to face your own health, financial, or relationship issues. Even Edgar Cayce did not listen to the advice of a reading that was given about his own health.

Discovering the Gift

Many professional psychics received encouragement to use their intuitive gifts from other psychics. John Edward and James Van Praagh, two well-known psychic mediums, were both advised that they had the gift to communicate with the dead by professional psychic mediums. Fortunately, they listened to the advice and worked on their gifts, helping thousands of people find solace in the fact that their loved ones are all right on the Other Side.

The psychic encounters occurred early in their lives. Edward discovered that he knew a lot about his family's history, and there was no logical explanation for how he could have known this information. Today, Edward has the ability to see, hear, and feel the energy of a person who has died. He then interprets what he feels for the person or persons whom the message from the Other Side is for.

Van Praagh had a more dramatic experience. When he was eight, he was praying in his room when he saw the Hand of God. Instead of shrinking away in fear, the boy found a peace that has stayed with him since his experience. As a medium, Van Praagh first feels the emotions and personalities of the deceased, and then receives a visual image of what he has felt.

Well-Known Mediums

Arthur Ford (1897–1971) met his spirit guide Fletcher in 1924, and he worked with him throughout his life. Ford was able to break Houdini's coded message that he had arranged to send to his wife after he died: "Rosabelle, believe." After Ford died, he wrote a book entitled *A World Beyond* through the automatic writing of Ruth Montgomery.

Another famed medium, Jane Roberts (1929–1984), channeled an entity whose name was Seth. Together they wrote a series of works sometimes known as *The Seth Material*.

Recognizing the Pain

There are many other scenarios as well. Sue developed her reading ability through the Spiritualist Church, where receiving messages from spirits was an accepted part of worship. As she became comfortable with her psychic abilities, Sue learned to trust her spirit guide, who gave her intuitive information in several different ways. She was able to tell what was wrong with a deceased loved one by feeling the pain in the area of her body that had caused the death of the spirit. At first she had to learn to protect herself from being overwhelmed by these feelings.

Once Sue made the adjustments she needed, she was able to learn to trust these feelings. As she progressed, she was also able to sharpen her focus in all five of her senses. Her images helped her produce accurate readings. One of her specialties is medical intuitiveness. She can give a diagnosis by reading it as it prints out backward across her visual eye screen in red letters.

It is important for a psychic to remember what or who is responsible for her intuitive information. Some struggle with the need to satisfy their egos and want all the credit for their "psychic gifts."

Seeing the Past

Mary's gift is different—she is able to visualize people as they were in a past life. She can describe what they were and what they did and how that has a direct bearing on their current lifetime.

Mary chose to use her gift as her profession. In her work, she helps clients resolve old karma and use the knowledge of their past lives to get in tune with their life today.

Other Psychic Profiles

Examples of psychic gifts abound. Here are a few other cases of how these psychics first discovered their gift. Dave Adam's grandmother told him that she could talk to the dead. She encouraged Dave to develop the same gift at an early age. Today, he has many visitors from the Other Side. When he knows that he is going to meet with a client, he will communicate with family members on the Other Side the night before so that he can get to know them. He has the ability to see guides, angels, animals, and deceased friends and family whenever he looks at a person.

Karen Lundegaard's gift is different. When she was a young child, she had playmates, including a fox named Foxie and a little girl named Lulu. Karen thought that everyone had the ability to see what she called "misty people," who came and went in her house. Her invisible friends helped her to see the future and hear what other people think.

Hollie began to have severe migraine headaches around the time that she started to open up to her psychic abilities. She needed help, and she went to a psychic who told her that in one of her previous lives she had been stoned to death for her psychic abilities. One of the stones hit her in the head, the same place where she gets her headaches. Once Hollie learned the reason for her pain, she tried to overcome it and began to work with her team of spirit guides.

FACT

Jeanne Dixon, known for predicting President John F. Kennedy's assassination, was told by a gypsy when she was eight years old that she would become a great psychic. Her information often came in the form of a dramatic vision.

Chapter 20

Let Your Psychic Ability Grow and Flourish

Finally, it's time to consider what you have learned about yourself and your abilities and how you may use your new-found knowledge in the future. In this chapter, you will have the opportunity to examine your responsibilities for using your intuitive gifts. You can begin to think of how you may keep yourself in tune to best meet this responsibility. Remember, helping others and continuing to learn more about your gifts is a part of your psychic responsibility!

What Have You Learned?

You have now had a chance to learn about and try many different psychic techniques. You have been shown how to identify and understand the intuitive gifts that you were born with and that you may already have been using throughout your life. You have developed ways to be in tune with your internal and external guidance systems. You may have been able to meet and identify your guides, angels, or other spirits that are there to help guide and protect you. You have also learned about the importance of staying grounded in the universal light.

You know of the possibility that you have a soul map to follow for growth during this lifetime, and you can now work with your Belief System. You have had a chance to compare yourself to the pros, and you have found that maybe your psychic ability is as good as theirs. Finally, you have had the opportunity to try and to experiment with many different types of psychic techniques and tools. By now, I hope, you have a good basic concept of your psychic strengths.

Staying on Course

Your next step is to decide what to do to continue your psychic development. The goal of this book is to help you identify your intuitive strengths. Now that you have had that chance, you have a wonderful opportunity to become in tune with your life map and your soul's journey. It is time to decide how you will put your psychic abilities to work. After all, it is part of your life plan.

You have probably been focusing your unconscious and your Universal Mind on the lesson of each chapter as you have gone through this book. Now focus on your internal and external guidance systems to let your psychic abilities become in tune with your life purpose.

An Exercise to Help You Find the Way

You can use your basic self-hypnosis technique to work with your unconscious and your Universal Mind to help determine the direction your psychic gifts will take. Find your comfortable place, loosen your clothes, take a deep breath, exhale, and relax. Focus on your third eye and let your eyes close. Continue breathing in and out slowly while you begin to work your way down through your chakras, opening and balancing each one until you return to your crown chakra. Now focus on the Universal Energy of peace and love as you begin to surround yourself with the Golden Light of the Universe. You may feel it wrapping around you like a protective bubble of golden love and peace.

When you are ready, slowly count yourself down from five to zero, focusing more and more on your connection to your Belief and your guides or angels. Use your self-hypnosis anchors to help deepen your trance and strengthen your connection to the Universal Mind. When you arrive at zero, take some time to reflect and enjoy the loving and peaceful energy of your universal connection.

Connect to Your Belief

Now ask your Belief to help you determine the way your psychic gifts should be used to benefit mankind. You may ask your guides or angels or other spirits to communicate with you in a way that you will recognize and understand. Ask that you may use this information to help you become in tune with your life map. Now give yourself a little time to be open for guidance and then suggest that after you count yourself back up to five that you will remain open to the messages and guidance from the Universe.

FACT

Once you have counted yourself back to five and have come back to the surface of your mind, you can prepare yourself for guidance from your inner and outer team. As you have learned, that guidance may manifest itself in many different ways. It may come from inside yourself or from something you hear from someone else. You may hear it more than once.

Your Psychic Responsibility

You can now call yourself a psychic. You have the unlimited power of the Universe at the tip of your third eye. All you have to do is shift your focus, and you are in instant contact. It can be very tempting to put this power to use for personal gain.

ALERT!

You have an inner guidance system that will let you know if you are going in a direction that is not in tune with your life journey. Pay attention to your warning system and take the time to get refocused on your life purpose.

So, what are you going to do with your new knowledge? Are you planning to use it for personal gain? Are you tempted to reach out for the riches and prosperity that you might have once thought were rightfully yours? Do you want to be able to gain an advantage on others so that you can manipulate and control them?

Yes, you can use your psychic abilities for personal gain, but for how long? Free will is your opportunity to go your own way instead of in the direction of your soul's journey. Remember what karma is. Are you willing to risk your investment in the future growth of your soul for momentary personal gain to satisfy your ego?

Prepare Physically

Part of your obligation is to keep yourself in tune physically for your psychic journey. If you are able, it is important that you find the time to stay as fit as possible. That means getting the right exercise and making the proper choice of healthful foods. The more you keep your physical body in condition to be a conduit for psychic energy, the better your connection to the Universal Mind will be. Your physical condition is a part of your psychic development.

Prepare Mentally

It is also important for you to keep yourself in as good a mental condition as possible for your upcoming psychic journey. Remember to keep a healthy mental perspective. Take the time to use your relaxation exercises to help keep your psychic energy in balance. Also use your mental anchors to trigger relaxed states during times when it is hard to escape the stresses that you encounter. The more time you can spend in a positive waking trance state, the more you will be mentally in tune with your psychic development.

Prepare Spiritually

The more grounded and comfortable you are with your personal belief, the more in tune with your spirituality you will be. Make sure that you are in touch many times a day with your spirit guides, your angels, or whatever you believe is there to help guide you on your soul's journey. The more you are open to your internal and external guidance systems, the more you will learn to rely on the power and strength of the Universal Energy. Remember always to be aware of keeping your chakra centers balanced and open to the peace and love of the Universe and to keep grounded in universal golden light.

Continue to Practice

Just as with any other talent, if you do not use your psychic talent it will eventually dwindle away. Now that you have identified your psychic gifts, it is time for you to work with them on a steady basis. You may have more than one area that you want to develop. Make sure that you develop a plan that is workable for you. Many times people get very excited at learning something new at first, but if they do not quickly establish a routine, they can easily lose interest and abandon their project.

Set aside a period of time everyday to work with your psychic ability. It doesn't have to be long, perhaps as little as fifteen minutes to start—the time you will need to take will depend on what you are working on and the potential need for companions in your work (whether you need to be alone, near people, or actually work with others). If you are using a self-hypnotic trance, you will not want to be interrupted. If you are reading people or energies, you will want to be in a place where you have access to different subjects.

Be aware that you may meet some resistance from other people, family, or friends. They may resent that you are spending time away from them. They may not believe in psychic abilities and may not be happy that you have that gift. They may not want you to mention the subject anywhere around them. You may have to find a way to balance your psychic development and your family and friends.

Disperse Psychic Energy Buildup

One of the hazards that you may face as you become more and more in tune with your intuitive abilities is psychic energy buildup. What this means is that when you take a large amount of Universal Energy into your body, it is possible to build up a surplus. If it does not find an outlet, it will manifest itself in different ways, such as with an intense electrical tingling. As an example, if you are using your hands for healing and are bringing in the energy for that purpose, it is possible that you feel prickly sensations in your hands.

ALERT!

Pay attention to how your psychic development is affecting you. When you remain focused on it for a period of time, are you able to clear it from your mind after you have finished a session? Are you able to sleep peacefully, or do you toss and turn?

It is always a good idea when you are working with energy to keep yourself grounded. There are several ways to do this. If the energy surplus is localized, such as in your hands or feet, the easy way is to touch the ground with the parts of your body that are overcharged. You can also shake your hands, your arms, or your fingers to help disperse the energy back into the Universe. Deep breathing is another excellent way as long as you let the energy flow out of your body when you exhale. If your entire body feels like it has been charged, you may want to exercise, go for a walk, or swim to help dissipate energy.

Washing your hands and arms in cold water, bathing your feet, or immersing your whole self are all good ways to get rid of surplus energy.

Remember that this charged energy is a healing energy and you can feel a sense of universal peace and health as you let it flow back out into the Universe. The goal is to keep yourself in balance and in tune so that you retain the proper amount of healing and psychic energy.

FACT

Instead of taking care of themselves, many people turn to chemical aids or alcohol to help them detune their psychic energy. Some turn to overeating and develop a serious weight problem. All of those things only suppress the energy rather than clearing it from their bodies.

Remember, It's Not Your Power

Another problem many novice psychics face is learning to develop and use their psychic abilities while keeping in mind where the source of their power and knowledge originates. As you continue working on developing your psychic abilities, continually ask yourself where your powers are coming from. Are they there for your responsible use and for the good of all? Or do you have the right to claim it as your own and use it for your personal short-term goals?

Owning something implies a certain amount of responsibility. If you impress on others that you have a psychic power, you will be expected to live up to your ability. Unfortunately your psychic power may not turn on and off like a light switch. Every time you receive psychic energy it may be a little different. Your connection to the Universe can sometimes be very strong and at other times very weak. Your job is to be ready to experience it when it is called for. The more you practice, the stronger your psychic connection will become.

If you take all the credit, then you will have to accept the failures that are bound to happen. If you acknowledge the ownership of the Universe, then there are no failures, only honest attempts to succeed. Once you have established clear universal ownership of your psychic abilities, not only in your mind but also in the minds of others, you will have the freedom to let it flow without the pressure to turn it on and perform.

Develop a positive belief habit as you progress in your psychic growth. The more you give acknowledgment to your Belief and your guidance systems, the easier it will be to avoid the problems of the ego and the conflict of ownership. This will free you up to stay in proper focus.

"I" or "Eye"?

The words you use to describe your psychic abilities and who owns them will either give you the freedom to experience or commit you to success or failure. When you say, "I have a psychic power," are you talking about yourself or the Universe?

It is okay to use the word as long as you mean your third eye or your universal connection. The Universe has incredible power as long as you accept what it has to offer. If you claim that it is yours instead, will you be able to handle the responsibility?

When you relate your third "eye" to your excitement over your psychic development, you can keep a balance with your ego "I." Whenever you are aware that you are having a psychic insight, remember to focus on your third eye for a brief moment and give thanks to the Universe for the miracle of knowing. When the insights are very good and you receive praise for your work, you can say "thank you" graciously and tell the person praising you that you will pass the message on to the true provider of your psychic information. At the same time you can feel the peace and love of the Universe radiating through you. Use this feeling as an anchor to your Belief.

It's Okay to Be Excited

It is okay to be excited over the discovery and development of your psychic gifts. It can be an amazing process. Every day can be a new adventure of learning and personal growth. However, don't expect that everyone else will be as excited about your intuitive development as you are. As long as you are bringing positive Universal Energy of peace and love, each person you connect with will have the opportunity to benefit from your enthusiasm. Focus your excitement onto the incredible power of the Universe, and remember to keep yourself in balance with it.

One Step at a Time

However, it is very easy to become so wrapped up in your new psychic adventure that it becomes the center of your focus. For a period of time you may not think of anything else. It may be in your mind every waking moment, and you may dream about it at night. You may grow to resent any outside interference that keeps you from immersing yourself in your psychic development.

ALERT!

As you grow in your psychic ability, you may not think the way you did before you started. This is because your sense imagery has developed, and you are in a state of change. You may feel distanced from those whom you used to be close to.

It is important to be able to find a balance between your psychic development and the rest of your world. Regardless of the transformation you are going through, you still need to be aware of family relationships and your work and other commitments. It is very possible that you will grow spiritually and find yourself out of place with many of your old friends and things you used to do. You may not be able to explain your new knowledge to others, no matter how hard you try.

If you try to progress faster than you should, you will become out of tune with your purpose. You may open up to more psychic energy than you bargained for. Remember to make sure that your chakras are always in balance and that your energy flow is positive. After all, you are only a part of a grand universal scheme that will unfold in its own way.

Always Be a Student

Always continue to be a student of the Universe. There is so much more that you can learn as you follow your soul's journey. Your teachers will appear when you are ready for the lesson. They may come at any time and from anywhere, while you are asleep, as an inner voice, or from someone you know or may have just met. Study, read, listen, and try out techniques to gain further knowledge.

Here are some suggestions to help you find support in your psychic journey:

1. Find or start a metaphysical discussion group in your area.
2. Use the Internet to develop positive metaphysical contacts.
3. Take a course in psychic development at a school such as Atlantic University.
4. Find a friend with similar interests.
5. Ask your Belief to help you connect with the right resources for your psychic development.

You will find a list of Web sites listed in Appendix B; use them to get help in further developing your psychic abilities.

How Does It Fit?

Whenever you investigate new knowledge and skills that can enhance your abilities, it is good to always ask yourself how someone else's philosophies or techniques fit you. How do their ideas compare with how you believe?

What is right for someone else may not be right for your psychic development. Remember that you are the one who intuitively knows whether or not a piece of information fits into your life map.

Your Greatest Reward

Our society teaches that you should always strive for personal gain and achievement. Many of the people who make this view their focus wind up at the end of their life journeys feeling a lack of a total fulfillment, regardless of their personal gains or the accumulation of wealth. On the way to reaching their personal goals, they have missed their soul's potential growth. They let their free will make the choices that put them out of touch with their life map.

FACT

As you near the completion of this book, now is an excellent time to use your communication with your guidance systems to help assess where you are in your life journey. How do you feel about your soul's journey? What can you do next to help stay on course?

It is very easy to feel inadequate and to develop low self-esteem when others flaunt their personal achievements in front of you. You may feel you have nothing to offer that will compare. You may have brought with you a past-life feeling that your personal gains are all that matters in life. You may be pushed by friends or family members to match the achievements of others whom you know. You may be open to ridicule and considered a failure if you do not meet their standards of success.

If you approach your life journey as a battlefield where the domineering force rules, you will always be in inner conflict. If you work with your guidance teams and believe that the result of your work will be in the best interests of all concerned, you will be opening your psychic abilities to help keep you in tune with your soul's potential growth. Your life need not seem as if it were a battlefield but can be instead a great adventure into the unknown. Every day can bring with it the potentials for amazing revelations.

ALERT!

Proceed slowly! It is always very tempting to go as fast as you can once you have an idea of what your life potential might be. Remember that you are only one piece of the universal puzzle. If you are open to your assignments, you will go at the correct speed.

It takes courage to take the risk and trust in your Belief to go against the flow. It is okay to know what others around you may not. Once you understand that you have access to the secrets of the Universe, you can feel free to use this knowledge to help others if they choose to allow themselves to learn. Remember, you are only a piece of the Universe, and your job is to focus on your assignment. The Universe will take care of everything else.

When you give someone a gift, you usually pick out something that you feel will be good for that person. If the recipient rejects it, you will probably be disappointed. The reality is that once they own the gift, they can do with it whatever they want. When you offer intuitive wisdom to someone, remember that it is no different from a physical gift that they can accept or reject. It is their choice, not yours.

Let Your Psychic Journey Begin

It is time for you to begin the incredible journey that lies ahead of you. You now have the knowledge and the tools to help you become in tune with your life purpose. You may want to refer to certain sections of this book until you feel confident and grounded in your Belief System. Remember that you may adapt any of the views stated here to fit how you intuitively feel. It is the purpose and significance of your journey that is important, not the attempt to take an approach that does not feel right for you.

It is hoped that you now know that you have a life purpose and that your psychic ability is a major part of it. If you accept the opportunity that you are offered, you may never view the world in the same way again. It may become rich in meaning and mystery and full of constant discovery.

Your friends, family, and coworkers may see something in you that they did not notice before. You may find that complete strangers are drawn to have a conversation with you. Every day you may notice miracles that have always existed around you but that you failed to see before. Life has the potential of taking on a complete new and exciting adventure for you. There is no way that you can successfully explain the incredible feeling of being in tune with your life map.

This book has within its covers a piece of your life map that is waiting for you to use to help you on your soul's journey. Your guides, angels, or spirits and the Universe have sent it to you. Every reader has been sent one. Have you discovered yours yet? Only you can recognize it. It is something that can help you rediscover and develop your psychic abilities that are a part of your soul's rich heritage. If you haven't discovered it yet, don't worry. It will be revealed to you when it is time for you to understand it if you so choose. Just be aware, go forward, and believe in your psychic gifts. Ⓔ

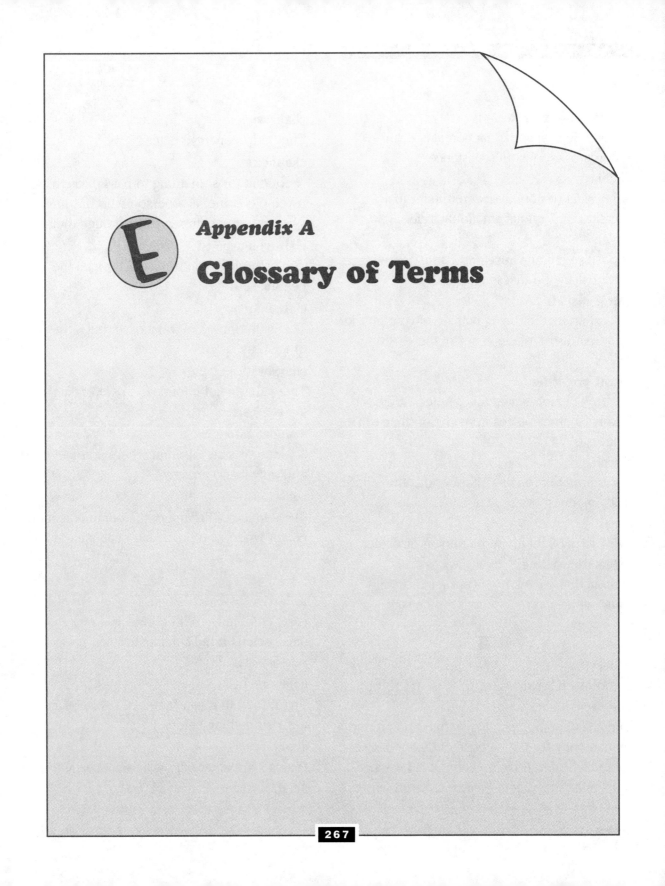

Appendix A

Glossary of Terms

A

Akashic Book of Records:
A mythological book that contains detailed records of every soul's existence.

anchor:
A physical or nonphysical reminder that recreates a previous emotional state.

angel:
A positive entity whose purpose is to help you. In Christianity, a messenger of God.

astral plane:
An experience of being outside of your physical body. An astral plane is not of the earth's plane.

astral projection:
When a person leaves the physical body and travels to other places in or out of the earth's plane.

astrology:
A system of predicting future events through studying the movement of celestial bodies.

aura:
The energy field around a person or object.

automatic writing:
Writing that comes from your unconscious mind while you're in a light trance state.

B

bobber:
A tool used for dowsing.

body scanning:
The ability to look psychically into and around a human body for the purpose of determining the subject's health. Body scanning can be experienced through any of the five different senses.

C

chakras:
The body's energy centers.

channel:
A conduit for something to pass through. A psychic channel is a person who has another spirit or entity communicate through them.

clairaudience:
The gathering of information through the hearing sense.

clairsentience:
The gathering of information through the sense of feeling.

clairvoyance:
The gathering of information psychically through the senses.

comfort zone:
A place or state of mind where you feel safe and little or no anxiety.

conscious mind:
The surface of the mind; the communication center where you process thoughts and ideas.

D

deductive psychic image:
A psychic image who comes from your **unconscious mind**'s ability to take in external sensory stimuli.

déjà vu:
The feeling that you have been someplace or done something before.

diamons:
Divine spirits that offer wisdom, usually through internal voices.

divination:
The ability to predict the future or find objects by information gathered through psychic abilities. Many different tools can be used to aid in divination.

dowser:
A person who uses a psychic tool to locate underground water, mineral deposits, or other unseen things.

dowsing:
A method of finding water or objects using psychic tools.

E, F

exorcism:
A rite to get rid of evil spirits, usually performed by a priest.

fairy:
A form of spirit resembling a small person; fairies are said to have magical powers.

free will:
The freedom to choose—to follow or reject the soul's purpose.

G

gatekeeper:
A strong and powerful guide who acts as your protector.

glyph:
A horoscope symbol for each sun and moon sign.

goal-focused psychic intuition:
A combination of deductive and random intuition.

guidance system:
The guidance system has two parts; internal and external. Your internal guidance system is the connection to and advice from whatever it is you believe in—God, angels, guides, or other beings. Your external guidance system is made up of the elements that go with you to help you on your soul's journey.

H, I

hologram:
A three-dimensional image.

horoscope:
A chart developed from your birth date that includes the patterns of the heavens at the exact time of your birth. Your personal horoscope is meant to be your guide to the future, providing predictions of what might happen.

hypnosis:
An altered state of consciousness in which the unconscious mind accepts suggestions.

I Ching:
An ancient Chinese method of divination consisting of sixty-four hexagrams, each with a different meaning.

intuition:
The ability to know things that is not related to conscious reasoning.

K, L

karma:
Unresolved situations from past lives that carry over into the current life.

kinesthetic:
Sense of touch or feeling.

life map:
Potential conditions for soul development that each person is born with; their **free will** to make life choices determines whether they will meet their potential.

life work:
The plan for your soul's development during your present lifetime.

L-rod:
A tool for **dowsing** that consists of two metal rods bent at a right angle and that swing easily with the use of tubes placed over the short ends.

lucid dream:
A dream that starts in your dream state and continues into your waking state.

M

magnetism:
Power that can bring about healing without using traditional medicine.

Major Arcana:
The twenty-two cards that do not belong to one of the four suits of cards in the **Tarot**. Each card has a specific theme and represents archetypal or major forces in your life.

manifest reality:
Everything that can be touched or seen or heard or smelled or tasted.

medical intuitive:
The psychic gift of knowing the health condition of others.

medium:
A person through whom the deceased can communicate with the living.

mental telepathy:
Nonverbal communication through the mind.

Minor Arcana:
Cards belonging to the four suits in the **Tarot** that represent four seasons, the directions, the elements, the four parts of your body, and the physical, mental, spiritual, and soul. They are meant to help you focus on your direction in your life journey.

miracle:
An occurrence with no explanation based on reality, usually attributed to a supernatural power that intervenes in the normal course of events.

N, O

near-death experience:
A form of **out-of-body experience**.

neurolinguistic programming (NLP):
A communication technique developed by Grinder and Bandler to change and improve thinking processes.

open channel:
An altered state of consciousness in which you are open to the information flow and energies of other entities.

Ouija board:
A board game that is designed to ask questions of spirits, who can answer with a "yes," "no," or by spelling out answers.

out-of-body experience:
When energy leaves your body and goes someplace else.

P

palmistry:
The ability to read the future by studying the lines and shapes of the palm of the hand.

pendulum:
A tool for dowsing that consists of a string or chain with a weight at the end.

phobia:
An anxiety disorder that is usually a fear of certain situations or specific objects.

postcognition:
A visual image that shows how an event from the past actually happened.

posthypnotic suggestion:
A suggestion given during a **hypnosis trance** that continues after the trance has ended.

power animal:
A spirit animal that acts as a guide.

precognition:
The knowledge of something that may happen in the future.

premonition:
The feeling that something is going to happen before it does.

psychic:
The ability to obtain information from sources that have no scientifically proven basis, such as intuition or the supernatural.

psychokinesis:
The ability to levitate, move objects, heal, and manipulate psychic energy.

Q, R

quatrain:
Poetry form in which each stanza consists of four lines and rhymes alternately.

random psychic intuition:
A psychic experience that comes at a time when it is unexpected and usually unwanted.

reframe:
The installation of a new habit into the **unconscious mind**.

Reiki:
A practice of transferring healing energy from the Universal Life Force through the practitioner to the subject. Dr. Mikao Usui developed this practice in the late 1800s.

remote viewing:
A form of **astral projection** in which the subject is psychically able to view a specific location and to report what he or she observes.

retrocognition:
Psychic information gathered from the past.

rune:
A letter of the ancient alphabet used by Germanic peoples from, approximately, A.D. 200 to 1200.

S

Sanskrit:
The ancient language of the Hindu people of India.

script:
The words used to help induce, deepen, and bring about a specific goal in a state of **hypnosis.**

scrying:
Using visual aids to help produce the proper **trance** to see into the future.

shaman:
A tribal medicine man, priest, or sorcerer.

spirit:
A nonphysical entity.

subconscious:
See **unconscious mind.**

synchronicity:
More than one thing that happens at the same time.

T

Tarot:
A deck of cards designed for psychic purposes—to help interpret past, present, and future events.

telekinesis:
The ability to get a psychic image from an object by touching it.

telepathy:
Communication of one mind with another by some means beyond normal sensory perception.

teleportation:
The mental movement of objects over a distance.

third eye:
The center of the forehead, which may feel tight and swollen by strong emotions and through which many believe the **Universal Mind** is contacted.

time bending:
Merging different time periods for the purpose of healing the past.

trance:
An altered state of consciousness in which the **unconscious mind** is open to suggestion and loses its ability to make critical decisions.

U

unconscious mind:
The storage area of the mind that contains all your past experiences; also referred to as the **subconscious**.

Universal Energy:
A form of energy that comes from your belief system.

Universal Flow:
The energy that is transmitted to and through you by the Universe or your Belief System.

Universal Mind:
The part of your soul where you enlist the unknown to give you strength and produce miracles. See **universal unconscious.**

universal unconscious:
Reached through the **unconscious mind** and believed to be the source from which you retrieve information and answers that have no scientific explanation; your Belief System.

unmanifest reality:
Something real that cannot be seen or touched or readily explained.

Appendix B

Additional Resources

Further Readings

Abadie, M. J., *The Everything® Tarot Book* (Avon, MA: Adams Media Corporation, 1999).

Ackerman, Diane, *The Natural History of the Senses* (New York: Random House, 1990).

Besant, Annie, *A Study in Karma* (Adyar, Madras 600020, India: Vasanta Press, 1987).

Brennan, Barbara Ann, *Hands of Light: A Guide to Healing Through the Human Energy Field* (New York: Bantam Books, 1988).

Browne, Sylvia, *Astrology Through a Psychic's Eyes* (Carlsbad, CA: Hay House, Inc., 2000).

DeBecker, Gavin, *The Gift of Fear: Survival Signals That Protect Us from Violence* (New York: Little, Brown & Company, 1997).

Ford, Arthur A., *A World Beyond* (Colorado Springs, CO: Fawcett Books, 1989).

Guiley, Rosemary Ellen, *Harper's Encyclopedia of Mystical & Paranormal Experience* (San Francisco: HarperSanFrancisco, 1991).

Hathaway, Michael R., *The Everything® Hypnosis Book* (Avon, MA: Adams Media Corporation, 2003).

Horan, Paula, *Empowerment Through Reiki* (Wilmot, WI: Lotus Light Publications, 1992).

Kirkpatrick, Sidney D., *Edgar Cayce: An American Prophet* (New York: Riverhead Books, 2000).

Legge, James, *I Ching: Book of Changes* (New York: Bantam Books, 1977).

MacGregor, Trish and Rob, *The Everything® Dreams Book* (Avon, MA: Adams Media Corporation, 1998).

Moody, Raymond A., Jr., *Life after Life* (New York: Bantam Books, 1975).

Ridall, Kathryn, *Channeling: How to Reach Out to Your Spirit Guides* (New York: Bantam Books, 1988).

Roberts, Jane, *The Seth Material* (Englewood Cliffs, NJ: Prentice-Hall, Inc., 1970).

Stearn, Jess, *The Search for a Soul: Taylor Caldwell's Past Lives* (New York: Berkley Books, 1994).

Tyson, Donald, *Scrying for Beginners: Tapping into the Supersensory Powers of Your Subconscious* (St. Paul, MN: Llewellyn Publications, 2000).

Washington, Peter, *Madame Blavatsky's Baboon: A History of the Mystics, Mediums, and Misfits Who Brought Spiritualism to America* (New York: Schocken Books, 1995).

Woods, Walt, *Letter to Robin: A Mini-Course in Pendulum Dowsing* (Oroville, CA: The Print Shoppe, 2001).

Music

Orfant, Bob and Robin, *Extraordinary* (Madison, NH: Coastline Productions, 1993).

Ibid., *Parrish* (Madison, NH: Coastline Productions, 1995).

Ibid., *Splendor* (Madison, NH: Coastline Productions, 1994).

Web Sites

- Association for Research & Enlightenment: *www.edgarcayce.org*

- Association for the Study of Dreams: *www.asdreams.org*

- Astrology on the Web: *www.astrology.com*

- Atlantic University (graduate program in transpersonal studies): *www.atlanticuniv.edu*

- Chakra: *www.spiritweb.org*

- Dowsers, American Society: *www.dowsers.org*

- Edgar Cayce Foundation: *www.edgarcayce.org*

- Hathaway, Michael R. (author of this book): *www.whitemountainhypnosiscenter.com*

- International Center for Reiki Training: *www.reiki.org*

- The International Society of Tarot: *www.tarotsociety.org*

- John Edward—the Official John Edward Web site: *www.johnedward.net*

- Light of the Soul—Links to Mediums: *www.lightofthesoul.net*

- Lundegaard, Karen (medium): *www.karenlundegaard.com*

- Maxfield Parrish (music): *www.maxfieldparrish.net*

- National Guild of Hypnotists: *www.ngh.net*

✑ National Spiritualist Association of Churches: *www.nsac.org*

✑ Parapsychology Foundation, Inc.: *www.parapsychology.org*

✑ Séance.com: *www.theseance.com*

✑ Van Praagh, James (medium): *www.vanpraagh.com*

✑ Yoga Network: *www.yoganetwork.org*

Index

THE EVERYTHING SERIES!

BUSINESS & PERSONAL FINANCE

Everything® Accounting Book
Everything® Budgeting Book, 2nd Ed.
Everything® Business Planning Book
Everything® Coaching and Mentoring Book, 2nd Ed.
Everything® Fundraising Book
Everything® Get Out of Debt Book
Everything® Grant Writing Book, 2nd Ed.
Everything® Guide to Buying Foreclosures
Everything® Guide to Mortgages
Everything® Guide to Personal Finance for Single Mothers
Everything® Home-Based Business Book, 2nd Ed.
Everything® Homebuying Book, 2nd Ed.
Everything® Homeselling Book, 2nd Ed.
Everything® Human Resource Management Book
Everything® Improve Your Credit Book
Everything® Investing Book, 2nd Ed.
Everything® Landlording Book
Everything® Leadership Book, 2nd Ed.
Everything® Managing People Book, 2nd Ed.
Everything® Negotiating Book
Everything® Online Auctions Book
Everything® Online Business Book
Everything® Personal Finance Book
Everything® Personal Finance in Your 20s & 30s Book, 2nd Ed.
Everything® Project Management Book, 2nd Ed.
Everything® Real Estate Investing Book
Everything® Retirement Planning Book
Everything® Robert's Rules Book, $7.95
Everything® Selling Book
Everything® Start Your Own Business Book, 2nd Ed.
Everything® Wills & Estate Planning Book

COOKING

Everything® Barbecue Cookbook
Everything® Bartender's Book, 2nd Ed., $9.95
Everything® Calorie Counting Cookbook
Everything® Cheese Book
Everything® Chinese Cookbook
Everything® Classic Recipes Book
Everything® Cocktail Parties & Drinks Book
Everything® College Cookbook
Everything® Cooking for Baby and Toddler Book
Everything® Cooking for Two Cookbook
Everything® Diabetes Cookbook
Everything® Easy Gourmet Cookbook
Everything® Fondue Cookbook
Everything® Fondue Party Book
Everything® Gluten-Free Cookbook
Everything® Glycemic Index Cookbook
Everything® Grilling Cookbook
Everything® Healthy Meals in Minutes Cookbook
Everything® Holiday Cookbook
Everything® Indian Cookbook
Everything® Italian Cookbook

Everything® Lactose-Free Cookbook
Everything® Low-Carb Cookbook
Everything® Low-Cholesterol Cookbook
Everything® Low-Fat High-Flavor Cookbook
Everything® Low-Salt Cookbook
Everything® Meals for a Month Cookbook
Everything® Meals on a Budget Cookbook
Everything® Mediterranean Cookbook
Everything® Mexican Cookbook
Everything® No Trans Fat Cookbook
Everything® One-Pot Cookbook
Everything® Pizza Cookbook
Everything® Quick and Easy 30-Minute,
    5-Ingredient Cookbook
Everything® Quick Meals Cookbook
Everything® Slow Cooker Cookbook
Everything® Slow Cooking for a Crowd Cookbook
Everything® Soup Cookbook
Everything® Stir-Fry Cookbook
Everything® Sugar-Free Cookbook
Everything® Tapas and Small Plates Cookbook
Everything® Tex-Mex Cookbook
Everything® Thai Cookbook
Everything® Vegetarian Cookbook
Everything® Whole-Grain, High-Fiber Cookbook
Everything® Wild Game Cookbook
Everything® Wine Book, 2nd Ed.

GAMES

Everything® 15-Minute Sudoku Book, $9.95
Everything® 30-Minute Sudoku Book, $9.95
Everything® Bible Crosswords Book, $9.95
Everything® Blackjack Strategy Book
Everything® Brain Strain Book, $9.95
Everything® Bridge Book
Everything® Card Games Book
Everything® Card Tricks Book, $9.95
Everything® Casino Gambling Book, 2nd Ed.
Everything® Chess Basics Book
Everything® Craps Strategy Book
Everything® Crossword and Puzzle Book
Everything® Crossword Challenge Book
Everything® Crosswords for the Beach Book, $9.95
Everything® Cryptic Crosswords Book, $9.95
Everything® Cryptograms Book, $9.95
Everything® Easy Crosswords Book
Everything® Easy Kakuro Book, $9.95
Everything® Easy Large-Print Crosswords Book
Everything® Games Book, 2nd Ed.
Everything® Giant Sudoku Book, $9.95
Everything® Giant Word Search Book
Everything® Kakuro Challenge Book, $9.95
Everything® Large-Print Crossword Challenge Book
Everything® Large-Print Crosswords Book
Everything® Lateral Thinking Puzzles Book, $9.95
Everything® Literary Crosswords Book, $9.95
Everything® Mazes Book
Everything® Memory Booster Puzzles Book, $9.95
Everything® Movie Crosswords Book, $9.95

Everything® Music Crosswords Book, $9.95
Everything® Online Poker Book
Everything® Pencil Puzzles Book, $9.95
Everything® Poker Strategy Book
Everything® Pool & Billiards Book
Everything® Puzzles for Commuters Book, $9.95
Everything® Puzzles for Dog Lovers Book, $9.95
Everything® Sports Crosswords Book, $9.95
Everything® Test Your IQ Book, $9.95
Everything® Texas Hold 'Em Book, $9.95
Everything® Travel Crosswords Book, $9.95
Everything® TV Crosswords Book, $9.95
Everything® Word Games Challenge Book
Everything® Word Scramble Book
Everything® Word Search Book

HEALTH

Everything® Alzheimer's Book
Everything® Diabetes Book
Everything® First Aid Book, $9.95
Everything® Health Guide to Adult Bipolar Disorder
Everything® Health Guide to Arthritis
Everything® Health Guide to Controlling Anxiety
Everything® Health Guide to Depression
Everything® Health Guide to Fibromyalgia
Everything® Health Guide to Menopause, 2nd Ed.
Everything® Health Guide to Migraines
Everything® Health Guide to OCD
Everything® Health Guide to PMS
Everything® Health Guide to Postpartum Care
Everything® Health Guide to Thyroid Disease
Everything® Hypnosis Book
Everything® Low Cholesterol Book
Everything® Menopause Book
Everything® Nutrition Book
Everything® Reflexology Book
Everything® Stress Management Book

HISTORY

Everything® American Government Book
Everything® American History Book, 2nd Ed.
Everything® Civil War Book
Everything® Freemasons Book
Everything® Irish History & Heritage Book
Everything® Middle East Book
Everything® World War II Book, 2nd Ed.

HOBBIES

Everything® Candlemaking Book
Everything® Cartooning Book
Everything® Coin Collecting Book
Everything® Digital Photography Book, 2nd Ed.
Everything® Drawing Book
Everything® Family Tree Book, 2nd Ed.
Everything® Knitting Book
Everything® Knots Book
Everything® Photography Book
Everything® Quilting Book

Everything® Sewing Book
Everything® Soapmaking Book, 2nd Ed.
Everything® Woodworking Book

HOME IMPROVEMENT

Everything® Feng Shui Book
Everything® Feng Shui Decluttering Book, $9.95
Everything® Fix-It Book
Everything® Green Living Book
Everything® Home Decorating Book
Everything® Home Storage Solutions Book
Everything® Homebuilding Book
Everything® Organize Your Home Book, 2nd Ed.

KIDS' BOOKS

All titles are $7.95

Everything® Fairy Tales Book, $14.95
Everything® Kids' Animal Puzzle & Activity Book
Everything® Kids' Astronomy Book
Everything® Kids' Baseball Book, 5th Ed.
Everything® Kids' Bible Trivia Book
Everything® Kids' Bugs Book
Everything® Kids' Cars and Trucks Puzzle and Activity Book
Everything® Kids' Christmas Puzzle & Activity Book
Everything® Kids' Connect the Dots Puzzle and Activity Book
Everything® Kids' Cookbook
Everything® Kids' Crazy Puzzles Book
Everything® Kids' Dinosaurs Book
Everything® Kids' Environment Book
Everything® Kids' Fairies Puzzle and Activity Book
Everything® Kids' First Spanish Puzzle and Activity Book
Everything® Kids' Football Book
Everything® Kids' Gross Cookbook
Everything® Kids' Gross Hidden Pictures Book
Everything® Kids' Gross Jokes Book
Everything® Kids' Gross Mazes Book
Everything® Kids' Gross Puzzle & Activity Book
Everything® Kids' Halloween Puzzle & Activity Book
Everything® Kids' Hidden Pictures Book
Everything® Kids' Horses Book
Everything® Kids' Joke Book
Everything® Kids' Knock Knock Book
Everything® Kids' Learning French Book
Everything® Kids' Learning Spanish Book
Everything® Kids' Magical Science Experiments Book
Everything® Kids' Math Puzzles Book
Everything® Kids' Mazes Book
Everything® Kids' Money Book
Everything® Kids' Nature Book
Everything® Kids' Pirates Puzzle and Activity Book
Everything® Kids' Presidents Book
Everything® Kids' Princess Puzzle and Activity Book
Everything® Kids' Puzzle Book
Everything® Kids' Racecars Puzzle and Activity Book
Everything® Kids' Riddles & Brain Teasers Book
Everything® Kids' Science Experiments Book
Everything® Kids' Sharks Book
Everything® Kids' Soccer Book
Everything® Kids' Spies Puzzle and Activity Book
Everything® Kids' States Book
Everything® Kids' Travel Activity Book
Everything® Kids' Word Search Puzzle and Activity Book

LANGUAGE

Everything® Conversational Japanese Book with CD, $19.95
Everything® French Grammar Book
Everything® French Phrase Book, $9.95
Everything® French Verb Book, $9.95
Everything® German Practice Book with CD, $19.95
Everything® Inglés Book
Everything® Intermediate Spanish Book with CD, $19.95
Everything® Italian Practice Book with CD, $19.95
Everything® Learning Brazilian Portuguese Book with CD, $19.95
Everything® Learning French Book with CD, 2nd Ed., $19.95
Everything® Learning German Book
Everything® Learning Italian Book
Everything® Learning Latin Book
Everything® Learning Russian Book with CD, $19.95
Everything® Learning Spanish Book
Everything® Learning Spanish Book with CD, 2nd Ed., $19.95
Everything® Russian Practice Book with CD, $19.95
Everything® Sign Language Book
Everything® Spanish Grammar Book
Everything® Spanish Phrase Book, $9.95
Everything® Spanish Practice Book with CD, $19.95
Everything® Spanish Verb Book, $9.95
Everything® Speaking Mandarin Chinese Book with CD, $19.95

MUSIC

Everything® Bass Guitar Book with CD, $19.95
Everything® Drums Book with CD, $19.95
Everything® Guitar Book with CD, 2nd Ed., $19.95
Everything® Guitar Chords Book with CD, $19.95
Everything® Harmonica Book with CD, $15.95
Everything® Home Recording Book
Everything® Music Theory Book with CD, $19.95
Everything® Reading Music Book with CD, $19.95
Everything® Rock & Blues Guitar Book with CD, $19.95
Everything® Rock & Blues Piano Book with CD, $19.95
Everything® Songwriting Book

NEW AGE

Everything® Astrology Book, 2nd Ed.
Everything® Birthday Personology Book
Everything® Dreams Book, 2nd Ed.
Everything® Love Signs Book, $9.95
Everything® Love Spells Book, $9.95
Everything® Paganism Book
Everything® Palmistry Book
Everything® Psychic Book
Everything® Reiki Book
Everything® Sex Signs Book, $9.95
Everything® Spells & Charms Book, 2nd Ed.
Everything® Tarot Book, 2nd Ed.
Everything® Toltec Wisdom Book
Everything® Wicca & Witchcraft Book, 2nd Ed.

PARENTING

Everything® Baby Names Book, 2nd Ed.
Everything® Baby Shower Book, 2nd Ed.
Everything® Baby Sign Language Book with DVD
Everything® Baby's First Year Book
Everything® Birthing Book

Everything® Breastfeeding Book
Everything® Father-to-Be Book
Everything® Father's First Year Book
Everything® Get Ready for Baby Book, 2nd Ed.
Everything® Get Your Baby to Sleep Book, $9.95
Everything® Getting Pregnant Book
Everything® Guide to Pregnancy Over 35
Everything® Guide to Raising a One-Year-Old
Everything® Guide to Raising a Two-Year-Old
Everything® Guide to Raising Adolescent Boys
Everything® Guide to Raising Adolescent Girls
Everything® Mother's First Year Book
Everything® Parent's Guide to Childhood Illnesses
Everything® Parent's Guide to Children and Divorce
Everything® Parent's Guide to Children with ADD/ADHD
Everything® Parent's Guide to Children with Asperger's Syndrome
Everything® Parent's Guide to Children with Asthma
Everything® Parent's Guide to Children with Autism
Everything® Parent's Guide to Children with Bipolar Disorder
Everything® Parent's Guide to Children with Depression
Everything® Parent's Guide to Children with Dyslexia
Everything® Parent's Guide to Children with Juvenile Diabetes
Everything® Parent's Guide to Positive Discipline
Everything® Parent's Guide to Raising a Successful Child
Everything® Parent's Guide to Raising Boys
Everything® Parent's Guide to Raising Girls
Everything® Parent's Guide to Raising Siblings
Everything® Parent's Guide to Sensory Integration Disorder
Everything® Parent's Guide to Tantrums
Everything® Parent's Guide to the Strong-Willed Child
Everything® Parenting a Teenager Book
Everything® Potty Training Book, $9.95
Everything® Pregnancy Book, 3rd Ed.
Everything® Pregnancy Fitness Book
Everything® Pregnancy Nutrition Book
Everything® Pregnancy Organizer, 2nd Ed., $16.95
Everything® Toddler Activities Book
Everything® Toddler Book
Everything® Tween Book
Everything® Twins, Triplets, and More Book

PETS

Everything® Aquarium Book
Everything® Boxer Book
Everything® Cat Book, 2nd Ed.
Everything® Chihuahua Book
Everything® Cooking for Dogs Book
Everything® Dachshund Book
Everything® Dog Book, 2nd Ed.
Everything® Dog Grooming Book
Everything® Dog Health Book
Everything® Dog Obedience Book
Everything® Dog Owner's Organizer, $16.95
Everything® Dog Training and Tricks Book
Everything® German Shepherd Book
Everything® Golden Retriever Book
Everything® Horse Book
Everything® Horse Care Book
Everything® Horseback Riding Book
Everything® Labrador Retriever Book
Everything® Poodle Book
Everything® Pug Book

Everything® Puppy Book
Everything® Rottweiler Book
Everything® Small Dogs Book
Everything® Tropical Fish Book
Everything® Yorkshire Terrier Book

REFERENCE

Everything® American Presidents Book
Everything® Blogging Book
Everything® Build Your Vocabulary Book, $9.95
Everything® Car Care Book
Everything® Classical Mythology Book
Everything® Da Vinci Book
Everything® Divorce Book
Everything® Einstein Book
Everything® Enneagram Book
Everything® Etiquette Book, 2nd Ed.
Everything® Guide to C. S. Lewis & Narnia
Everything® Guide to Edgar Allan Poe
Everything® Guide to Understanding Philosophy
Everything® Inventions and Patents Book
Everything® Jacqueline Kennedy Onassis Book
Everything® John F. Kennedy Book
Everything® Mafia Book
Everything® Martin Luther King Jr. Book
Everything® Philosophy Book
Everything® Pirates Book
Everything® Private Investigation Book
Everything® Psychology Book
Everything® Public Speaking Book, $9.95
Everything® Shakespeare Book, 2nd Ed.

RELIGION

Everything® Angels Book
Everything® Bible Book
Everything® Bible Study Book with CD, $19.95
Everything® Buddhism Book
Everything® Catholicism Book
Everything® Christianity Book
Everything® Gnostic Gospels Book
Everything® History of the Bible Book
Everything® Jesus Book
Everything® Jewish History & Heritage Book
Everything® Judaism Book
Everything® Kabbalah Book
Everything® Koran Book
Everything® Mary Book
Everything® Mary Magdalene Book
Everything® Prayer Book
Everything® Saints Book, 2nd Ed.
Everything® Torah Book
Everything® Understanding Islam Book
Everything® Women of the Bible Book
Everything® World's Religions Book

SCHOOL & CAREERS

Everything® Career Tests Book
Everything® College Major Test Book
Everything® College Survival Book, 2nd Ed.
Everything® Cover Letter Book, 2nd Ed.
Everything® Filmmaking Book
Everything® Get-a-Job Book, 2nd Ed.
Everything® Guide to Being a Paralegal
Everything® Guide to Being a Personal Trainer
Everything® Guide to Being a Real Estate Agent
Everything® Guide to Being a Sales Rep
Everything® Guide to Being an Event Planner
Everything® Guide to Careers in Health Care
Everything® Guide to Careers in Law Enforcement
Everything® Guide to Government Jobs
Everything® Guide to Starting and Running a Catering Business
Everything® Guide to Starting and Running a Restaurant
Everything® Job Interview Book, 2nd Ed.
Everything® New Nurse Book
Everything® New Teacher Book
Everything® Paying for College Book
Everything® Practice Interview Book
Everything® Resume Book, 3rd Ed.
Everything® Study Book

SELF-HELP

Everything® Body Language Book
Everything® Dating Book, 2nd Ed.
Everything® Great Sex Book
Everything® Self-Esteem Book
Everything® Tantric Sex Book

SPORTS & FITNESS

Everything® Easy Fitness Book
Everything® Fishing Book
Everything® Krav Maga for Fitness Book
Everything® Running Book, 2nd Ed.

TRAVEL

Everything® Family Guide to Coastal Florida
Everything® Family Guide to Cruise Vacations
Everything® Family Guide to Hawaii
Everything® Family Guide to Las Vegas, 2nd Ed.
Everything® Family Guide to Mexico
Everything® Family Guide to New England, 2nd Ed.
Everything® Family Guide to New York City, 3rd Ed.
Everything® Family Guide to RV Travel & Campgrounds
Everything® Family Guide to the Caribbean
Everything® Family Guide to the Disneyland® Resort, California Adventure®, Universal Studios®, and the Anaheim Area, 2nd Ed.
Everything® Family Guide to the Walt Disney World Resort®, Universal Studios®, and Greater Orlando, 5th Ed.
Everything® Family Guide to Timeshares
Everything® Family Guide to Washington D.C., 2nd Ed.

WEDDINGS

Everything® Bachelorette Party Book, $9.95
Everything® Bridesmaid Book, $9.95
Everything® Destination Wedding Book
Everything® Father of the Bride Book, $9.95
Everything® Groom Book, $9.95
Everything® Mother of the Bride Book, $9.95
Everything® Outdoor Wedding Book
Everything® Wedding Book, 3rd Ed.
Everything® Wedding Checklist, $9.95
Everything® Wedding Etiquette Book, $9.95
Everything® Wedding Organizer, 2nd Ed., $16.95
Everything® Wedding Shower Book, $9.95
Everything® Wedding Vows Book, $9.95
Everything® Wedding Workout Book
Everything® Weddings on a Budget Book, 2nd Ed., $9.95

WRITING

Everything® Creative Writing Book
Everything® Get Published Book, 2nd Ed.
Everything® Grammar and Style Book, 2nd Ed.
Everything® Guide to Magazine Writing
Everything® Guide to Writing a Book Proposal
Everything® Guide to Writing a Novel
Everything® Guide to Writing Children's Books
Everything® Guide to Writing Copy
Everything® Guide to Writing Graphic Novels
Everything® Guide to Writing Research Papers
Everything® Improve Your Writing Book, 2nd Ed.
Everything® Writing Poetry Book